P9-DTM-631

Canadian Writers and Their Works

CANADIAN WRITERS AND THEIR WORKS

FICTION SERIES · VOLUME EIGHT

EDITED BY

ROBERT LECKER, JACK DAVID, ELLEN QUIGLEY

INTRODUCED BY GEORGE WOODCOCK

ECW PRESS, 1989

CANADIAN CATALOGUING IN PUBLICATION DATA

Main entry under title:

Canadian writers and their works: essays on form,
context, and development : fiction

Includes bibliographies and indexes.
ISBN 0-920802-43-5 (set). — ISBN 1-55022-032-2 (v. 8)

1. Canadian fiction (English) — History and criticism.*
2. Authors, Canadian (English) — Biography.* I. Lecker,
Robert, 1951–   . II. David, Jack, 1946–   .
III. Quigley, Ellen, 1955–   .

PS8141.C37 1982   C81161.009   C82-094802-0
PR9190.2.C37 1982

V. 8
62,085

Copyright © ECW PRESS, 1989.

The publication of this series has been assisted by grants from the Ontario
Arts Council and The Canada Council.

This volume was typeset in Sabon by ECW Production Services, Sydenham,
Ontario. Printed and bound by University of Toronto Press, Downsview,
Ontario.

Published by ECW PRESS, 307 Coxwell Avenue, Toronto, Ontario M4L 3B5.

The illustrations are by Isaac Bickerstaff.

CONTENTS

CAMROSE LUTHERAN COLLEGE
LIBRARY

PREFACE

Canadian Writers and Their Works (CWTW) is a unique, twenty-volume collection of critical essays covering the development of Canadian fiction and poetry over the past two centuries. Ten volumes are devoted to fiction, and ten to poetry. Each volume contains a unifying Introduction by George Woodcock and four or five discrete critical essays on specific writers. Moreover, each critical essay includes a brief biography of the author, a discussion of the tradition and milieu influencing his/her work, a critical overview section which reviews published criticism on the author, a long section analyzing the author's works, and a selected bibliography listing primary and secondary material. The essays in each volume are arranged alphabetically according to last names of the writers under study.

This is Volume Eight of the Fiction Series of *Canadian Writers and Their Works*. Other volumes in the series will be published as research is completed. The projected completion date for the entire series is 1990.

The editors wish to acknowledge the contributions of many people who have played an important part in creating this series. First, we wish to thank the critics who prepared the essays for this volume: Keith Garebian, Judith Skelton Grant, Barbara Godard, Lawrence Mathews, and George Woodcock. We are also indebted to the production and design teams at both The Porcupine's Quill and ECW Production Services, and to Pat Kenny and Stephanie Termeer, who keyboarded the manuscript in its initial typesetting phase. Our sincere thanks also go to Scott Mitchell, and his associate Jamie Gaetz, for their excellent technical editing.

RL / JD / EQ

Introduction

GEORGE WOODCOCK

WHERE LITERATURE is concerned, the urge to find significant arrangements is always present, whether it is among the writers themselves or among their critics and editors. And in writing the introductions to the volumes in this series, I have always begun with the assumption that in offering a volume to me the editors had been led in their selection by at least a sense of affinity between the authors who were included. Thus I have always begun by trying to identify the common elements or the significant contrasts. Sometimes the pattern has emerged immediately with felicitous clarity; sometimes I have had to search hard to find it.

In the case of the present volume, the equations are there, but almost equally strong are the discordances, which are as much of generation as of gender when one looks at this group of four, two men and two women, half of them (Mavis Gallant and Norman Levine) born in the 1920s and half (Audrey Thomas and Leon Rooke) in the 1930s. One might also bring up the contrast between natives and immigrants, for Gallant and Levine are Canadians born and Thomas and Rooke are Americans by origin. But this point is somewhat neutralized by the fact that Gallant and Levine have lived most of their writing lives in Europe, while Thomas and Rooke have come to literary maturity in Canada, however much at times the vestiges of their American pasts may seem to cling.

I suppose the one element that does unite these four writers is a matter of formal preference; though all of them have written novels, novellas, and stories, they seem uniformly to be most successful in the briefer structures. But in each case, this success may be rather deceptive, for the difficulties evident in their longer works can be rewarding even in their often imperfect solutions, since these works represent serious attempts to grapple with the role of fiction in our age when writers still hover between modernism and post-modernism, between realism and metafiction, and are enriched rather than diminished by the range of possibilities.

One can divide the four writers here presented in two different ways apart from generation and gender. First there are those — Levine and Thomas — who are engaged in that haunted borderland between autobiography and fiction which has attracted many writers at least since Aphra Behn wrote *Oroonoko; or, The Royal Slave* (1688) by transmuting and embellishing the experiences of her childhood in Guiana. It is a borderland that some of us, like the present writer, have known from the autobiographical side: how much, in a successful memoir, actual experience must be rearranged and essentially fictionalized to make it authentic. Writers like Levine and Thomas pick up on the other side of the interface and constantly arrange and fictionalize material taken from their own experience.

Yet there is an obvious difference between a writer like Norman Levine, who adopts something very like the original documentary approach of Daniel Defoe, presenting what purports to be a straightforward narrative of ordinary existence, and one like Audrey Thomas, who is ready to use any metafictional or surrealist technique she can lay her mind on to project what in the end seems to her the most intriguing literary problem of all — the extent to which, in trying to remain faithful to art as well as experience, the writer is forced to adopt devices that inevitably remove her or him from the realm of actuality and even from that of veracity. Thomas once said — and who among us can refute her? — "Writers are terrible liars. There are nicer names for it, of course, but liars will do. They take a small incident and blow it up, like a balloon. . . . "[1] They also find, if they are writers like Thomas, with notable literary erudition and a recognition of the way in which the act of writing becomes a closed, self-reflexive process, that even if they have not adopted the extreme aestheticist doctrine of art for art's sake, they are involved in a process where the true presentation of feeling becomes entangled with the postmodernist problems of literary communication; with endlessly equivocal relations among character, writer, and reader, that "*hypocrite lecteur*" who, as Baudelaire saw so long ago, is the unpredictable joker in any literary game.

If the writing of Levine and Thomas derives so much from personal experience, presented plain by Levine and coloured by Thomas, both Gallant and Rooke rely far more on worlds of the imagination outside direct personal experience. But here also there is a clear division which mirrors that between Levine and Thomas.

Gallant may not — except in the Linnet Muir stories — examine her own personal life, but she does rely greatly on her perceptions of a world she regards with constant curiosity, creating characters and situations out of fugitive and fragmentary encounters and chance-heard conversations, so that it is hard to tell in her stories where observation ends and invention begins. What she shares with Leon Rooke is the fact that her own life is not the palpable centre of her fictional world; she faces, and in her own way deals with, the problem of otherness by making it the basis of her fictional approach, which rests essentially on the creation of alienated characters in a great variety of predicaments.

But Gallant differs from Rooke, as Levine does from Thomas, in the sense that in broad terms — the terms of Flaubert in one case and Graham Greene in the other — they are both realists. They set out to create and to portray with appropriate artifice the lives of credible people who may or may not resemble their authors. Plausibility and verisimilitude are old-fashioned goals they retain as the great premodernist literary masters did before them. Proust would recognize a kindred spirit in his admirer Gallant, and Gissing, I suspect, would acknowledge a fellow in Levine.

I do not suggest that Gallant and Levine ignore the problems of communicating through writing or the ambiguities of the relations between the writer and his literary predecessors or between the writer and his readers; occasionally, in fact, as in her novella "The Pegnitz Junction," Gallant does seem, in her playful parody of contemporary German writers and in her manipulation of telepathic awarenesses, to be encroaching on metafictional and extrarational areas of post-modernism where Thomas and Rooke are more evidently comfortable. But she and Levine clearly regard these problems mainly as challenges to their skills and assume that by writing clearly and well, they can communicate their insights and stir their readers' imaginations. To writers like Thomas and Rooke, on the other hand, the problems of communication, and the sense that writing is an autonomous activity, fed by life yet in some way self-perpetuating and self-modifying, can never be avoided, though this does not mean that their work is without moral, as well as aesthetic, content.

Norman Levine is the least immediately spectacular of the four writers. He offers a plain and unembellished prose; his people tend to sadden, rather than inspire, one with their resigned ineffectuality.

9

If they seem at times affirmative or assertive, we feel it to be out of character; at best one can say of them, as Lawrence Mathews does in the essay he contributes to this volume, that they show "awkward incompleteness paradoxically linked with dignity." Levine's admiration for Graham Greene, which led him to entitle his one travel book *Canada Made Me* in a none too oblique tribute, emerges in a shared preoccupation with "the failures, . . . the seedy.''[2] In comparison with the highly imaginative and sometimes exotic fiction of the three other writers we are discussing, his stories seem flat in tone and often banal in conception. His prose never lacks in clarity, and, as Mathews remarks, he always seems to be "speaking in his own voice," with no metafictional trickery, and he would probably reject with some indignation Thomas' view of the writer as liar. He early came to the conclusion that, again to quote Mathews, ". . . poetry can be discovered in precise observation of the ordinary . . . ," and in fiction the ordinary remained his province. His rejection of avant-gardism of any kind probably marks him off from most of his contemporaries. His rather staid and old-fashioned realism is shown in his admiration for Graham Greene because Greene showed so clearly the "visible world" around one, and in his preference for the Joyce of "The Dead" over the Joyce of *Ulysses*.

Levine's writing has indeed been so evasively modest that even his admirers, at least in Canada, find it hard to pick the right words to praise him. Robert Weaver, with the best will in the world, ended up writing an essentially neutral account of him in *The Oxford Companion to Canadian Literature*. Frank Davey rather pointedly left him out of his "guide to English-Canadian literature since 1960," *From There To Here*, and W. J. Keith could find only faint praise for him in his recent *Canadian Literature in English*.

But there is no doubt that something in Levine's unassuming writing at times, as I once remarked, "stirs one's empathies and quietly saddens one.''[3] Margaret Keith in her piece on him in *Contemporary Novelists* remarks perceptively that his language is "so empty of implication that it becomes mysterious," and she adds:

> In his low-keyed world even tiny incidents stand out like figures against a landscape of snow. They may mean nothing or anything, but to him they have an importance which the reader feels, but never entirely understands.[4]

Perhaps it is this inadvertent mystery that explains the curious fact of Levine's considerable reputation in both West and East Germany in comparison with the low-keyed approval he has received in both Canada and England. Of course, the reputations that English-speaking writers have acquired in continental Europe often bear little relation to the intrinsic merits of their writing. Byron and Wilde were both esteemed more than their literary betters because the exile into which their lifestyles forced them seemed a reproach to Perfidious Albion. Mazo de la Roche in her day was far better known in France than any Québécois writer because her facile romancing struck a responsive popular cord. Edgar Allan Poe gained a vast French reputation through the advocacy of Baudelaire, and there seems little doubt that Levine owes his success in Germany largely to the good fortune that his work attracted the attention of Heinrich Böll, who actually became his translator. And what may have attracted Böll was a prose so clear and neutral, and so lacking in idiomatic individuality, that it would be easily rendered into German.

Mathews speaks well for Levine but perhaps weakens his advocacy by sometimes claiming too much. He objects to Terry Goldie's remark that ". . . the major writer must have major things to say. Levine does not."[5] Mathews goes on to suggest that Levine's later writings do bring in what one might regard as major themes, such as freedom. But to be a major writer, one does not have only to enunciate in some unobtrusive way one or more of the grand human themes. One has to enunciate them in a major way, and there is nothing in the forms or the concepts or the language of Levine's writing that has enough originality or grandeur to seem in any true way "major." Change a word, and what Archibald Lampman once said of himself could best define Levine: "I am a minor poet of a superior order, and that is all."[6] And that, for most writers, in the end is enough.

The richness and complexity that Mavis Gallant has given to the short story can only be seen in terms of contrast to the grey understatement of Levine's fiction. Which is not to accuse Gallant of overstatement, but to draw attention to the variety and depth of perception and the range of expression shown in the hundred-odd stories and the handful of novels and novellas she has published since she set out in 1950 for her long and chosen exile in Europe.

Gallant's realism is much more than a matter of presenting plausible settings or even of creating credible speech patterns for an astonishing variety of characters, though she does both with great virtuosity. It is essentially a psychological realism, and there is nothing accidental about the fact that Marcel Proust is Gallant's favourite author. Psychological realism, as I see it, differs from the naturalist realism of a writer like Levine in that it is responsive to what Proust used to call the "intermittencies of the heart" and is therefore much more fluid in its handling of time and much more experimental in its rendering of memory. So, while Gallant may seem straightforward in her prose, she is in fact very subtle in the variations she achieves in the patterns of spoken and unspoken speech, and in the devices she employs to create the temporal patterns of her fictions, particularly in her longer stories, and in her novels, like *A Fairly Good Time*, in which a variety of devices — journals, letters, interior monologues, and recollective flashbacks — are used very skilfully to illuminate the central story of the failure of a marriage between a Canadian girl and a member of a stuffily conservative French family. Judith Skelton Grant in her essay in this volume writes interestingly on the "circling structures," the "loops," by which, in so many of the stories, time comes back on itself so that a formal, as well as a psychological, ordering of the story is created.

What emerges from such structures is an order that avoids continuity, and this accords with Gallant's belief — perhaps not derived from, but certainly resembling, Proust's "intermittencies" — that life is discontinuous and not a tightly knit structure of cause and effect; such a belief has made her happier, and better, with the short story than with the longer fictional forms.

The sense of life as discontinuous already introduces a kind of alienation, from one's past, from one's other selves, and undoubtedly it is connected closely with the fact that, as Grant remarks, "exile, expatriation, and rootlessness" become "recurrent in [Gallant's] fiction." We have already seen alienation, in the form of a difficulty in entering a foreign culture, as the basic theme of her larger and more successful novel. And the sense of being a stranger, often unable to make adjustments to the home that destiny has chosen for one, is recurrent in her stories.

Of course, this feeling of alienation and impermanence echoes far back into Gallant's life; she says of the seventeen shifts she made in her childhood from school to school that they "did something positive for me — there's no milieu I don't feel comfortable in, that I don't immediately understand."[7] But, one begins to speculate as one reads her stories, is it really *the milieu* that she understands? Is it not rather the experience of being recurrently a stranger in new places? Admittedly she has developed an extraordinary eye for background detail, but within her meticulously observed and recorded settings, she writes better of the transient than of the inhabitant, and on the occasions when she does write well of the inhabitant, we usually find that he is somehow alien in his own country.

Thus, though her stories are frequently about Anglo-Saxons — British as well as Canadians and sometimes Americans — leading empty and often spiteful lives in France or Italy, she also shows in one of her collections, *The Pegnitz Junction*, how a whole people, the post-Nazi generation of Germany, have been alienated — not from their native land but from the past which they are trying desperately to forget. Even when she turns back to her own county and countrymen in *Home Truths*, she shows how Canadians are often "foreigners" even when they do not live abroad. The most impressive stories in this volume are the semi-autobiographical Linnet Muir pieces, and these concern the failure of a young woman, returning to Montreal, to find her emotional bearings even in the city where she was born and spent her childhood.

It may be perilous to generalize over a large group of stories that show a great variety of situation, characterization, and thematic approach, but most of Gallant's fiction does concern people who have built up some kind of protection from the world, and who in the end are made to realize how precarious their defences are against the inherent discontinuousness of existence, and how hiding from life and trying to make themselves impervious to change has only increased their vulnerability. Gallant's stories are witty and often humorous in their way of expression yet pathetic in their unfolding effect; they are detached in viewpoint, so that at times they seem positively callous, yet they are so involving that one's final emotion is always something nearer to compassion than to contempt. Gallant has sometimes been called a satirist, but the satirist writes in the hope that mankind can be reformed, whereas Gallant seems sadly to know that the people she writes of will never become wiser or better.

Many of Gallant's stories have highly complex structures, not only involving elaborate manipulations of time and memory, but also the interplay of varying points of view. Sometimes the handling of incident, the way the visible and audible world cuts away from the inner world and back again, is almost cinematic in its effect and reminds one of Gallant's early training in the National Film Board, but in other stories there is often a distinctly dramatic feeling in the arrangement of scenes and the strength of dialogue. Indeed, Gallant seems to write with a special kind of relationship to most of the other arts, for she has a sharp eye for the visible world, and her stories often take on a marvellously visual quality so that the words seem like a translucent veil over what is seen. This offers an extraordinary double effect, so that the scene is observed as clearly and concretely as the background to a Pre-Raphaelite painting, yet one is always moving through it into the characters' states of mind, which are so convincing because they are related constantly to the physical here-and-now.

Because she has lived so long away and in her early writing years published so much abroad rather than in her home country, Canadians have been slow in recognizing Gallant's excellences. In the first edition of the *Literary History of Canada: Canadian Literature in English* (1965), her name is mentioned twice, but nothing is said about her writing, and in the second edition (1976), William H. New discusses her and Levine together, presumably because they were both exile writers; I doubt if he would do the same, now we have become more aware of the power and versatility of Gallant's writing. How far we have now gone in recognizing this undeniably major writer is shown by W. J. Keith when he remarks, in *Canadian Literature in English*, on "the number of accomplished women writers who have achieved distinction since the 1950s" and then quietly adds: "Of these . . . Mavis Gallant is perhaps supreme."[8]

It is a daringly emphatic statement, but it should not be dismissed without consideration, for as a stylist Gallant's only real rival among Canadian women writers was Marian Engel, and in narrative skill and psychological insight, Gallant certainly has no superiors.

Keith notes also that in spite of Gallant's stance as "a writer in the English language" without local ties, there is "a recognizably Canadian detachment about her authorial stance," yet he credits her with being in her own special way an international writer who "has brought an uncommon polish and sophistication into the literature of her native country and has also introduced an independent

Canadian perspective to the literary world of both Europe and the United States.''' And, indeed, one has to go back to Sara Jeannette Duncan in the late nineteenth century to find a Canadian writer whose position was comparable with hers, but even Duncan could not rival Gallant's awesome fictional skill.

It was André Gide in *Les Caves du Vatican* who first developed the idea of the "*acte gratuit*," the motiveless deed, as a factor challenging the fiction bound by causality of the naturalists, like Edmond and Jules de Goncourt and Emile Zola, who had preceded him. But Gide's rebellion against the necessitarian patterns of late nineteenth-century fiction was somewhat negated by his own stylistic classicism, and though in other novels, like *Les Faux-Monnayeurs* with its elaborate mirror pattern of diaries within diaries and writers writing about writers, he anticipated the metafictional trends of recent years, there was still a disturbing quality of artifice about his attempts to project the disorderliness and discontinuity of life.

Nobody to my knowledge, and certainly not Keith Garebian in the essay he contributed to this volume, has thought of mentioning Gide in connection with Leon Rooke. But the comparison does suggest that others have been before where our post-modernists are now treading. Garebian quotes Rooke as saying: "I don't like resolving situations because most situations are not resolved. I like the open ending. I like the reader to say, 'This is the ending,' and the other reader to say, 'No, this is the ending.'"'' André Gide would have agreed; the open-ended novel was his aim also. And when we come to the features of Rooke's work described by Garebian as "the rejection of ethical absolutes" and "the rejection of the traditional satirist's faith in the efficacy of satire as a reforming instrument," the links with the Gide of *L'Immoraliste* as well as of *Les Caves du Vatican* are clearly evident.

I am not suggesting the links are direct. I have no evidence that Rooke ever read Gide, though given his academic background, it seems unlikely that he did not. But the literary background he emerged from, that of the fictional tradition of the Southern states, was essentially North American, though in its own way as permeated with decadence as the symbolist background from which Gide himself emerged. Certainly it was not Canadian, and there is no sign that past Canadian writers have influenced Rooke any more than the Canadian environment in which he has lived for almost two decades has had any deep effect on his fiction, except in liberating him from the setting of his youth and enabling him to develop at a distance the strain of writing on which he had started even before he came northward. Rooke, as Garebian points out, has deliberately dissociated himself from any definition by region: "Place (locale) in fiction," Rooke has said, is "a vastly over-rated virtue."[11]

Rooke calls himself a New Traditionalist, which means that he is quite willing to pick up traditional elements from the cultural debris in which the post-modernists like to rummage, and incorporate them into his experimental structures. Doubtless this literary scavenging has contributed to the variety and the inventive oddity which his works display, particularly as one reads the plot summaries to which Garebian devotes so much of his essay. Certainly, more than any other writer I know of in Canada, Rooke is a virtuoso of the metafictional, presenting the disorder of existence with kaleidoscopic vividness and fragmentation.

Yet, in the end, as with Gide, how much it all seems a work of brilliant contrivance! The post-moderns have never really reconciled, any more than their grandly imperfect predecessor did, their rejection of pattern in life with the acceptance of another pattern that comes inevitably when one introduces the process of fiction as subject into the fiction itself.

Such movements, it seems to me, though they are inevitably part of the general flow of literature, are side channels that eventually flow back into the mainstream and enrich it by immersion, as happened with Gongorism in seventeenth-century Spain, with the decadent movement of the *fin de siècle*, with Vorticism which spilled over from art to writing, and with surrealism. They depend too much on theory and artifice to dominate the mainstream or materially change its course, but they contribute greatly through the experimentation that originally sets them apart.

One thing a writer like Rooke demonstrates, as Gallant does in another way, is that there are standards and loyalties other than local ones. By their very presence, such artists disprove the nationalist contentions that Canadian literature must interpret Canadian life and project what purport to be Canadian values. They place our writing in the broader setting to which as work in English it also belongs.

Audrey Thomas has seized upon the best of several worlds. She is a psychological realist of — as Frank Davey once remarked — "an extreme kind," but in addition, as Davey also said, she is a "technical adventuress."[12] She has a strong natural scholarliness, which is perhaps why she never fitted into the normal academic world, and this has given her an awareness of the uses of words and literary structures that she has put to good use as she turns meta-fictional devices to the service of her psychological realism. In addition, she works always in the valley where autobiography and fiction come together, so that her works are never far from life but never become literal presentations. Barbara Godard says appropriately of her that, "Like many other expatriates, she has used writing to bring order to her varied existence, giving herself a context through words."

In this sense, without being any less imaginative, Thomas is certainly less inventive than writers like Gallant and Rooke, who mostly portray sharply differentiated others, even if in the end, one recognizes that the others project their own potentialities. She differs from them also in defining herself as a regionalist, and, interestingly enough given her American youth and the African travels of her young womanhood, she does so in the most local way, not — as she has insisted — as a "Canadian writer," but as a "B.C. writer," celebrating in this way the fact that British Columbia has been not only the place where her writing matured, but also the setting that has inspired some of the best of her writing.

Given the fact that, in *Mrs. Blood* and elsewhere, Thomas has written often of her African experience, there is always a temptation to see her in similar terms to other Canadian writers, like Dave Godfrey and Margaret Laurence, on whose fiction periods in Africa have also had profound influence. But the resemblances are limited, for while Laurence and Godfrey were fascinated by African society and by the political developments as colonial Gold Coast changed into independent Ghana, Thomas was already concerned deeply with the way in which feminine psychology and feminine physicality reacted on each other, and with the perhaps not entirely alien subject of the process of literary creation, with its periodicities and its gestational cycles.

During the two decades since the appearance of her first book, *Ten Green Bottles* (1967), Thomas has demonstrated in her writing a great formal variety and a great range of perception. Her six novels vary from the powerful study of a divided personality in

Mrs. Blood through the almost classical *Bildungsroman* of *Songs My Mother Taught Me* to the sophisticated use of a collage technique that, in the highly experimental *Blown Figures*, perpetually invites the reader to vary the plot. In her volume of two novellas, *Munchmeyer and Prospero on the Island*, the post-modernist problems of the relations between writer and character, work and reader, are worked out in interlacing structures. *Munchmeyer* is a kind of mirror work in which it is hard to tell what is meant to be real action and what is the novelist hero's fantasy. The situation is complicated by the fact that *Munchmeyer* has actually been written by Miranda, the protagonist of *Prospero on the Island*, so that it is in fact a work within a work, which she discusses with Prospero, an elderly painter living on the same British Columbian island.

In Thomas' fiction, forms shade off one into the other, so that her novels take episodic shapes that resemble collections of related stories, while her stories tend to fall into linked groups. They vary over an immense range from fairy tales to studies of childhood awakening, from sharp-edged comedies of manners to troubled studies of the relationships of women and men and the relationships between women, whether they are friends or mothers and daughters. Perhaps it is the fact that she has come so honestly to a feminine viewpoint based on a recognition of sensibilities differing according to gender that has saved Thomas from falling into the arid didacticism which has marred so much feminist fiction, just as it mars any determinedly partisan writing.

Constant throughout Thomas' writing is the fact of suffering, and an acute awareness of suffering's psychological results — its power to distort perceptions and memories alike. A recurrent situation brings us — sometimes in the setting of an actual madhouse or its hospital ward equivalent — to the appalling borderland between sanity and madness, and here, in its most concentrated form, appears the terror that shadows all Thomas' fiction. Yet the essential quality of her work is not the sense of nightmare that haunts all her psychologically complex characters with their feelings of loss, their postlapsarian guilt, and their inevitably imperfect grasp of experience, but is rather the precarious balance between fear and the joy of existence which so intermittently — but more frequently and securely in her later fiction — they achieve. There are in Thomas few of the superbly "well-made" structures or of the impeccable surfaces one admires in Gallant's stories, largely because she does not seek to make her work what in a double sense she might consider "finished." She is always starting again; she herself has said, "All my novels are one novel, in a sense. . . . Each one extends, in a different style, offering more information, from a different perspective, what is basically the same story."[13] And in the process of perfecting these variations, she has taken her place among the best and least predictable of our writers.

NOTES

[1] "Initram," in *Ladies and Escorts* (Ottawa: Oberon, 1977), p. 88.

[2] Norman Levine, *Canada Made Me* (London: Putnam, 1958), p. 255.

[3] George Woodcock, "A Saddening Novel of Exile by a Canadian Expatriate," rev. of *From a Seaside Town*, by Norman Levine, *Toronto Daily Star*, 12 Sept. 1970, p. 67.

[4] "Levine, (Albert) Norman," in *Contemporary Novelists*, 4th ed., ed. D. L. Kirkpatrick (London: St. James, 1986), p. 536.

[5] Rev. of *Thin Ice*, in *Canadian Book Review Annual 1979*, ed. Dean Tudor, Nancy Tudor, and Kathy Vanderlinden (Toronto: Peter Martin, 1980), p. 167.

[6] Letter to Edward William Thomson, 29 Aug. 1895, Letter 89, *An Annotated Edition of the Correspondence between Archibald Lampman and Edward William Thomson (1890–1898)*, ed. and introd. Helen Lynn (Ottawa: Tecumseh, 1980), p. 149.

[7] Geoff Hancock, "An Interview with Mavis Gallant," *Canadian Fiction Magazine*, No. 28 (1978) [*A Special Issue on Mavis Gallant*], p. 23.

[8] W. J. Keith, *Canadian Literature in English* (New York: Longman, 1985), p. 157.

[9] Keith, p. 159.

[10] Geoff Hancock, "An Interview with Leon Rooke," *Canadian Fiction Magazine*, No. 38 (1981), p. 133.

[11] "Leon Rooke," in *Canada Writes: The Members' Book of the Writers Union of Canada*, ed. K. A. Hamilton (Toronto: Writers Union of Canada, 1977), p. 295.

[12] "Audrey Thomas," in *From There to Here: A Guide to English-Canadian Literature since 1960* (Erin, Ont.: Porcépic, 1974), p. 254.

[13] Quoted in John Hofsess, "A Teller of Surprising Tales," *The Canadian* [*The Toronto Star*], 6 May 1978, p. 17.

*Mavis Gallant
and Her Works*

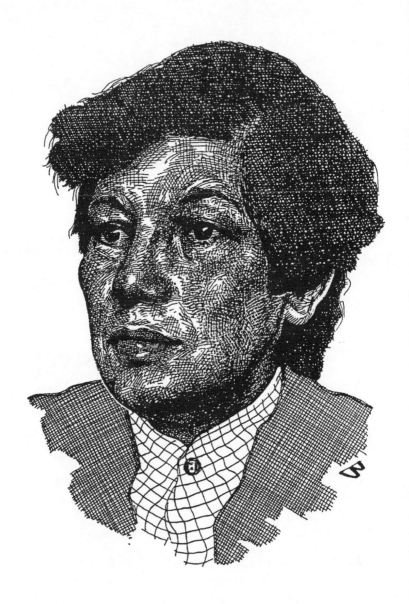

Mavis Gallant (1922–   )

JUDITH SKELTON GRANT

Biography

BORN 11 AUGUST 1922 in Montreal, Mavis Gallant lived until she was eight on Sherbrooke Street opposite McGill University in a grey stone house with a bow window.[1] This is one of the places etched in her memory. Another is Châteauguay, Quebec, where she summered from her seventh through her tenth year in a white clapboard house with a gallery. Her father was British (Scots and English); her mother, Canadian (but raised in the United States) of mixed heritage — German, Breton, Rumanian. She spoke German and some French. Gallant herself learned to speak French from her French Canadian nurse at the same time as she learned to speak English from her parents. An important result of her parents' attitudes was that she became "European-minded"[2] and ended up with "no national or religious prejudice whatever."[3]

Two aspects of Gallant's childhood made her an observer, a person acutely aware of differences, a quick study in new situations. One was her father's occupation. Stewart Young was a painter (and remittance man) "at a time in Canada when if you said your father painted, people would say, 'Yes, but what does he *do*?'"[4] The other was her schooling. By the time she completed high school, she had attended seventeen different schools in Quebec, Ontario, Connecticut, New York State, and one other state. Of the French schools, where she "was the only English Canadian and the only Protestant" and where she "suffered enormously" though not "in a tragic way" (Markle, 22 Jan. 1965), the Pensionnat Saint-Louis-de-Gonzague, a convent boarding school of "an extremely severe Jansenist kind,"[5] which she entered at the age of four, looms large in her memory. Her father disappeared from her life when she was about nine (he died at the age of thirty-two or thirty-three a year or so after she last saw him, possibly a suicide[6]). After her mother (who was a musician, though not professionally) remarried and moved to Toronto and then to New York, Gallant viewed school as a place where she was dumped.[7] Not surprisingly she was unhappy at school. Yet these recurrent plunges into new school situations "did something positive for me — there's no milieu I don't feel comfortable in, that I don't immediately understand" (Hancock, p. 23).

In 1941, disliking her stepfather and unwilling to depend on him financially any longer, Gallant returned on her own to Montreal. She worked briefly as a woman's social secretary, then helped in the woman's real estate business, before taking the job with Canadian National Railways described in "Between Zero and One" (1975; *HT*, pp. 238–60).[8] Next she worked for the National Film Board in Ottawa in the negative-cutting room before becoming a staff writer for *The Standard* [Montreal] from 1944 to 1950. (From 1943 through 1946, she was married to John Gallant, a Winnipeg musician. The marriage, which ended in divorce, was briefer than the dates suggest since her husband was in the armed forces overseas for much of the time.)

The matter of vocation was settled early. Gallant says that she always wanted to be a writer (Hancock, p. 21). She recalls dictating well-known carols and nursery rhymes as a little girl of four to her father, who would write them out for her. Then for years she would build a city called Marigold using books and furniture and peopling it with figures cut from newspapers. She would push them around quickly with her finger, making them perform, as she spoke all the dialogue for their long adventures to the background music of opera records. By the time she was twelve or thirteen, she was writing. She tried little stories but didn't get far with them. What did flow easily was poetry, but eventually "la poésie m'a quittée."[9] Then from eighteen or nineteen until she was twenty-five, she wrote little scraps of plays, learning to work with dialogue. At the same time, she began to write short stories.

Getting her work published proved surprisingly easy. Soon after she joined *The Standard* in 1944, she gave (after being asked) two stories to Kit Shaw, the paper's librarian. F. R. Scott (a friend of Shaw's) promptly published them in *Preview*. The fiction editor of *The Standard* asked for a story, liked what she gave him, and published it in December of 1946. He sent it to the CBC; it was read on the air. Though Gallant found such ready publication reassuring, she didn't pursue these avenues because they were not what she wanted — to succeed as a writer in the larger English-speaking world.

In 1950 she was ready to leave her job at *The Standard*. She was disillusioned by her discovery that she was not paid as much as men in comparable positions and by the fact that, though she had helped to establish a press club, the men promptly voted to exclude women.[10] She'd had her brush with commercial reality: she was taken off film criticism because a chain of art theatres objected to her impact on theatre-goers, and her radio column was taken from her because advertisers did not like her views. Her job had come full circle: assignments she'd done when she first joined the paper had begun to recur. She felt that she must make her move before her thirtieth birthday and before contributing to the paper's new compulsory pension plan inhibited her psychologically from leaving. Montreal was also becoming less attractive. It was the place where her ex-husband lived and where she suffered the stigma of divorce. She liked neither the current political climate in North America nor the increasing materialism. There was a strong pull outward too. She was yearning to travel, to get to Europe, to try her wings now that her writing had matured, and was afraid that travel might be restricted because of the Korean War. She preferred to take a cut in living standard, which living on her writing would entail, elsewhere than Montreal where she'd been reasonably paid. She gave notice. Challenged by a fellow reporter (envious of her willingness to make a leap of faith or perhaps just concerned that she might not be able to sell her stories), she typed up one of her many manuscripts and sent it to *The New Yorker*. *The New Yorker* found the story too Canadian, asked for a second story, and accepted it. (Thus began a long, fruitful relationship. *The New Yorker* has been the first publisher of most of Gallant's stories and has had a first reading contract with her at least since 1964.[11] Gallant has published with the magazine longer than any of their other current writers of fiction.[12])

Reassured by *The New Yorker*'s reaction to her work, Gallant set off for Europe and has lived there ever since. Between 1950 and 1954, she spent time in London, Paris, Salzburg, and in Italy, Spain, Yugoslavia, Alsace, and Sicily. She was not a tourist merely passing through; she *lived* in these places, taking a flat, doing her own cooking, meeting people. In 1954 she leased a gardener's cottage in Menton-Garavan near the French-Italian border. Here she found the colonies of foreigners (mostly English) left over from before the war who became the subject of many of her stories. Then in 1960 she took a Paris flat in the sixth arrondissement as her permanent base. She kept her cottage for a time and subsequently, from the early 1960s until the mid-1970s, leased a villa in the south of France instead. She travelled a great deal, notably and often to Germany during the 1960s. She has also returned to Canada on at least eleven separate occasions during the past thirty years, including a year as writer-in-residence at the University of Toronto during 1983–84. She has said that she never writes about a place she has not visited.[13]

Only a little can be said about her friendships. She has as many French Canadian as English Canadian friends. Morley Callaghan and Mordecai Richler are among the latter. Most of her Paris friends are French-speaking, though they come from many different countries. In spite of Geoff Hancock's statement to the contrary,[14] Roland Barthes and Simone de Beauvoir were not among them. That many of her friends are painters is a legacy from her father, for she feels "completely at home as soon as I walk into someone's studio" (Markle, 22 Jan. 1965). Joe Plaskett is one such friend in Paris.

Some of the people who matter deeply to Gallant have had books or a story dedicated to them. Her first collection, *The Other Paris: Stories* (1956), names Elaine Hennessy, a close English friend who is no longer living. Her first novel, *Green Water, Green Sky* (1959), is dedicated to Diarmuid Russell, her agent in New York for a time, now dead. She singles out William Maxwell, a good friend and her first editor at *The New Yorker*, in *My Heart Is Broken: Eight Stories and a Short Novel* (1964). Doyle Klein, the dedicatee of her second novel, *A Fairly Good Time* (1970), a writer at *The Standard* during Gallant's time there, stood as an older sister to her. Neither *The Pegnitz Junction: A Novella and Five Short Stories* (1973) nor *The End of the World and Other Stories* (1974) is dedicated, but *From the Fifteenth District: A Novella and Eight Short Stories* (1979) names "H. T.," a Paris friend who appears in Gallant's two-part essay "The Events in May: A Paris Notebook" (1968; *PN*, pp. 9–95). *Home Truths: Selected Canadian Stories* (1981) cites Nellie McMillan, Gallant's "oldest and closest and dearest Canadian friend" (Grant), who died of cancer in 1983. The story "With a Capital T" (1978; *HT*, pp. 317–30) is "For Madeleine and Jean-Paul Lemieux," French Canadian friends she mentions several times in interviews. Gallant wanted her play *What Is to Be Done?*

(1983) to be dedicated to the British critic and documentary film producer Edgar Anstey but didn't make her wish known in time. Her most recent story collection, *Overhead in a Balloon: Stories of Paris* (1985), is for "G. de D. M.," and her *Paris Notebooks: Essays and Reviews* (1986), for Josie Peron.

Gallant has won awards for several individual stories.[15] She is an Officer in the Order of Canada (1981), received the Governor General's Award for fiction for *Home Truths* (1981), was given the 1983 Canada-Australia Literary Prize, and in 1984 was awarded two honorary degrees, a doctor of letters by York University in Toronto and a doctorat en lettres by l'Université Sainte-Anne in Nova Scotia. Obviously, Gallant's fear as she ventured forth in 1950 to try her luck as a writer that, like her father, she might have the vocation but not the talent, was unfounded. Her own assessment of her achievement is characteristically modest and blunt: "I never thought that I had a very large talent. I thought that I went to the limit of what I could do. I never made the mistake of thinking of myself as a Dostoevsky. I've not neglected anything, I don't think, that I could [have developed]."[16]

Tradition and Milieu

Since many aspects of "tradition and milieu" have received little critical attention to date, this section will be suggestive, not definitive. No one has looked seriously at influences on Gallant's writing, for example, though Gallant has herself thrown out interesting hints. She is convinced that "the writers who help you look at the world are those you read when young," and that after a certain age, no one "can change your way of looking" (Hancock, p. 21). It thus behooves us to consider what we know about her formative years.

There were several biases in her early reading. Because her father was British and her mother an Anglophile, she was given British books to read during her childhood. In addition, her mother's family put her in touch with German literature, and her schooling, with French literature. As an adolescent she was influenced by an American psychiatrist who helped to raise her. He had been an assistant to Sigmund Freud and had been analyzed by him. "He never talked very much to me about it, but the library was there, you know, so I read a lot. And I went through a period when that

27

was gospel. It was almost like a code, until, well, you know, you get older, and that's that. You get out of it."[17] Naïveté concerning Freud's system was certainly past by the time she began to write for *The Standard* in 1944, and her continuing interest in psychology is evident in many articles.[18] Between the ages of fifteen and twenty-five, Gallant read much of Katherine Mansfield's work. During her teens she read American and English poetry avidly, memorizing passages that mattered to her. During the same period and into her early twenties, she was attracted to socialism. Like her character Linnet Muir in "In Youth Is Pleasure" (1975; *HT*, pp. 218–37), she probably treasured Zinoviev and Lenin's *Against the Stream* and "a few beige pamphlets from the Little Lenin Library" (*HT*, p. 221) and had by heart Stephen Vincent Benét's "Litany for Dictatorships," "Notes to Be Left in a Cornerstone," and "Ode to the Austrian Socialists."[19] (Meeting refugees from war-torn Europe dispelled Gallant's illusions about socialism.)

When she began writing fiction at eighteen or nineteen, she was reading the Russians — Chekhov, Gogol, Turgenev, Dostoevsky — in translation. In her view, her early stories (like the two published in *Preview* in 1944) "read really as if they had been translated out of the Russian."[20] She feels she was particularly influenced by Chekhov. Curiously, the major link in her mind between the stories and Chekhov appears to be the refugee characters whose cultural background and assumptions made them see things differently from her and whose point of view she tried to imagine (Grant; and Hancock, p. 31).

After the Russians, she read "a wave of French" (Hancock, p. 21) — Stendhal, Flaubert, Colette, Maupassant, Mérimée — and she saw at least one of Sartre's plays. Of Proust, her favourite writer, she had read *Swann's Way* and *Within a Budding Grove* before she left Canada. (Subsequently she read his work through, and she rereads him more than any other author.) She was reading widely in English too during her years in Montreal. She read Nabokov's *The Real Life of Sebastian Knight* in this period, for example. Francean Campbell reported her as saying that the writers who influenced her most in her formative years were Thomas Wolfe, John Steinbeck, and Richard Wright,[21] but Gallant denies this, declaring that she "never had any time" for either Wright or Steinbeck and that her enchantment with Thomas Wolfe lasted only a couple of months (Grant). When she went to London in 1950, it was with her "head full of Dickens," whom she'd first read as a child. She also held a temporary conviction that E. M. Forster was "god" (Grant). Gallant's literary roots are clearly spread widely in European and English literature.

Gallant has continued to read Russian, French, and German writers, and to read broadly in English. She reads French writers in the original French but the Russian and German in English translations. Though this reading has probably not changed her way of seeing (as her earlier reading may have done), it has had some impact on her work. The novella "The Pegnitz Junction" (1973; *PJ*, pp. 3–88) is full of "parodies and take-offs and skits"[22] of German writing. And her reading coupled with her broad experience of Europe makes her a knowledgeable interpreter primarily of the French, but occasionally of other Europeans, for North Americans, in articles, reviews, and essays which have appeared primarily in *The New Yorker* and in *The New York Times Book Review*.[23] Her long-awaited book (in preparation since the early 1970s and still not finished) on the case of Alfred Dreyfus, the Jewish French officer who was unjustly imprisoned for treason in the 1890s, is also intended for a North American audience. Though widely read in European literatures, she is not associated with any literary movement in Europe. While she reads much French literature, current French notions about "her" genre, the short story, repel her. When Geoff Hancock observed that she did not appear to hold "the traditional view of the short story, that it rises and falls, has a dramatic resolution or a plot," Gallant replied: "Well, I don't think the story should be a fragment. A short story is not just something snatched out of a larger fiction, or something you don't know what to do with, that you turn into a story because it's not good for anything else. That's the French view and I don't agree with it at all" (Hancock, p. 48).

Some reviewers have suggested *The New Yorker* itself as an influence. But the range and diversity of the fiction published in *The New Yorker* is so great that it is not surprising that their various attempts at defining its characteristics make amusing and contrastive reading.[24] Early on, Gallant herself worried that *The New Yorker* "would put a kind of hand on me . . . that there would be so much editing that my work would cease to be mine" (Hancock, p. 33). Experience revealed that the magazine's editors queried things rather than changing them, so that she retained control of her work. The one exception concerns the story "Orphans' Progress" (1965; *HT*, pp. 56–62). According to Gallant, as well as querying many more points than usual (thirty-three in an eight-page story), *The New Yorker* found the story's first paragraph "too sexual" for its readers. After a long correspondence, she acceded to the magazine's demands; she made many revisions and agreed to change the offensive first paragraph. "It is the only major change I have ever made because of an objection of that kind, and I have always regretted having done so."[25] She acknowledges a great debt to her first editor there, William Maxwell. Maxwell was careful not to change her way of writing as the edited typescripts of her stories attest (almost all editing in them is copy editing), nor did he influence her indirectly through his writing (indeed, Gallant did not realize for some years that her editor and the writer William Maxwell were the same person). In fact, he was the only person with whom she felt comfortable discussing writing, something they did usually through letters, and occasionally in conversation, when she was in New York or he in Paris. He gave her the subtle encouragement young writers need, to become more rigorous in her writing. She thinks that possibly he functioned for her as Leonard did for Virginia Woolf, giving her what "women very often need because we have perhaps too much sensibility," and she feels that without his influence she might have become "a very, very minor Elizabeth Bowen" (Grant).

Gallant's place in the Canadian literary tradition is not entirely clear. During the 1940s when she was in Montreal, she belonged to no group of writers. She seldom showed her work to anyone. Indeed, she does not feel that there *was* a literary movement to which she might have belonged then (Hancock, p. 42). She did not know Ethel Wilson, P. K. Page, Irving Layton, Louis Dudek, or Anne Marriott, all of whom wrote for John Sutherland (who published the story *The New Yorker* rejected in *The Northern Review* in 1950). And of course she has been at some distance from the Canadian literary scene since 1950. In his Introduction to Gallant's *The End of the World and Other Stories*, Robert Weaver linked Gallant to Margaret Laurence, Mordecai Richler, and Norman Levine, all of whom had "lived abroad for long periods without forfeiting their identity as Canadian writers." But he felt that Gallant, unlike the others, "has come to seem the complete expatriate" (*EW*, p. 7). Since then, journalists have regularly called

Gallant an expatriate and have referred to those three writers (and recently to Elizabeth Smart and Sinclair Ross as well). (Curiously only Gallant herself has thought to mention Anne Hébert, who has lived in Paris since the mid-1950s.[26]) But the group is dropped virtually as it is raised, so little do these writers have in common. The obvious niche for Gallant in Canadian literary tradition is not "expatriate" but "important contemporary writer of short stories." Her "place" in that tradition, however, has not yet been fully clarified. She seems not to have been influenced by earlier writers of the short story in Canada, and it is too soon to tell whether she will influence others.

With her work rooted in Western literature, her stories published and anthologized in Canada, the United States, and Britain, and her fiction set in Canada, the United States, and many countries in Europe, Gallant is truly a supranational phenomenon. Her mode, as John Metcalf points out in "The Curate's Egg,"[27] is the "modern" short story. In a recent article, Suzanne C. Ferguson argues that the main formal characteristics of the modern short story are:

> (1) limitation and foregrounding of point of view, (2) emphasis on presentation of sensation and inner experience, (3) the deletion or transformation of several elements of the traditional plot, (4) increasing reliance on metaphor and metonymy in the presentation of events and existents, (5) rejection of chronological time ordering, (6) formal and stylistic economy, and (7) the foregrounding of style.[28]

A story need not possess all seven characteristics to be "modern." There is a considerable range in the degree to which one story or another exhibits any one of the seven.

Critical Overview and Context

In 1979 the short-story writer Merna Summers observed that a new book by Mavis Gallant is "usually heralded by a spate of articles demanding to know why Mavis Gallant is so little known in Canada." Yet, "the fact is, most serious readers do know Gallant's work."[29] Summers was right. From the mid-1960s to the present, there have been recurrent outbursts of indignation at Canadian ignorance of Gallant, by writers, journalists, critics, and academics whose articles reveal that they have long followed her work. These same "serious readers" have ensured that Gallant's work has been included in more than twenty Canadian short-story anthologies since 1960, that she has been interviewed over the years by local newspapers and on Canadian television and radio, and that she has been cited regularly in reference works on Canadian literature, on writers, and on the short story since 1965. But "serious readers" are a special and small group. Only recently has Gallant begun to be familiar to a general audience in Canada, or to acquire the kind of Canadian public recognition accorded to writers like Alice Munro, Margaret Atwood, and Margaret Laurence.

There were good reasons for Gallant's relative obscurity in Canada. She has lived in Europe since 1950, and most of her stories appeared first in *The New Yorker*. Her first three collections of short stories, like her two novels, were published in the United States and soon after in England, but not in Canada. It seems likely that Canadian newspapers and journals were not sent copies of these books for review since her first collection received no Canadian reviews, and the other books, only a handful each. Nineteen seventy-four marked a minor shift in the Canadian awareness of Gallant when *The End of the World and Other Stories* was added to the New Canadian Library (although unremarked by Canadian critics). *My Heart Is Broken* was reprinted the same year by Paper-Jacks. Nineteen seventy-seven brought the first Gallant bibliography,[30] and 1978 the first Canadian critical journal issue devoted to her work[31] and the first brief critical book on her writing.[32] These prepared the way for the real turning point in Canadian public awareness of Gallant when the "Canadian" publication of *From the Fifteenth District* in 1979 drew reviews right across the country. (There is an irony here since Random House actually "made" the book and Macmillan of Canada simply bought the American plates.) In 1981 came *Home Truths*, a collection specifically Canadian in focus. Gallant's consequent publicity tour was her first in Canada. Her play *What Is to Be Done?* was performed in Toronto in the fall of 1982 (and again in Montreal in the fall of 1984). Between 1981 and 1983, all of her books except *The Other Paris* appeared in Canadian paperback editions. During 1983–84, while writer-in-residence at the University of Toronto, she travelled extensively in Canada to speak and give readings. She was interviewed widely and finally became much better known to Canadians.

The lion's share of commentary on Gallant's work lies in reviews of her books. American reviewers of *The Other Paris* in 1956, aware of her as a *New Yorker* writer, understandably thought she was American and compared her work to that of Eudora Welty, Jean Stafford, Hortense Calisher, Flannery O'Connor, and Henry James. American reviewers of subsequent collections continued to place her work against the backdrop of American writing.

By the time *Green Water, Green Sky* appeared in 1959, reviewers recognized that Gallant was a consummate craftsman. Constance Pendergast's four-paragraph review in *Saturday Review* is particularly useful since it mentions almost all the elements of Gallant's technical agility which reviewers have admired over the years. She points to the exactness of Gallant's imagery, noting her ability to select the "single sharp detail," and she commends Gallant for her technical ability, her skilful handling of time, her economical prose style, her shrewd insight, and her "illuminating wit."[33] Pendergast's comments, like those of many later reviewers, read like excerpts from Ferguson's discussion of the modern short story's "formal and stylistic economy" and its "foregrounding of style" (Ferguson, p. 15), encompassing such factors as economy of language, poetic density, exact diction, use of simile and metaphor, verbal polish, and selection of *le mot juste* (Ferguson, p. 21).

With the publication of *My Heart Is Broken*, reviewers began to see Gallant as a significant writer of her time. Exile, expatriation, and rootlessness, themes typical of the modern short story, began to be perceived as recurrent in her fiction. Though characteristic of modern fiction, the lack of an authoritative omniscient narrator in Gallant's stories and the limitation of point of view to that of a character or characters in the narrative divided the reviewers of *My Heart Is Broken* into two camps. Elizabeth Janeway is typical of one group when she argues that "there is intention in the grouping of events; we know it at once by the way they 'compose.' But having clumped her plantings, Miss Gallant leaves them to speak for themselves. She will not generalize. She will not force a pattern."[34] Janeway admires Gallant's refusal to point the moral. Eve Auchincloss puts the opposing view, arguing that Gallant's deliberate "withholding of judgment . . . begs the question: why then write the story?" Gallant's stories fail to move because neither the characters nor their author risk emotional involvement and thus "nothing is really changed by these encounters; nothing is added to the sum of life."[35] The split between reviewers who feel Gallant's stories confront the reader with difficult, complex moral issues and those who are disturbed to find her work emotionally shallow (or "cool" and unjudgemental) recurs in reactions to *A Fairly Good Time*,[36] *The Pegnitz Junction*,[37] and *From the Fifteenth District*.[38]

Gallant's *A Fairly Good Time* drew many reviews, among them one by R. V. Cassill on the brilliant handling of gossip in the novel, which made me notice the gossip elsewhere in Gallant's writing.[39] Among those who reviewed *The Pegnitz Junction*, Aviva Layton wrote most intelligently about what distinguishes this book from Gallant's earlier collections of stories — namely, that these stories are all rooted in postwar Germany and share a central metaphor.[40] For most reviewers, *From the Fifteenth District* stood as Gallant's best work to date in the complexity and breadth of its vision, in the mastery of its style, in its maturity and balance. They were impressed by the range of Gallant's characters and by the sweep of European history captured in unheroic lives from the 1930s to the present. Ronald Hatch used his long review to comment on self-aware characters in four stories ("The Moslem Wife" [1976; pp. 36–74], "Baum, Gabriel, 1935–[ ]" [1979; pp. 139–61], "Potter" [1977; pp. 169–212], and "Irina" [1974; pp. 225–43]) who have limited but real freedom.[41] And Grazia Merler used hers to argue that changes in the handling of time and narration (see Ferguson — characteristics 1, 2, and 5) are the best index of the evolution of Gallant's art.[42] *Home Truths* inspired a number of interesting reviews. Several sought to isolate underlying threads in the collection beyond the obvious presence of Canadian characters or background.[43] Many pointed to the Linnet Muir stories as the major achievement of the volume. Ronald Hatch saw Linnet Muir as a character through whom Gallant explores personal freedom and its limits.[44] The present author drew attention to differences between *The New Yorker*'s and this collection's text of the story "Orphans' Progress" and looked at links between Gallant's early journalism and these stories.[45] *What Is to Be Done?*, Gallant's first play, was warmly received, both in the theatre and in book form. Nonetheless several commentators noted that the play lacks dramatic structure and narrative tension, betraying Gallant's inexperience with the form.[46]

A modest number of articles and one book offer some signposts to Gallant's work. Two essays are general in their thrust, though each of them focuses on a particular area of Gallant's fiction. Robertson Davies' "The Novels of Mavis Gallant" is an appreciation of Gallant's style and her "classic" art.[47] George Woodcock's "Memory, Imagination, Artifice: The Late Short Fiction of Mavis Gallant" deepens and enriches our understanding of many aspects of Gallant's work which reviewers had recognized as characteristic, such as her isolated characters, her polished style, her interest in memory, her realism, and her powerful use of images in *The Pegnitz Junction*.[48] Two other critics tackle technical aspects of Gallant's writing with mixed results. Grazia Merler's attempt to define "key qualities of the author's creative imagination" (p. 7) and her identification of "five main narrative patterns or basic situations" (p. 25), in *Mavis Gallant: Narrative Patterns and Devices*, are undercut by inaccurate and blunt readings of individual stories. On the other hand, her concluding chapter, where she examines "The Pegnitz Junction" (1973; *PJ*, pp. 3–88), "The Moslem Wife" (1976; *FFD*, pp. 36–74), and "Potter" (1977; *FFD*, pp. 169–212) as stories of reversed situation and character, and of controlled narrative tone and level, is persuasive and insightful. Michel Fabre's "'Orphans' Progress,' Reader's Progress: Le 'on dit' et le 'non-dit' chez Mavis Gallant" offers a fine series of reflections on Gallant's narrative procedures and on her manipulation of point of view and tone in the story "Orphans' Progress" (1965; *HT*, pp. 56–62). Unfortunately, Fabre based his analysis on the heavily modified *New Yorker* text, unaware that Gallant had been pushed by her *New Yorker* editors to make changes that she later regretted. By the time his article was translated into English two years later, Fabre had discovered that the *Home Truths* text of "Orphans' Progress" differed from the *New Yorker* text, but he assumed wrongly that he had been working on the "original version" and dealt with the *Home Truths* text only in a footnote.[49]

Several articles are thematic, or partly so. In the first academic critical article on Gallant's work, Peter Stevens seems to be setting out to examine in Gallant's three novels the characters' need for escape from the closeness and domination of families. Actually he treats this theme only briefly in his rambling discussion of each book.[50] More recently, David O'Rourke suggests that the stories in *My Heart Is Broken* are unified "through a repetition of theme and technique which approaches pattern." His article, too, is weak. He feels that in each story, "the sterility of an old order, frequently manifested by a pseudo-aristocratic gentility and symbolized by the season of winter, is contrasted with a vitality traditionally assigned to the working class and youth."[51] But Gallant treats the "ideal" represented by the working class and youth ironically. Some interesting thinking about Gallant has been done by Ronald Hatch and Neil Kalman Besner, both of whom are interested in the rhythm of Gallant's career. Hatch looks at two themes and finds changes in the way Gallant handles them in the 1970s. In "The Three Stages of Mavis Gallant's Short Fiction," he sees Gallant's early stories and her German stories as indictments of "liberal humanism" or "romantic individualism." For him the story "Irina" (1974; FFD, pp. 225–43) offers the first indication of the more hopeful attitude found in the Linnet Muir stories later in the 1970s.[52] In "Mavis Gallant and the Expatriate Character," Hatch examines expatriation in Gallant's work, again finding a change in the 1970s when some characters "turn their situations of exile to their advantage."[53] In his excellent doctoral thesis "Mavis Gallant's Short Fiction: History and Memory in the Light of Imagination," Neil Kalman Besner charts a line of development in Gallant's fiction from characters in early stories who miss the significance of revelatory moments, through characters dimly aware of such moments, to characters who explore the significance of such moments. His sense of the shape of Gallant's career is similar to Hatch's.[54] Like Besner, Janice Kulyk Keefer sees history as central in Gallant's work. She uses the first of two recent articles to prepare the ground for the other, as she argues that most criticism of Gallant's work — that focused by national concerns, that concerned with style and technique, and that which acknowledges her technical polish while attacking her for her narrow view of life and for her ironic tone — ignores or downplays what makes Gallant a major writer, namely, "her acute social, political and historical sense."[55] In her second article, "Mavis Gallant and the Angel of History," she demonstrates that Gallant has been exploring the meaning of historical events and setting forth history as lived experience throughout her oeuvre.[56] She finds Gallant's depiction of women central to her engagement with history. Like Besner and Hatch, she discovers in the stories in From the Fifteenth District rays of hopefulness which are new to Gallant's work.

Information about Gallant and her work can also be found in the interviews she has granted since 1955.[57] In the absence of a biography or an autobiography, these interviews are the primary source of biographical data on Gallant. Also, Gallant has been depositing her papers at the Thomas Fisher Rare Book Library at the University of Toronto. Of particular interest are the brief notes Gallant includes with each bundle of typescripts.

Gallant's Works

To date Gallant has written over one hundred stories. She has also written three novels, a novella, satires, a play, essays, and journalism of various sorts (book reviews, movie reviews, a radio and television column, articles). The writing that has given her an international reputation and that she will be remembered for, however, is her stories. Her novels and novella have not made her a comparable reputation in the genre of the novel. Her brief satires are slight. Her play is charming but certainly not a major addition to drama. The journalism she wrote while at *The Standard* is competent, rather than brilliant. Her more recent journalism is much richer, as are several of her essays — especially "The Events in May: A Paris Notebook" (1968; *PN*, pp. 9–95), concerning what happened in the city during May 1968 when a massive student protest resulted in civil disorder, police brutality, and strikes, and her powerful piece on the Gabrielle Russier scandal, "Immortal Gatito: The Gabrielle Russier Case" (1971; *PN*, pp. 96–141).[58] But even these splendid exercises are important not of themselves but for what they reveal about Gallant, the writer of short stories. I am not, therefore, going to discuss the satires, play, essays, or journalism in their own right, though I will refer to them from time to time. The novels and novella are another matter. Though they are not landmarks in the genre of the novel, when they are read as part of the stream of the fiction Gallant has created over the years, they strike the reader as being among the finest things she has done. Moreover, read against the background of the stories, they seem similar in thrust and form, and different only in their greater length. They are of a piece with her story writing and are as important as the best stories from the periods to which they belong.

The genre Mavis Gallant uses most of the time, the short story, is the fictional prose form most comfortable to her. From time to time, she has claimed that she writes stories rather than novels because she cannot financially afford to wait the eighteen months or more necessary for the writing of a novel. This is true in the sense that Gallant has never saved. When she has money, she likes to spend it, living cheerfully with the consequences of such improvidence — "champagne one day" and "no butter" the next.[9] Another reason she has mentioned is that her travels around Europe deprive her of the necessary stretches of unbroken time (Girard and Valette, p. 83). But, of course, she is not forced to travel; rather, travelling is part of her way of life. Clearly the novel does not draw her powerfully enough to make her reorganize her life to accommodate its demands.

A more fundamental reason for not choosing the novel as her basic form is that she doesn't believe that the novel reflects what life is like. As she told Jean Royer, for her,

> Dire 'La vie est un roman'; cela est un mensonge. Parce qu'il n'y a pratiquement pas de liens entre les choses de la vie. Vous-même n'êtes plus le même. Oui, dans un certain sens, vous êtes encore vous. Le Jean Royer de 10 ans est encore en vous mais il est très réduit. Et, ou vous le protégez pour ne pas le blesser, ou vous dites: 'Il s'est trompé sur toute la ligne, je ferai autrement.' On n'est pas toute sa vie exactement les mêmes . . . . [J]e ne crois pas que la vie est un roman continu. Même en lisant Proust, que j'admire beaucoup: sa suite d'oeuvres est bien découpée et le narrateur n'est pas toujours exactement le même, si on lit bien. (Royer, pp. 19, 36)

This belief that life is discontinuous appears in her fiction also. In *Green Water, Green Sky*, for example, the cousins George and Florence encounter each other as children only every two or three years, with the result that "every time it was like meeting a different person" (p. 13). In *A Fairly Good Time*, Shirley Perrigny, seeing her husband on television some time after he left her, was struck by "his newness": "He was freshly minted. She could recognize his face but not his expression. She remembered his voice but not his clothes, and his professional manner daunted her" (p. 193). Given Gallant's conviction that life is not a continuity, it is not surprising that she dislikes writing the bridging passages that link one episode to the next in a novel. In her view, only the great masters of the form can handle such passages convincingly. As she said: "Le roman a besoin de tisser des liens entre les événements, et il faut être Stendhal ou, mieux encore, Flaubert, pour réussir à rendre chaque passage intéressant" (Girard and Valette, p. 83). Such connective tissue, like descriptive passages, is part of the superfluity she associates with the novel, an excess she usually finds unnecessary and boring (Girard and Valette, p. 86).

The short story, on the other hand, both attracts and is congenial to her. Gallant feels that the short story accurately reflects the fact that life is not continuous and coherent but "largely accidental,"[60] full of discrete things with no, or only passing, connection. Life is not a novel but "une suite de nouvelles. Avec certains liens" (Royer, p. 36). Again and again she has turned a rich situation or a complex pattern of relationships into a number of stories rather than shaping her material into a novel. I have in mind interrelated stories like the three about Willi and Ernst ("Willi" [1963], "Ernst in Civilian Clothes" [1963; PJ, pp. 131–47], and "A Report" [1966]), or like the six about Linnet Muir ("In Youth Is Pleasure" [1975; HT, pp. 218–37], "Between Zero and One" [1975; HT, pp. 238–60], "Varieties of Exile" [1976; HT, pp. 261–81], "Voices Lost in Snow" [1976; HT, pp. 282–94], "The Doctor" [1977; HT, pp. 295–316], and "With a Capital T" [1978; HT, pp. 317–30]). Other such related stories are the two about the gallery owner Sandor Speck and his assistant, Walter ("Speck's Idea" [1979; OB, pp. 1–48] and "Overhead in a Balloon" [1984; OB, pp. 49–71), the four about Henri Grippes, Victor Prism, and Mary Margaret Pugh ("A Painful Affair" [1981; OB, pp. 101–10], "Larry" [1981; OB, pp. 111–17], "A Flying Start" [1982; OB, pp. 118–29], and "Grippes and Poche" [1982; OB, pp. 130–50]), the four about Édouard B. and his sharply contrasted wives, Magdalena and Juliette ("A Recollection" [1983; OB, pp. 151–60], "Rue de Lille" [1983; OB, pp. 161–65], "The Colonel's Child" [1983; OB, pp. 166–75], and "Lena" [1983; OB, pp. 176–87]), and sisters Berthe and Marie Carette ("The Chosen Husband," "From Cloud to Cloud," and "Florida" [all 1985]). Shaping her material as stories rather than novels allows Gallant to suppress the connective material she so dislikes. As she said of the stories about Édouard B. and his wives, "Il ne me reste que les quatre temps forts, j'ai éliminé le reste" (Girard and Valette, p. 83).

Yet, how different are these linked stories from Gallant's novel *Green Water, Green Sky?* After all, three of its four sections were published initially as stories. And as in the linked stories, Gallant gives us only "temps forts" in this novel, leaving us to deduce the connective material between them. On the other hand, the four sections of the novel together comprise a unity as they tell the story of Flor's life. They present a story with a beginning, middle, and end, a shape emphasized by the presence of Flor's cousin George in the opening section where we are given the roots of Flor's problem and again in the closing section which takes place after Flor, now mad, is institutionalized.

Almost none of the linked story groups has this kind of overarching unity and completeness. The stories about Willi and Ernst take off in different directions, each focused on a different character. The stories about Linnet Muir, though more closely linked because they have the same narrator and take place in the same period and in the same city, likewise lack unity as a group. The telling of Linnet Muir's life is only one of a number of impulses shaping her stories. In "Varieties of Exile" (1976; *HT*, pp. 261–81), for example, though we learn something about her life, the story is moulded around various exiles she encounters — refugees, married women, remittance men. The series has a beginning in "In Youth Is Pleasure" (1975; *HT*, pp. 218–37) where Linnet tells us about the start of her adult life, but there is no story that provides an ending. The stories about Sandor Speck and his assistant, Walter, likewise lack unity as a pair, since the one is focused on Speck's machinations as he prepares to mount an art show, and the other on Walter's living arrangements. The four stories about Henri Grippes, Victor Prism, and Mary Margaret Pugh on the other hand do have an odd unity. They proceed in wildly different ways: as an altercation between the two writers concerning their relations with Miss Pugh, as a conversation between Miss Pugh's brother Larry and their ne'er-do-well father, as the tale of the fortunes of a projected dictionary of literary biography, and as encounters between Grippes and his tax officers. But along the way, we gain a surprisingly detailed picture of the lives of the men and their patroness. Yet, even when measured against unconventional models like William Faulkner's novels, we can't consider these stories a novel. What they reveal about the three central characters' lives is too scrappy, too discontinuous; the forms of the various stories make the stories pull away from each other; and their combined length (only fifty pages in *Overhead in a Balloon*) is too short. Ironically, given that Gallant deliberately chose to give us only "les quatres temps forts" in the lives of Édouard B. and his two wives, it is this series which is closest to being an unacknowledged novel. This series has a beginning (indeed a beginning for each relationship) and an end (again for each relationship). In the story "Rue de Lille" (1983; *OB*, pp. 161–65), the series also has something of a middle, where much is conveyed in very short compass. But it lacks extension. Together the stories in the series amount to less than forty pages in *Overhead in a Balloon*. In Gallant's most recent series, concerning the Carette sisters, the overarching story is less comprehensive than that in the two preceding groups, but it is too soon to speak with certainty since the series may not be complete. Even though the writing of interconnected stories might seem to suggest that Gallant is moving away from the short story towards the longer fictional form of the novel, examination of the linked stories she has written to date reveals that she is still centred in the short story.

Let me turn now to consider three characteristic features of Gallant's writing — her circling structures, her presentation of character and situation as "puzzles" to be solved, and her use of reflection. These are not new to Gallant; most writers probably make some use of each of the three at some time. Since Gallant stamps the third most powerfully hers, I will look at it at greater length. What makes them worthy of special consideration in Gallant's work is that they constitute almost a signature. It would be most unusual to read two randomly chosen Gallant fictions without encountering one (and probably more) of the three. I shall begin with her circling structures.

The backbone of a Gallant fiction is usually a sequence of happenings in a character's life or in two or three characters' lives. With very few exceptions, Gallant gives us the events of a story's "time present" in order. But in many stories, the flow of events is interrupted as the narrator or a character introduces information or events from the past or (very occasionally) from the future. These interruptions feel like loops, or circles, or perhaps spirals since they return readers to their point of departure or one step past their point of departure. In some instances, it is as if time present were the last scene of a five-act play and all the background information and action leading up to that scene were supplied in a series of asides. Occasionally there is just one loop. Then, time present may occupy only a brief opening passage and the conclusion, with the middle of the story circling back to relate events leading up to the story's opening paragraphs and its resolution. Or time present may occupy much of a story's length with a single loop into the past lodged in its middle. Sometimes there are loops within loops; sometimes the interruptions are relatively minor, mere thoughts entertained by a character. The variations are many.

I am not the only reader of Gallant's stories to say that they circle and spiral. In his 1978 interview with her, Geoff Hancock commented that her stories "have a spiral to them, not a straight linear sense until recently" (Hancock, p. 45). And Gallant replied that her first *New Yorker* editor, William Maxwell, told her in a letter written probably in the early 1960s, "'You've finally stopped going around and around.' But he had never said to me, 'Don't go round and round.' I had no idea I was doing it" (Hancock, p. 46). Both Maxwell and Hancock make it sound as if all of Gallant's stories had circling structures for a time and that after a particular point (early 1960s, or mid-1970s) their story lines straightened out. But this impression is inaccurate. Roughly half of Gallant's stories circle in some way, while the balance proceed in straightforward chronological sequence; the two types of arrangements occur right through her writing. ("Modern" though Gallant's loops are in their departure from "chronological time ordering," most of her stories proceed in part or wholly in temporal sequence. Gallant uses the techniques of the modern short story only when they suit her purposes.)

Part of the reason that so many of Gallant's stories circle in some way may be that her own thinking is not linear. Talking about how a story grows in her mind (and not about how she eventually structures it), Gallant says that a story "builds around its centre, rather like a snail" (Hancock, p. 45). But even if the circles begin that way, that is certainly not the only reason they are there in the finished story. Her circles have many different functions. In a few instances, they introduce a special kind of material that Besner explores in his thesis — key moments from the past of a few of Gallant's characters, moments whose import must be faced if those characters are to develop. In his view, such characters in her early stories fail to grapple with the implications of such past experience, those in slightly later stories partially meet the challenge, and a few in stories from the 1970s accept it, come to terms with the past, and grow in consequence. Usually though, Gallant's circles have to do with such things as pacing, intensity, introducing information for the greatest impact, engaging readers' curiosity and making them think. Only a story-by-story analysis can give a full sense of the effects Gallant achieves with her circling, but several examples will give a sense of how she uses them.

Gallant often uses looping to avoid the monotony of temporal ordering, to group her material meaningfully, to introduce disparate information economically. In a series of such loops through the whole of a short story like "Jorinda and Jorindel" (1959; *HT*, pp. 17–28), or at the beginning of long stories like "The Cost of Living" (1962; *MHB*, pp. 157–93) and "In Youth Is Pleasure" (1975; *HT*, pp. 218–37), she supplies the reader with a great deal of information in very little space. The story "Jorinda and Jorindel" is typical of what Gallant can achieve with this kind of looping. In time present a party guest's exclamation merges with the child Irmgard's dream about a fairy-tale witch, who captures Jorindel in order to turn him into a bird. She wakes with her braids undone, discovers a guest asleep in the hammock outside, goes to the kitchen where her nurse is having tea with the cook, has her hair braided, moves into the breakfast room where she stands next to her mother's chair and hears the adults talking. As the story ends, she thinks about her dream of the night before, recalling it differently than she had at the beginning of the story, but when she wants to discuss it, her parents cut her off. There is much more to the story, however, than these events of time present. The things Irmgard sees and hears as she moves from one minor event to the next prompt little memory excursions, concerning the guest, the cook, the maid, and her summer with the orphan Freddy and with her cousin Bradley. By the time she recalls her dream at the end of the story, the reader has a clear sense of the various elements that have shaped Irmgard's summer and an understanding of why she might dream about a witch capturing and transforming Freddy, or Bradley, or herself.

Excursions away from a story's time present, even when inventively handled, tend to slow a story's momentum. They ask the reader to turn aside from the story's forward flow to attend to things required as background for the main action. Aware of their impact on pace, Gallant places them with care. In many cases such loops occur only in the first third of a story (see "Acceptance of Their Ways" [1960; *MHB*, pp. 3–13] and "A Recollection" [1983; *OB*, pp. 151–60] as early and late examples), not only because they supply information needed at the beginning of the story, but because there they don't impede the story's movement towards its conclusion. The story "Bernadette" (1957; *MHB*, pp. 14–41) is a fine example of a story which begins slowly and gradually gathers momentum through Gallant's careful manipulation of loops. She runs a large risk by departing for five-and-a-half pages from time present after only four sentences. But it is a risk she justifies brilliantly. The loop is technically difficult — it establishes its own time present (a Sunday in October) from which two other little sub-loops depart and return — but the information imparted concerning the Knights' backgrounds, their relationship, and their personalities is vivid with characters' conversation and with astute narrative comment. It is handled with such flair that the reader doesn't resent rereading it and pondering its implications. The remaining narrator-controlled loops — two brief (a paragraph or less each) and one longer (two pages) — carry the reader to the story's tenth page. For its remaining eighteen pages, the story flows forward unimpeded, necessary aspects of the past appearing briefly in characters' thoughts.

Gallant also uses loops to help establish other kinds of story rhythms besides simple acceleration. Midstory loops, for example, may offer a resting point, a time for reassessment, for pulling things into perspective, before a narrative moves on to its conclusion. Shirley Perrigny's forty-page examination in *A Fairly Good Time* of the past events that resulted in her losing her husband and her job functions this way. Midstory loops may also contribute to a ruminative, balanced rhythm as they do in "Malcolm and Bea" (1968; *EW*, pp. 106–19), one of several of Gallant's stories divided into numbered sections. Each of that story's five parts has its own shape and completeness, encouraging readers to progress in a measured way, considering and weighing what they are being shown. This is as true of the first, second, and fifth sections, which take readers through several scenes of an afternoon and evening of the same day, as it is of the third part, which loops back a number of years to examine the sequence of events leading up to Malcolm and Bea's marriage, and of the fourth part, which circles back to a conversation Malcolm had with a neighbour earlier that same day.

Gallant is amazingly inventive and fresh in the ways she uses the loops, but I will include just one further example. On occasion she employs them to create the feel of a thinking mind darting off on side issues, using mental shorthand, leaping from one subject to another, linking things by association rather than logic. She doesn't actually duplicate a mind thinking; that would be a sure way to bewilder readers. Rather she gives a sense of a mind's movement, carefully including just enough data so that readers can, with some careful thinking, deduce how to place what they are being told. Part 1 of *Green Water, Green Sky* and "The Cost of Living" (1962; *MHB*, pp. 157–93), for example, both create a sense of a mind thinking by establishing the story's time present and then circling away into events which precede *and* follow. Since they expect readers to keep several streams of information in mind simultaneously, such stories are intellectually demanding, but Gallant intends that they be so. Loops introducing past and future events are just one of many techniques she uses to make her readers stand back from a story and grasp its patterns before making judgements.

We have seen that many of Gallant's stories are characterized by circling structures. Another recurrent feature in her fiction is the presentation of character and situation as "puzzles" to be solved. This tendency may have its source in Gallant's own experience. Her moves from one to another of her seventeen schools repeatedly plunged her into new contexts which she had to grasp quickly if she were to fit in. As a reporter travelling all over Quebec and as a traveller about Europe, she was likewise presented again and again with fresh human conundrums to understand. She was a passer-through, a visitor, an outsider, needing to figure out the lay of the land. Something of this perspective surely surfaces in Gallant the writer, who says of her characters: "... les personnages ne sont pas vos créations, ils existent d'eux-mêmes, et ils se révèlent à vous. Vous les décodez comme vous décodez les personnes que vous rencontrez" (Girard and Valette, p. 86). Whatever the origin of her interest in human puzzles, her underlying purpose in presenting them in her stories appears to be to prod her readers to be active as they read — to weigh, to assess, to make connections — rather than passively to let a story wash over them.

Gallant draws her readers' attention to human puzzles in many ways, and she tries to move readers to solve them. Sometimes she simply uses the word puzzle or an equivalent to alert readers to the presence of a conundrum. The story "The Statues Taken Down" (1965), for example, moves towards the moment when Dorothy's younger brother Hal "stolidly tried to put together the egg puzzle he had bought in the early days, at the Palais-Royal. He had all the

pieces, nothing was missing, but still could not make it whole."
Earlier Dorothy had fitted together the bits and pieces of information
about her parents' relationship that she had collected from several
sources. The pattern she had constructed no longer seemed plausible. So now she "pulled everything she knew apart and started
from the beginning."[61] Another story, "Baum, Gabriel, 1935–( )"
(1979; FFD, pp. 139–61), shifts the image a bit. There Gabriel "still
imagined that everyone's life must be about the same, something like
a half-worked crossword puzzle. He was always on the lookout for
definitions and new solutions. When he moved close to other people,
however, he saw that their lives were not puzzles but problems set in
code, no two of which ever matched" (p. 144). Other fictions use the
word "riddle" or imply that there is a mystery because they use
words like "clues."[62]

Gallant also draws attention to human conundrums by means of
characters who are aware of a mystery, and who then react to its
presence in some way. Their words, thoughts, and actions provoke
readers to tackle the problem themselves. The least serious of these
characters are the gossips. No one would listen to them were there
not some enigma, some unknown factor, which their gossip pretends
to explain. One of Gallant's characters says, "Gossip implies at least
a theory about behaviour," and human behaviour, as another
observes, is "the only riddle worth a mention."[63] Everyone knows
that the "theory" gossip offers is suspect. Yet often there is little else
to go on. It is thus a perfect instrument for pushing readers not only
to see that there is a puzzle but to do some thinking about it. The
gossip in fictions like "By the Sea" (1954), "Poor Franzi" (1954; OP,
pp. 54–68), "Careless Talk" (1963), "Its Image on the Mirror"
(1964; MHB, pp. 55–155), "The Sunday after Christmas" (1967), A
Fairly Good Time (1970), and "The Moslem Wife" (1976; FFD,
pp. 36–74) provokes readers to sift its abundant chaff for its odd ker-
nel of truth by considering it in relation to other evidence.

Gossips offer casual hypotheses concerning human conundrums
in public. Many of Gallant's characters privately assess the
situations around them in thoughts that Gallant makes available as
she moves point of view from one character to another. Like gossip,
these interpretations point to the fact that there is a puzzle while
offering a solution that may or may not be accurate. The fact that
readers know that such interpretations are subjective and prone to
error pushes them to tackle the puzzle themselves. If readers should

forget, Gallant has many ways of reminding them of the limitations of such opinion. In "Night and Day" (1962), she has an amnesiac accident victim revise his assessments of the situation in which he finds himself day by day as his memory returns, as he is gradually weaned from morphine and regains his health. In "Luc and His Father" (1982; *OB*, pp. 72–100), she introduces passages from a young visitor's diary which wildly misinterpret scenes that readers have already witnessed. But these are unusual examples. More typical is the way she handles Berthe's assessments of what Uncle Gildas, Louis Driscoll, and Marie Carette did, thought, and felt in "The Chosen Husband" (1985). The verbs "could not have," "could never be," "may have frightened," "must have said," "seemed to think," and the words "probably" and "perhaps,"⁶⁴ reveal that her thoughts are only conjectural. Readers inevitably find themselves speculating on how far to accept Berthe's views as accurate, weighing what they know of her character and about the situation.

In addition to prodding readers to think about character and situation by means of the public statements of gossips and the private assessments of other characters, Gallant challenges readers to consider the activities of individuals who are so rivetted by a human mystery that they enter on something approximating an "investigation." The problems that command their attention are various. Sometimes the enigma is the bewildering behaviour of adults. The child Dorothy in "The Statues Taken Down" (1965) tackles one such puzzle. Often those who look into the curious actions of adults failed to solve the puzzle as children (as Dorothy fails) and so return to it as adults — Irmgard in "Rose" (1960), Stefan in "One Aspect of a Rainy Day" (1962), and Linnet Muir in "In Youth Is Pleasure" (1975; *HT*, pp. 218–37), "Voices Lost in Snow" (1976; *HT*, pp. 282–94), and "The Doctor" (1977; *HT*, pp. 295–316). Sometimes the mystery concerns a person whose life is entwined with that of the investigator. Thus Amalia asks endless questions about the woman who helped her escape with her husband from Rumania years before ("Questions and Answers" [1966]), Malcolm yearns to understand his wife, Bea ("Malcolm and Bea" [1968; *EW*, pp. 106–19]), and Shirley wants to comprehend why her husband Philippe left her (*A Fairly Good Time*). Sometimes characters try to ferret out every detail of another person's life at least partly because they want to be like the other person. In "Acceptance of Their Ways" (1960; *MHB*, pp. 3–13), for example, Lily Littel, desiring to be a gentlewoman, puts herself to school to Mrs. Garnett and Mrs. Freeport, deliberately noting every nuance of their behaviour. The narrators in "The Cost of Living" (1962; *MHB*, pp. 157–93) and "Its Image on the Mirror" (1964; *MHB*, pp. 55–155) want to absorb, not just the manners, but the thoughts, feelings, and inner reality of the person who most fascinates them. In order to solve their chosen mystery, such sleuthing characters together sift a surprisingly broad range of evidence, evidence that they seek out or that comes their way. They examine documents like letters and photographs; indirect sources like novels, articles, and research projects; memories; gossip and informed opinion; family background and national conditioning; and on and on. (Consider, for example, Shirley Perrigny's ruminations in *A Fairly Good Time* under the heading "Why P. Left Me and How I Lost My Job" [pp. 211–51], ruminations which, though wide-ranging, constitute only part of the "evidence" brought into play in the novel as a whole.)

Readers of one of Gallant's detection stories are moved (like readers of ordinary detective stories) by the sheer interest of the problem to match wits with the sleuth and to try to solve it themselves. In some stories, they are led to see the investigator too as a puzzle worth investigation. Their speculations about these puzzles often bring them to conclusions different than those of the story's sleuthing character. They come to see the gentility which is Lily Littel's goal, in "Acceptance of Their Ways" (1960; *MHB*, pp. 3–13), not as worthwhile and admirable, but as shabby and pettily tyrannical. They suspect that, in "Rose" (1960), Irmgard is wrong to regard her recollection of her cousin Rose and her grandmother as a hallucination, and that rejecting the memory is less upsetting than accepting its implications — that her proper grandmother loved this illegitimate cousin more than her. They see that Stefan's silent, unwilling involvement in the general strike in France in "One Aspect of a Rainy Day" (1962) brings deeper understanding of his brother Günther's silence during the oath of allegiance to Hitler years before; but they find Stefan's downplaying of his experience at the end of the story deeply disturbing. They notice inconsistencies in the tales told by the narrators in "The Cost of Living" (1962; *MHB*, pp. 157–93) and "Its Image on the Mirror" (1964; *MHB*, pp. 55–155) and note that jealousy occasionally distorts what both narrators report, and so on. In a very few cases, they find themselves matching wits with an investigator who is as wise or wiser than they. It is clear, for example, that when Linnet Muir finds that she cannot solve the puzzle of her father's death in "In Youth Is Pleasure" (1975; *HT*, pp. 218–37), she makes the right decision: she lets the unresolvable conundrum go by *choosing* an interpretation that seems appropriate and gets on with her own life. As readers move from one detection story to the next, they realize that the underlying goal of many of these investigations is quite different from their declared objectives. As the fortune teller tells Amalia *vis-à-vis* her obsessive questions about her friend Marie in "Questions and Answers": "... it's another way of talking about yourself."[65] The ultimate goal is self-knowledge and self-definition, but few characters have even a partial sense that this is what the search is about.

Gallant has one further ploy to make her readers see characters and situation as puzzles and to involve them in solving them: she makes her readers play detective themselves. Concerned as they are with their own problems, the various observers of Flor in *Green Water, Green Sky*, for example, provide only hints concerning the novel's central question, "Why does Flor go mad?" Readers must draw the clues into a pattern. Likewise they have to put together the bits and pieces supplied by the little boy Dennis and by Roy McLaughlin to understand the tragedy awaiting the war bride and her son in "Up North" (1959; *HT*, pp. 49–55). Stories like "Saturday" (1968; *HT*, pp. 29–48), "The Captive Niece" (1969), "Good Deed" (1969), "The Rejection" (1969), "The Prodigal Parent" (1969; *EW*, pp. 120–25), "New Year's Eve" (1970; *EW*, pp. 130–41), "The Pegnitz Junction" (1973; *PJ*, pp. 3–88), and "Baum, Gabriel, 1935–( )" (1979; *FFD*, pp. 139–61) challenge the reader to figure out what they are about, to find the thread that binds the elements into a meaningful whole.

A third recurrent feature in Gallant's writing is her use of reflection. Since reflection often appears in images, it gives some sense of Gallant's handling of the modern story's heightened, economical style. Her characters regularly glimpse themselves or others in store windows, in people's sunglasses, in windows blackened by night, in magnifying makeup mirrors, in dressing-table three-way mirrors, in long mirrors, in a fortune teller's magic hand mirror, in someone else's eyes, in a car's rear-view mirror, in mirrored rooms, in looking glasses, in the dusty glass of bookcases, and in pier glasses. They do so because Gallant herself is fascinated by the possibilities inherent in mirroring and reflection. When playing "associations" during her interview with Fletcher Markle, her response to "mirror" was: "Love mirrors. I have a book about them. Not so much looking at oneself as, oh, the whole philosophy of mirrors, the image, the thing going on and on, the eternal thing, you know" (Markle, 29 Jan. 1965). Many instances of reflection in her fiction (and in her essays and journalism, though I won't be discussing these) supply a vivid detail concerning the character reflected but fall into no discernable pattern and evince no recurrent way of using reflection. A paper could be focused on these alone. Other examples of reflection fall into categories and patterns. Because the latter reveal Gallant's habitual cast of mind *vis-à-vis* reflection, I will concentrate primarily on them.

She uses reflection to comment on characters who are self-centred, self-involved, or concerned with their appearance. In these instances a narrator wryly observes the person or people looking at him- or themselves, noting the exuberant egoism of children (as the children admire their reflections in "Jorinda and Jorindel" [1959; *HT*, pp. 17–28]), the peacock vanity of a self-centred adult (as the magnate preens himself before a mirror in "An Alien Flower" [1972; *PJ*, pp. 167–93]), the self-containment of a woman who has learned to depend only on herself (as Marian objectively contemplates her own image in "Thieves and Rascals" [1956]), the self-conscious dramatizing of an aspiring actress (as Sylvia appeals to her mirrored self in the midst of conversation in "The Cost of Living" [1962; *MHB*, pp. 157–93]), or the inaccessibility of a woman to her husband (as Bea envisions her essential self as a slight figure carrying a beautiful, untouched object on a June day and walking towards not her husband but herself in "Malcolm and Bea" [1968; *EW*, pp. 106–19]).

Several times, Gallant has people function as mirrors (the word mirror appears in three of the following examples and is implied in the fourth). Sometimes she has characters reflect back the image other characters wish to project, or sometimes the image they return is their own view. Wishart gives back Bonnie's chosen image in Part III of *Green Water, Green Sky*; Janet reflects to Digby an image unlike any he had perceived hitherto in other mirrors, an image which inspires decisiveness and self-confidence, in "Two Questions" (1961); and her first father-in-law reflects Shirley Perrigny as "a great lump of a Campfire Girl" in *A Fairly Good Time* (p. 239). A related but broader mirroring appears in "Jorinda and Jorindel" (1959; *HT*, pp. 17–28) where the mother selectively reflects life for her daughter, giving light to some things, darkening others.

Gallant also uses reflection to underline family continuity (an instance of mirrored images "going on and on"?) by having individuals find in their own reflections a mirroring of their parents. Thus, looking into a mirror, a woman suddenly glimpses her mother's expression (Shirley in *A Fairly Good Time*) or a man sees himself gesturing or moving in a way that recaptures his father (Thomas Bestermann in "The Latehomecomer" [1974; *FFD*, pp. 117–38]). Sometimes characters find in their reflections a reassuring point of familiarity in an otherwise alien situation. There is a moment in *A Fairly Good Time*, for example, when Shirley Perrigny, a Canadian living in Paris, experiences tremendous relief on sighting a familiar figure, sensing that this person knows her and will not make mistakes. The person is her own image in a mirror. The title character in "The Chosen Husband" (1985) is drawn to his own reflection as the only familiar object in the room where he first meets the girl he will marry, though, unlike Shirley, he knows he is looking at himself.

There are many ways a writer might have gone about making these varied points. Why, apart from her delight in mirrors, does Gallant make them by means of reflection? She probably chooses this method because, as characters contemplate their own images, there is a curious meeting of outer and inner, of the outer appearance that others see and the inner, viewing self. Much can be revealed graphically and economically in such moments about the delicate balance between a person and the surrounding world. Gallant, who often draws attention by means of shifts in point of view to the difference between characters' views of their "selves" and the way they appear to others, uses reflection as another method to comment on the subtle relations between the self and the world.

Mirrors also function as truth tellers in Gallant's fiction. Sometimes, as in Chekhov's "The Lady with the Pet Dog," mirrors tell characters like Bonnie in Part II of *Green Water, Green Sky*, Jean Price in "Its Image on the Mirror" (1964; *MHB*, pp. 55–155), or Piotr in "Potter" (1977; *FFD*, pp. 169–212) that they are growing old. Sometimes mirrors have other unpleasant truths to tell. The looking glass over the sink in "Sunday Afternoon" (1962; *MHB*, pp. 203–17) gives back the girl's curlers and bathrobe, the glass in "A Report"

(1966) reveals that M. Monnerot's German military costume is comprised of ill-assorted components, and the bathroom mirror in "The Captive Niece" (1969) reflects the girl's frightened, small face. Very occasionally the truth captured is one of beauty, as in Molly's glimpse of her nude mother in "The Remission" (1979; *FFD*, pp. 75–116). These are all relatively minor revelations, mere blips in the story line, but sometimes the truth revealed in a mirror precipitates a story's turning point or draws a conclusion. Thus, the young wife in "Autumn Day" (1955; *OP*, pp. 31–53) who briefly hates her husband for supposing that either an apartment or a child will solve her uncertainty and misery, notices his helplessness and unhappiness in the mirror and for the first time wonders how marriage feels to him. They look at each other in the mirror, really seeing each other at last, and the reader senses that now their marriage has a chance of succeeding. In "Sunday Afternoon" (1962; *MHB*, pp. 203–17), Ahmed considers making a move towards Veronica, only to decide that his friendship with Jim is worth more to him than the girl. Veronica, who has been aware of Ahmed's wandering thoughts, senses, as she watches the men's reflections in the window, that the upshot of the incident is that the men draw closer together. In "The Ice Wagon Going Down the Street" (1963; *MHB*, pp. 246–73), Peter Frazier, who has taken a drunken girl home from a party at his hostess' and his wife's behest, suddenly realizes, as he sees himself comforting the girl in the mirror over the fireplace, that in this situation lies the potential for disaster. The potential is real, but he and the girl both turn away from it. What is it about seeing something in a mirror that precipitates such moments of insight? It has to do, I think, with the objectivity born of seeing things at one remove, so that emotions do not blur perception of the other person or of the situation. In the last two examples, it also has to do with seeing things composed as a scene, a scene which in the first instance significantly excludes Veronica and in the second includes Peter Frazier.

In several longer stories and in all her novels, Gallant introduces not just a single moment of mirroring but a number of interrelated instances. Indeed, she points to the importance of reflection and mirroring in the titles of two of her three novels — *Green Water, Green Sky* and "Its Image on the Mirror." In these longer fictions, she sometimes uses a series of reflections to mark ground gained or lost. In his thesis, Besner looks at one such series in "The Moslem

Wife" (1976; *FFD*, pp. 36–74). Another series that helps establish the trajectory of a story occurs in "Speck's Idea" (1979; *OB*, pp. 1–48), where the stages in Sandor Speck's mounting of a show in his art gallery are underlined by changes in his reflection. Gallant makes no fuss about these references to his reflection, but it is clear that she expects each instance to be noticed. When Speck notes that "his features, afloat on a dusty pane, were not quite as pinched as they had been the other night, but the image was still below par for a man considered handsome" (p. 21), or when he feels much later that "he was a saner, stronger, wiser person than the Sandor Speck who had seen his own tight smile on M. Chassepoule's window only two months before" (p. 47), Gallant expects that her readers will recall the moment close to the beginning of the story when Speck saw his smile reflected in Chassepoule's window: "It was pinched and tight, and he looked a good twenty years older than thirty-nine" (p. 7).

Two other series perform a similar function in two of the sections comprising Gallant's first novel, *Green Water, Green Sky*. Early in Part II, Flor steals glimpses of herself in shop windows to assure herself of her own existence. As she retreats into insanity later in the story, mirrors and mirroring become more disturbing. Reflected in a long glass, she looks unreal, disconnected from life — like "a pale rose model in a fashion magazine" or "a porcelain figure, intended to suggest that . . . the dream of love is preferable to love in life" (p. 77). And the mirror which "witnessed" her (p. 77) seems to be more a centre of consciousness than Flor herself. In Part III, Wishart invents a double persona: "the sardonic Englishman in America, the awfully decent American in England" (p. 98). In a store window, he admires his reflection because it seems to confirm that he has projected his persona successfully; later he believes that the miniature of this reflection which he sees in Bonnie's sunglasses is the view of him she accepts, only to discover still later that she had never believed in it.

In Part I of *Green Water, Green Sky*, Gallant uses mirroring in a different way, to help readers understand her character Flor. The title of the novel is drawn from Flor's recollection of a day in Venice ten years before. She reminds her cousin George of that day: "Everything was so clear and green, green water, even the sky looked green to me." Flor's eyes are then associated with water, for they are "green as the lagoon had been" (p. 17). On that day ten years before, Flor had told George that she would be loyal to her mother in "a cry of despair, love and resentment so woven together that even Flor couldn't tell them apart" (p. 11). Ever since, whenever George thinks of Flor, he recalls "love and resentment, . . . one reflecting the other, water under sky" (p. 19). Moreover, an incident on the childhood day hinted that this intertwining of love and resentment is linked with death. Fourteen-year-old Flor, her eyes "green as water" (p. 6), threatened to push seven-year-old Georgie into the water, a threat which made him remember the time he had fallen into a pond, "the heavy green water closing out the sky . . . the mossy water over his mouth. He must have been on his back; there was a memory of sky" (pp. 6–7). The person who "drowns," of course, is not George but Flor, as Gallant implies in Part II by having Bob Harris recollect Flor's "drowned face" (p. 37) and by having Flor herself think of narrowing shores, encroaching seas, and boats drifting away from the shore as she withdraws into madness.

Reflection plays an important role in Gallant's second novel too. The title, "Its Image on the Mirror" (1964; *MHB*, pp. 55–155), is drawn from the lines of Yeats' "The Shadowy Waters" which frame the novel, standing as its epigraph and recalled in its final paragraph:

> What is love itself,
> Even though it be the lightest of light love,
> But dreams that hurry from beyond the world
> To make low laughter more than meat and drink,
> Though it but set us sighing? Fellow-wanderer,
> Could we but mix ourselves into a dream
> Not in its image on the mirror!
>
> (*MHB*, p. 55)

The love in the novel, which is so ungraspable, is the familial love the story's narrator, Jean Price, feels primarily for her sister, Isobel, and, in diminishing intensity, for her mother, her brother, Frank, and her father. It is a love that is almost always veiled or muffled. On the one occasion when Jean tries to show her sister the depth of her feelings by reaching out to take her hand, her sister promptly withdraws. The mirror of the epigraph is evoked near the beginning of the story when Jean, visiting her parents in the old family home, notices a ghost watching her watching herself in the glass in her old bedroom. She implies that the ghost is either that of Frank, who was killed in the Second World War, or that of Isobel, now married and living in Venezuela and "equally lost" (p. 60). At the end of the story, she decides that the ghost is not Frank's, so presumably it is Isobel's.

Mirroring and reflection are also present as ideas. The family members share genes and thus appearance; they have experiences and background in common and thus attitudes. The notion of one reflecting another appears again and again. Jean is like her mother. She tells us:

> As I grow older I see that our gestures are alike. It touches me to notice a movement of hands repeated — a manner of folding a newspaper, or laying down a comb. I glance sharply behind me and I know I am reproducing my mother's quick turn of head. Our voices are alike. We have the flat voice of our part of the country; our r's fall like stones. (p. 65)

Frank and Isobel as children are alike in many ways. For the sisters, who are of the same generation and the same sex, likeness often moves towards identity, as when Jean thinks she will die if Isobel dies, or is attracted to the men her sister loves, or is mistaken for her sister. Ironically, as well as likeness, there is also difference, indeed opposition: the one sister bohemian, the other dutiful; the one emotional, the other contained; and so on. The narrating sister vacillates, shifting between attraction and repulsion, describing similarity and difference, until the story fetches up at the moment when she reaches out and finds herself more distant than ever.

Familial reflection plays a role in the novel *A Fairly Good Time* also, primarily in Shirley's mirroring of her mother's attitudes, gestures, training, habits, and beliefs, which culminates in the moment when Shirley looks into "the pretty gilt-framed mirror in the hall" and notices that "her face bore an unexpected resemblance to her mother's" (p. 262). There is also a larger system of resemblances in national similarities. To Italians, Shirley and her first husband, Peter Higgins, look like each other. People mistake them for sister and brother. "Only a North American could have guessed what our families were, what our education amounted to, and where he had got the money to spend on travelling" (p. 231).

Reflection also looms large in Shirley's attempt to come to understand her second husband, his view of her, and their marriage.

Sometimes the actual word *mirror* is used; sometimes reflection and mirroring are present as ideas. For example, Philippe writes an article concerning their honeymoon trip to Berlin. Shirley, pregnant, throws up regularly on the trip. He intends to include her illness as something "both poignant and comic," but significantly in the end, ". . . he eliminated Shirley altogether. In the long first-person account of the trip that appeared in *Le Miroir* it was clear that Philippe had traveled alone" (p. 38). Though it is the newspaper which is called "The Mirror," the article is also a kind of mirror, one that reflects only what Philippe finds acceptable. Indeed, all Philippe's articles for *Le Miroir* reflect something of Philippe, as do his pieces of research and his more private papers. Another place where mirrors and reflections appear in *A Fairly Good Time* is in the pages of a typescript novel written by Philippe's friend Geneviève:

> I looked at myself in the mirror   I saw the delicate
> face and soft unruly   Upstairs I saw my face in the
> Venetian dressing table with its charming   the face of
> Saint Veronica after she
>   . . . I saw my small face in the black wind-screen   I
> looked like Lazarus risen from the dead   bruised arms
> . . . I saw my small blanched face in the bowl of a spoon . . . .
> (pp. 20–21)

Geneviève's view of herself is revealed in such excerpts, but more importantly her typescript reflects her view of Philippe (brilliant journalist, spiritual guide) and Shirley (North American slut, dead of drink and disaster).

My final example of reflection is drawn from one of Gallant's recent stories about art and artists. This is a singular, rather than a reiterated, use of reflection, but it is of particular interest for two reasons. As an instance of Gallant using reflection in concert with another kind of image, it touches, albeit briefly, on another area — images related to reflection — which would reward investigation. Also, since Gallant incorporates something of her own experience into her story, this particular example of reflection allows a brief glance at Gallant the writer.

The images Gallant uses in association with reflection in the story in question, "Grippes and Poche" (1982; *OB*, pp. 130–50), concern windows. Long important in Gallant's work, windows are occasionally linked with reflection. Like mirrors, windows can be used to say something about the relationship of inside and outside. Sometimes Gallant has characters who are inside a room look through a window at the world beyond, perhaps seeing something that parallels their own experience (Veronica Baines looking at the threesome in the café across the street at the beginning of "Sunday Afternoon" [1962; *MHB*, pp. 203–17]), perhaps seeing a person who is to join them inside (the Carette women watching the arrival of the stranger who is to marry Marie in "The Chosen Husband" [1985]), perhaps choosing to leap through to the outside (Luc briefly attempting to get beyond his parents' control in "Luc and His Father" [1982; *OB*, pp. 72–100]). Sometimes she has a character look from a darkened street through a window at a lighted room, hungering to share the life within ("Its Image on the Mirror" [1964; *MHB*, pp. 99, 149]), or has characters within a lighted room feeling their private emotions exposed to those who watch from the street ("Its Image on the Mirror," p. 131). All it takes is a shift in lighting to transform a window from a transparency giving access to the outside to a reflector giving back the room and its occupants within. Gallant capitalizes on the possibilities of this shift at the end of "Sunday Afternoon."

In "Grippes and Poche" Gallant uses windows and reflection to say something about the origins of a writer's characters. Here, "a series of novels offered themselves" to the French writer Henri Grippes as "shadowy outlines behind a frosted-glass pane. He knew he must not let them crowd in all together, or keep them waiting too long. His foot against the door, he admitted, one by one, a number of shadows that turned into young men, each bringing his own name and address . . ." (*OB*, p. 136). The young men become the central figures in a series of novels. Gradually, though, "the frosted-glass door was reverting to dull white; there were fewer shadows for Grippes to let in" (*OB*, p. 145), and the series draws to a close. But in time, Grippes' imagination offers up a new character, a woman who materializes initially in a church, walks out into the street, and then "move[s] off in a gray blur. There was a streaming window between them Grippes could not wipe clean" (*OB*, p. 149). He imagines her entering a dark dining room, and there he resolves to keep her until she tells him her name and, presumably, becomes the central character in a novel.

Grippes has no idea where the young male characters come from. "At the same time, it seemed to Grippes that their wavering, ruffled reflection should deliver something he alone might recognize. What did he see, bending over the pond of his achievement?" (*OB*, p. 138). What he sees finally is that O. Poche, the taxation officer to whom he reports for many years and about whom he knows only that he eventually marries, is the ultimate inspiration for the series of male characters. When he no longer has to visit Poche, that source dries up. Speculating about the possible consequences of Poche's seeming misinterpretation of the tax rules, Grippes blunders on a new source of inspiration. He imagines Poche's superior, the woman tax officer to whom he reported only once, telling him to repay the money Poche has mistakenly allowed him. As he contemplates this woman, his imagination offers up the woman in the church, the woman who will probably become a character.

By means of these window and reflection images, Gallant captures two sides of a writer's experience with characters. On the one hand, characters seem to have an independent existence (an independence perhaps reinforced in Gallant's own experience by the fact that many of her characters are inspired by people she glimpses in public places such as railway stations or restaurants).[66] The seeming exteriority of characters is caught in the various shadows presenting themselves *outside* the "frosted" or "streaming" window. On the other hand, the fact that characters are created by the writer is captured in the shadows being ushered inside, and in the image of the writer peering at reflections in "the pond of his achievement."

All three characteristic features of Gallant's writing — her loops, her puzzles, her use of reflection — appeal primarily to the mind rather than the emotions. They thus contribute to the sense that some reviewers have that her work is cool, cerebral, emotionless. Here it is worth noting that Gallant is not necessarily in a dispassionate frame of mind as she writes a story. Asked about "Ernst in Civilian Clothes" (1963; *PJ*, pp. 131–47), she (though antimilitarist) talked about how shabbily the legionaires, who had risked their lives for their country, were treated when the French Foreign Legion was disbanded. She continued:

If you take someone who's a little girl who's been ill-treated, naturally you're on her side, but take a man who's an ex-Nazi who has been unjustly treated, your sympathies are against him. But if you believe in justice, they've got in the end to be for him . . . . And that's why I took that particular thing. I was in a white-hot rage when I wrote that.[67]

I suspect that she was just as angry when she wrote stories like "Going Ashore" (1954; *OP*, pp. 69–103), "Rose" (1960), or "Orphans' Progress" (1965; *HT*, pp. 56–62), where children are not cared for, are lied to, or are handled insensitively. Doubtless, other powerful emotions lie behind other stories. But, with the exception of humour, Gallant keeps her own feelings out of her stories so that they do not blur her exposition of the complexities of a situation. Moreover, she presents her material in such a way as to keep readers' own emotional responses at bay to ensure that they are alert to all shades of the tale presented to them. That accomplished, I suspect Gallant wants feeling to play its part. And it does, despite the claims of some reviewers. Many of her stories elicit strong feeling as one looks back on them.

Apart from relatively recent bibliographies, little scholarly work has been done on Gallant. As a result, critics have only begun to tap such resources as Gallant's early journalism or her writing for *The New York Times Book Review*. The material in the Thomas Fisher Rare Book Library at the University of Toronto remains barely utilized; the information in interviews and reviews is largely unassimilated; publishers' and agents' files are unexamined. Little is known even about something as basic as the collecting of Gallant's stories into the volumes that are the basis of many people's knowledge of her work. Yet knowing who controlled the various aspects of assembling a volume of stories, and knowing what was chosen, what rejected, and why, are important. If, for example, an author has done her own collecting, she may be underlining connections and relationships in her arrangement of stories, pointing directions in her choice of title, revealing that she values some stories more than others, as she chooses what to include and what to reject. An editor or publisher assembling a collection may likewise be underlining connections and so on, but we value an editor's or publisher's opinion differently than an author's. No matter who has drawn a volume together, it is important to know the principle of selection and the field from which the choice was made, so that it is clear just what the collection represents.

CAMROSE LUTHERAN COLLEGE
LIBRARY

Gallant's general position on the assembling of collections is that this is a publisher's, rather than an author's, job; decisions concerning which stories to include, how to arrange them, and what to call the resultant volume are in her view a publisher's.[68] However, as we shall see, she actually involves herself far more than this would suggest. According to Gallant, Houghton Mifflin chose and arranged the stories in her first collection, *The Other Paris* (1956). The arrangement is not chronological. Her publishers also titled the volume, choosing to call it after a story which Gallant had submitted untitled to *The New Yorker*.

The resultant collection gives a good sense of Gallant early in her career as a professional writer. It includes all but two of the stories Gallant published after she left *The Standard* in the summer or fall of 1950 until 1955. The two omitted are weaker than those chosen. Because the collection includes almost all of her early work, it is fair to use it as a basis for characterizing that work. At that point in her career, her stories are set in many places in Europe and in Quebec. Many of her characters are children, adolescents, or young adults, and the stories she creates about them are about innocence, illusion, and romance encountering reality. A few characters grow in understanding, but more retreat or are defeated. Two stories — "The Other Paris" (1953; *OP*, pp. 1–30) and "The Picnic" (1952; *OP*, pp. 104–21) — give some hint of the capacity Gallant developed as a mature writer to show us something of the clash of the values and assumptions of different cultures through the interaction of individual characters.

The next volume to appear, the novel *Green Water, Green Sky* (1959), is not a collection in the usual sense, although three of its sections were originally published as stories. Gallant *did* control the contents of her novel: she planned the four stories as a group, and she decided in what order they should be arranged. This volume represents a short, concentrated phase of Gallant's writing: three of its four sections appeared in *The New Yorker* in June, July, and August of 1959, and the novel was published the same year. Like *The Other Paris*, it is set in several places in Europe (as well as a couple in the United States). It gives the first sample of Gallant's interest in unusual mental states, an interest which reappears occasionally through the balance of her career in characters who are mad, refuse to speak, or suffer from amnesia.

According to Gallant, an editor chose and arranged the stories in her next collection, and gave the volume its title, *My Heart Is Broken* (1964). Again the arrangement is not chronological. Gallant recalls that an effort was made to alternate long with short stories. It is possible that she asked that "Its Image on the Mirror" (1964; *MHB*, pp. 55–155) and "The Cost of Living" (1962; *MHB*, pp. 157–93) be placed next to each other. If she did not ask for this pairing, then the arrangement is astute since the two fictions are associated in Gallant's mind. She told Fletcher Markle that "The Cost of Living" tackled "the same idea in a shorter form" as "Its Image on the Mirror" and that the two depicted "the same relationship between sisters, one attempting to enter into the life of another. The theme of both is domination . . ." (Markle, 29 Jan. 1965).

This collection is different in kind from *The Other Paris*. The earlier volume drew together virtually all the stories from one period. This one selects eight stories from the twenty-eight (I do not include the three stories of *Green Water, Green Sky* in my count) that appeared after the publication of *The Other Paris* in 1956 until 1963, to accompany the short novel or novella[69] "Its Image on the Mirror," which was too brief to publish alone. It has a number of strengths both because and in spite of its limited list of stories. All the stories in it are excellent; none of the half-dozen or so light-weight stories from the period is included. Even though it contains few stories, it reveals that Gallant's range of settings in Europe and Quebec is wide. Now many of her characters are not just away from home temporarily, but are expatriates, wanderers, exiles. Though some of her characters are young and just getting involved in relationships and work, many more are middle-aged and engaged in established patterns of behaviour. The lives of these older characters typically receive a jolt in the course of the story before they settle into familiar grooves once more. As a group the stories of this volume are less hopeful than those of *The Other Paris*. The story "Bernadette" (1957; *MHB*, pp. 14–41) and the short novel "Its Image on the Mirror" join "The Other Paris" (1953; *OP*, pp. 1–30) and "The Picnic" (1952; *OP*, pp. 104–21) as fictions where Gallant depicts not just characters but cultures, in this case different segments of the Quebec mosaic. Inevitably though, the volume does not provide an accurate picture of Gallant's writing during the period it is drawn from. It includes a disproportionate number of longer stories. It finds no place for stories concerning children, though several of those excluded —

"Jorinda and Jorindel" (1959; *HT*, pp. 17–28), "Up North" (1959; *HT*, pp. 49–55), and "Rose" (1960) — are excellent. It gives no hint of budding interests. Gallant's concern about the way adults distort children's memories ("The Old Place" [1958], "Willi" [1963]) and her sense that the world divides into those who remember and those who don't ("Ernst in Civilian Clothes" [1963; *PJ*, pp. 131–47]) begin in this period. Her first grapplings with what happened in Germany before, during, and after World War II also appear during this time in "One Aspect of a Rainy Day" (1962), "Willi," and "Ernst in Civilian Clothes."

Gallant did play a role in the creation of *The Pegnitz Junction* (1973). When Random House forwarded a list of possible stories for a new collection, she recommended that only German stories, including a long piece she had just written ("The Pegnitz Junction," [1973; *PJ*, pp. 3–88]), be used. She wanted "The Latehomecomer" (1974; *FFD*, pp. 117–38) in the volume, but it could not be included because *The New Yorker* did not publish it in time.[70] She insisted that the book be called *The Pegnitz Junction* instead of "Ernst in Civilian Clothes," her editor's title. Though the name she selected is clearly appropriate because it points to the collection's central metaphor, she came to regret her choice; Americans apparently had sufficient trouble pronouncing "Pegnitz" to diminish sales.

Though its stories were written over a decade, this collection is more cohesive than either *The Other Paris* or *My Heart Is Broken*. It is unified by its focus on Germans and by its many-faceted concern with the effect on Germans of the years dominated by Hitler. It is not a complete collection of the German stories, however. It omits not only "The Latehomecomer" but also the stories "Willi" (1963) and "A Report" (1966). One can see why: were all three stories about Willi and Ernst included, they would form a little eddy in the collection, countering the general flow of the volume; Random House selected the richest of the three, "Ernst in Civilian Clothes" (1963; *PJ*, pp. 131–47). In spite of the collection's concern with Germans, its stories represent well Gallant's continuing capacity to set her fictions in diverse places in Europe and North America. What the collection does not offer is a balanced view of Gallant's story writing between 1963 and 1972, selecting as it does only five stories with a particular slant from the twenty-nine of that period. *The Pegnitz Junction* includes medium, long, and *very* long stories, but none of the many short short stories Gallant wrote throughout this period. It gives no hint that she wrote about Canadians at home and abroad. She wrote stories about children, underlining adult irresponsibility towards them. She wrote fictions about people forming relationships deluded by "love" and about marriages between people who have little to say to each other. The role of language in a child's or an adult's sense of self, something mentioned briefly in stories throughout her career, was central to several in this period. And art and artists, present in early stories like "One Morning in June" (1952; *OP*, pp. 173–89), "Wing's Chips" (1954; *OP*, pp. 141–51), and "A Short Love Story" (1957), got their first probing attention in "Bonaventure" (1966; *HT*, pp. 135–72), a story about a musician.

The End of the World and Other Stories (1974) was the brainchild of Robert Weaver, who wished to draw attention to Gallant at a time when few people in Canada appeared to be aware of her work.[71] He sent Gallant a tentative list of selections, some from her two early collections and the balance uncollected stories. He had thought that the out-of-print collected material might be easier to acquire but discovered that she was most enthusiastic about him using uncollected stories. He suspects that the stories from the just-published *Pegnitz Junction* were off limits and thinks that he probably looked for specifically Canadian stories because the volume was to be in the New Canadian Library series. Gallant asked that "Bernadette" (1957; *MHB*, pp. 14–41) not be included. The result of the mixed impulses and constraints under which Weaver laboured is a book comprised of three selections from *The Other Paris*, three from *My Heart Is Broken*, and seven stories with Canadian settings or characters published between 1967 and 1971. As a collection it falls between several stools: it does not assemble the best of Gallant's work, it has only a partial national focus, and it does not reveal her full range.

Random House put together Gallant's next collection, selecting and arranging the stories (as usual the order is not chronological) and giving it the title *From the Fifteenth District: A Novella and Eight Short Stories* (1979). (There is no novella.) The result is Gallant's best collection to date. Its stories are drawn from one period (they all appeared between the publication of *The Pegnitz Junction* in 1973 and August 1979); it has a regional focus (Europe) and a historical impulse (World War II and its impact on small lives). It is a collection where the sum is greater than the individual parts, for the volume conveys the sweep of history. It is the culmination of Gallant's keen interest in the way political movements touch ordinary people, evinced earlier in "Señor Pinedo" (1954; *OP*, pp. 199–216), "Sunday Afternoon" (1962; *MHB*, pp. 203–17), and the German stories. It encompasses many of Gallant's continuing preoccupations: children victimized by adults, cultural clash, memory and forgetfulness. Though its powerful overall impression is the volume's major achievement, its individual stories are also among Gallant's best. At no point does Gallant's command of detail, her capacity to convey experience in all its intensity, flag. The collection gives an all but complete sense of Gallant's European stories from this period since it omits only one (which was significantly weaker than the others), but the complete range of her 1970s fiction is not represented, however, since the Montreal-based Linnet Muir stories are not included.

Gallant influenced her next collection in several important ways. Douglas M. Gibson, then with Macmillan of Canada, conceived of a book called *Home Truths* (1981) which would collect all of Gallant's Canadian stories.[72] When he wrote to Gallant with the idea, his list of proposed stories included the Linnet Muir series and stories from her various collections. Though doubtful about Canadian interest in such a book and apprehensive that the title might arouse resentment, Gallant was receptive to Gibson's proposal probably (and here I am making an assumption) because it gave her a way to publish the Linnet Muir stories as a group. (She had planned to publish the series separately, once she had enough stories for a volume. Three visits to Montreal between 1975 and 1978 had unfortunately dissipated her memory of the Montreal of the 1940s, which was the setting for the series, so that she was unable to complete the last two "half-written" stories.[73]) She asked that several stories on Gibson's list, including "Bernadette" (1957; *MHB*, pp. 14–41), be dropped, forwarded a list of uncollected stories with Canadian backgrounds or Canadian characters for Macmillan to choose from, and recommended that the original typescripts housed in the Thomas Fisher Rare Book Library be used as text instead of the edited *New Yorker* versions. Gallant suggested (but did not insist on) the order of the Linnet Muir stories. A note concerning "Bonaventure" (1966; *HT*, pp. 135–72) and "Virus X" (1965; *HT*, pp. 173–216) in the Thomas Fisher Rare Book Library which Macmillan's editors probably saw while looking at Gallant's typescripts may have moved them to place the stories side by side. In it Gallant wrote: "The idea for both emerged at about the same time, and both took a very long time to write. They are the most intensely Canadian of any of my stories; oddly enough, Canadians have overlooked them."[74] Macmillan accepted Gallant's suggestions,[75] including the tentative one about the ordering of the Linnet Muir stories, made a final selection, and arranged the volume. (As usual the arrangement is not chronological.)

The result is a retrospective volume. Apart from Gallant's 1981 Introduction, the Montreal memory stories which appeared between 1975 and 1978 are the most recent writing in the volume. The other stories were published between 1956 and 1971, although at least three of these were written much earlier than 1956. In her Introduction Gallant says that she wrote "Thank You for the Lovely Tea" (1956; *HT*, pp. 2–16) in New York when she was eighteen, and both "Jorinda and Jorindel" (1959; *HT*, pp. 17–28) and "Up North" (1959; *HT*, pp. 49–55) in Montreal during the 1940s. Many of the stories in the collection's first two sections are fine examples of Gallant's writing and deserved rescue from *The New Yorker*'s files. But as one might expect, the strongest of the book's three sections is the one called "Linnet Muir" since its six stories were written in the 1970s at the height of Gallant's powers. One of these stories, "The Doctor" (1977; *HT*, pp. 295–316), like the earlier "Bernadette" (1957; *MHB*, pp. 14–41) and "Its Image on the Mirror" (1964; *MHB*, pp. 55–155), vividly depicts facets of Quebec's cultural mosaic. The book as a whole is unified by its Canadian focus, but Macmillan was restrained from assembling either a "complete Canadian stories" or a "best Canadian stories" by Gallant's request that certain stories from earlier volumes not be included.

Gallant exercised considerable control over her most recent collection.[76] The stories in *Overhead in a Balloon* (1985) were forwarded to Macmillan by Gallant's agent. (Gallant herself, then, may have selected them.) According to Gibson, Gallant suggested that linked stories be grouped together, a request that caused some departures from chronological arrangement. She chose the volume's title.

This volume includes *all* the stories which appeared after the publication of *From the Fifteenth District* in 1979 up to the end of

1984 (namely, three groups of interrelated stories and "Luc and His Father" [1982; *OB*, pp. 72–100]) plus the satire "The Assembly" (1980; *OB*, pp. 188–96), all of them set in Paris. One of Gallant's longtime interests gets major treatment in the volume: in the stories about the gallery owner and his assistant and in the ones about the two men of letters and their patroness, her ongoing interest in art and artists (present earlier in artist characters, the story "Bonaventure" [1966; *HT*, pp. 135–72], and the Linnet Muir series) is taken several steps further as she takes a wry look at art shows, scholarship, patronage, criticism, and publication and a searching look at creativity. The volume differs from earlier collections in several ways. It is the first collection to be set in one place and the first one to be dominated by linked stories. Where some stories from *My Heart Is Broken* and later volumes have portrayed long stretches in characters' lives, here, in several of the interrelated stories, we are given the beginning, middle, and end of a number of careers and relationships. There is also a satirical/humorous element in *Overhead in a Balloon* in "The Assembly" (one of fourteen brief, funny satires Gallant published during 1980–82) and in three stories. Gallant wrote the brief satires (pieces she says she can toss off "before breakfast" [Grant]) at the prompting of her *New Yorker* editor as a way of keeping "her name in front of *New Yorker* readers"[77] during a period when she was pouring her energy into her play *What Is to Be Done?* and her still uncompleted book on Dreyfus. Writing them moved her to try to take satirical humour into the short story, something she did with splendid success in three of the stories about Miss Pugh, Grippes, and Prism. That the satires sparked a successful experiment in Gallant's story writing is their chief importance; of themselves they are slight, and there is no need to regret that more of them were not included in the collection.

What can be concluded from all this? First of all, because the principles of selection differ, and Gallant exercises her influence quite unpredictably, the various forces shaping a collection must be known before anything meaningful can be said about it. What does it mean to isolate a theme in *My Heart Is Broken*, for example, when it includes only a few of many stories Gallant wrote over an eight-year period, and when an editor selected the stories in the volume? Secondly, the two books which have usefully underlined Gallant's long preoccupation with Germans and Canadians —

namely *The Pegnitz Junction* and *Home Truths* — both, for different reasons, omit material which should be considered before anything is said about her fictional depiction of those national groups. Thirdly, Gallant's development as a writer can be traced only partly through the collections drawn together so far. Only two fully represent her story writing for a particular period — *The Other Paris*, covering the years 1952 to 1955, and *Overhead in a Balloon*, 1979 to 1984 — though, if the Linnet Muir stories from *Home Truths* are read with *From the Fifteenth District*, it is also possible to get a good sense of Gallant's fictional output from 1973 to 1979. That leaves the period from 1956 to 1972 represented only haphazardly in a number of different collections where selections were made on many different grounds. Lastly, factors other than the quality of individual stories may make a particular collection more, or less, compelling. *The Other Paris* is less beguiling as a collection than are *The Pegnitz Junction*, *From the Fifteenth District*, *Home Truths*, and *Overhead in a Balloon*, not just because it contains less expert, early stories, but because no common thread binds its stories together. Again, *Home Truths* and *Overhead in a Balloon* are less successful as collections than *The Pegnitz Junction* and *From the Fifteenth District* because the latter two are united both by their national and regional focuses and by their political preoccupations. *Home Truths* has nothing comparable to "the Hitler years" influencing all its characters, and excellent though Gallant's Introduction is, it is unable to draw everything under its umbrella as her novella "The Pegnitz Junction" does the stories in *The Pegnitz Junction*. *Overhead in a Balloon* is likewise less satisfying than *From the Fifteenth District*, partly because its little groups of two, three, or four interrelated stories tend to pull away from the unifying effect of their common setting of Paris. Some collections are more memorable *as collections*, then, because their disparate parts unite to create a satisfying larger whole. This is a special bonus. But it should not draw attention away entirely from the individual stories. Gallant has produced fine stories throughout her career. Perhaps what would be most helpful at this juncture would be a complete, chronologically arranged edition of Gallant's stories, which would make it easier for readers to see the way her technique and subject matter have shifted and evolved, and which would invite readers to assess her stories one by one.

NOTES

[1] Biographical details were culled from many interviews and places where Gallant has written about her life. There were two important sources in addition to those mentioned in the notes: Joanne Philpott, "The Writing Comes First," *The Globe and Mail*, 26 July 1984, p. L6; and Mavis Gallant, "Profile — Mavis Gallant," in *Writers and Writing* (Toronto: Ontario Educational Communications Authority, 1981), pp. 61–67.

[2] Earl Beattie, "Interview with Mavis Gallant," *Anthology*, CBC, 24 May 1969.

[3] Judith Skelton Grant, personal interview with Mavis Gallant, 26 Jan. 1984. In all further references, this interview is abbreviated as "Grant."

[4] Fletcher Markle, "Interview with Mavis Gallant," *Telescope*, CBC, 22 Jan. 1965. All further references to this interview (Markle, 22 Jan. 1965) appear in the text.

[5] Geoff Hancock, "An Interview with Mavis Gallant," *Canadian Fiction Magazine*, No. 28 (1978) [*A Special Issue on Mavis Gallant*], p. 28. In all further references, this work is abbreviated as "Hancock."

[6] Marci McDonald, "Exile in Her Own Write," *Macleans*, 19 Nov. 1979, p. 12.

[7] Howard Engel, "Interview with Mavis Gallant," *Stereo Morning*, CBC, 28–29 Oct. 1981.

[8] All references to Gallant's collected stories, essays, or reviews are to the first volume in which the story, essay, or review appeared, preceded by the year in which the piece was first published, and appear in the text. The following abbreviations are used:

The End of the World and Other Stories	EW
From the Fifteenth District	FFD
Home Truths: Selected Canadian Stories	HT
My Heart Is Broken	MHB
The Other Paris	OP
Overhead in a Balloon: Stories of Paris	OB
Paris Notebooks: Essays and Reviews	PN
The Pegnitz Junction	PJ

Uncollected stories, essays, and reviews are identified only by the date they were first published. Publication details of primary sources are available in the bibliography.

[9] Jean Royer, "Mavis Gallant: 'La vie n'est pas un roman,'" *Le Devoir* [Montréal], 21 May 1983, p. 19. All further references to this work (Royer) appear in the text.

[10] See Karen Lawrence, "From the Other Paris: Interview with Mavis Gallant," *Branching Out*, Feb.–March 1976, pp. 18–19.

[11] Robert Fulford, "On Mavis Gallant's Best Fiction Yet: The Memoirs of a WASP in Wartime Montreal," rev. of *My Heart Is Broken*, *Maclean's*, 5 Sept. 1964, p. 45.

[12] Anne-Marie Girard and Claude Pamela Valette, "Entretien avec Mavis Gallant," *Les Cahiers de la Nouvelle: Journal of the Short Story in English*, No. 2 (Jan. 1984), p. 83. All further references to this work (Girard and Valette) appear in the text.

[13] Zoe Bieler, "Visiting Writer Finds Montreal Changed in the Past Five Years," *The Montreal Star*, 30 Aug. 1955, p. 26.

[14] Geoff Hancock, "Mavis Tries Harder," *Books in Canada*, June–July 1978, pp. 5–6.

[15] "The Other Paris" (1953; *OP*, pp. 1–30) was chosen by Harvard University as the Best Short Story of 1953; "With a Capital T" (1978; *HT*, pp. 317–30) won the *Canadian Fiction Magazine*'s Annual Contributor's Prize in 1978; and "Luc and His Father" (1982; *OB*, pp. 72–100) was selected as the best short story published in *The New Press Anthology: Best Canadian Short Fiction £1* (1984).

[16] Graeme Gibson, "Interview with Mavis Gallant," *Anthology*, CBC, 31 Aug. 1974.

[17] Fletcher Markle, "Interview with Mavis Gallant," *Telescope*, CBC, 29 Jan. 1965. All further references to this interview (Markle, 29 Jan. 1965) appear in the text.

[18] See, for example, B184, B201, B211, and B286 in Judith Skelton Grant and Douglas Malcolm, "Mavis Gallant: An Annotated Bibliography," in *The Annotated Bibliography of Canada's Major Authors*, ed. Robert Lecker and Jack David, V (Downsview, Ont.: ECW, 1984).

[19] Gallant has said in a number of places that the character Linnet Muir is based on her young self. She told Maxine Crook, who had read the Montreal stories as straight autobiography, that she "took responsibility" for Linnet Muir and for her father in "In Youth Is Pleasure," but that the remaining characters were partly or wholly fictional ("Interview with Mavis Gallant," *Morningside*, CBC, 8 Dec. 1976).

[20] Crook.

[21] Francean Campbell, "Meet Mavis Gallant, Maybe," *The Montreal Star*, 26 Sept. 1970, p. 17.

[22] Debra Martens, "An Interview with Mavis Gallant," *Rubicon*, No. 4 (Winter 1984–85), p. 158.

[23] Many of these have been collected in *Paris Notebooks: Essays and*

Reviews (1986). For others, see Grant and Malcolm, B362–B364, B366, B368, B388, B393, B395. See also "What Did Sartre Do during the Occupation?" rev. of *The Left Bank: Writers, Artists and Politics from the Popular Front to the Cold War*, by Herbert R. Lottman, *The New York Times Book Review*, 4 April 1982, pp. 3, 26–27; and "Paris Truths: On the Street Where She Lives," *Destinations*, 1, No. 4 (Winter 1986), 42, 44, 46, 48.

[24] See Grant and Malcolm, D9, D12, D17, D20, D33, D76, D78.

[25] Mavis Gallant, ts. note concerning "Orphans' Progress," May 1980, Mavis Gallant Collection, Thomas Fisher Rare Book Library, Univ. of Toronto.

[26] William French, "Rewards at Home End the Era of the Literary Exile," *The Globe and Mail*, 1 June 1982, p. 13; Hancock, p. 35.

[27] "The Curate's Egg," *Essays on Canadian Writing*, No. 30 (Winter 1984–85), pp. 35–59.

[28] Suzanne C. Ferguson, "Defining the Short Story: Impressionism and Form," *Modern Fiction Studies*, 28 (Spring 1982), 14–15. All further references to this work (Ferguson) appear in the text. Ferguson is concerned to explain why the modern short story differs more radically from its predecessors than does the modern novel, but I shall refer only to what she says about the story. My attention was drawn initially to Ferguson's article by Neil Kalman Besner's "Mavis Gallant's Short Fiction: History and Memory in the Light of Imagination," Diss. British Columbia 1983, pp. 15–18.

[29] "An Attempt to Find the Origin of the Worm," rev. of *From the Fifteenth District*, *The Edmonton Journal*, 27 Oct. 1979, p. 14.

[30] Douglas Malcolm, "An Annotated Bibliography of Works by and about Mavis Gallant," *Essays on Canadian Writing*, No. 6 (Spring 1977), pp. 32–52.

[31] Geoff Hancock, ed., *Canadian Fiction Magazine*, No. 28 (1978) [*A Special Issue on Mavis Gallant*].

[32] Grazia Merler, *Mavis Gallant: Narrative Patterns and Devices* (Ottawa: Tecumseh, 1978). All further references to this work appear in the text.

[33] "Love's Grim Remains," rev. of *Green Water, Green Sky*, *Saturday Review*, 17 Oct. 1959, p. 19.

[34] "We Exit Wondering," rev. of *My Heart Is Broken*, *Saturday Review*, 18 April 1964, p. 45.

[35] Rev. of *My Heart Is Broken*, by Mavis Gallant, *The Keepers of the House*, by Shirley Ann Grau, and *Extreme Magic*, by Hortense Calisher, *The New York Review of Books*, 25 June 1964, p. 18.

[36] Elizabeth Janeway, in her review of *A Fairly Good Time*, *The New*

York Times Book Review, 7 June 1970, pp. 5, 34 sees Gallant as confronting her readers with complex moral issues, while Judith Rascoe, "This Side of Happy," rev. of A Fairly Good Time, The Christian Science Monitor, 4 June 1970, p. 7; and Christopher Lehmann-Haupt, "Books of the Times: Vanishing Creams," rev. of A Fairly Good Time, by Mavis Gallant, and One or Another, by Rosalyn Drexler, The New York Times, 5 June 1970, p. 33, find Gallant's novel emotionally shallow or unjudgemental.

[37] Among those who see Gallant's work as posing complex moral issues is Kildare Dobbs, "Train Trip Becomes a Journey of Life," rev. of The Pegnitz Junction, The Toronto Star, 2 June 1973, p. 73; among those who fault her work as cool and unjudgemental are Aviva Layton, "Missed Connections," rev. of The Pegnitz Junction, The Montreal Star, 9 June 1973, p. C3; and William H. Pritchard, rev. of The Pegnitz Junction, The New York Times Book Review, 24 June 1973, p. 4.

[38] Among those who see Gallant as eschewing easy generalization and posing tough moral problems are: Timothy Foote, "Coin's Edge," rev. of From the Fifteenth District, Time [Canadian ed.], 26 Nov. 1979, pp. 75–76; V. S. Pritchett, "Shredded Novels," rev. of From the Fifteenth District, by Mavis Gallant, and In Between the Sheets and Other Stories, by Ian McEwan, The New York Review of Books, 24 Jan. 1980, pp. 31–32; and W. H. New, "The Art of Haunting Ghosts," rev. of From the Fifteenth District, Canadian Literature, No. 85 (Summer 1980), pp. 153–55. Arguing that Gallant's stories are ultimately cool, unjudgemental, forgettable are: Diane Joy Charney, rev. of From the Fifteenth District, Library Journal, Aug. 1979, p. 1587; Anatole Broyard, "Books of the Times," rev. of From the Fifteenth District, The New York Times, 2 Oct. 1979, p. C9; Brigid Elson, rev. of From the Fifteenth District, by Mavis Gallant, and 79 Best Canadian Stories, ed. Clark Blaise and John Metcalf, Queen's Quarterly, 87 (Spring 1980), 160–61; and R. P. Bilan, rev. of From the Fifteenth District, in "Letters in Canada 1979: Fiction 2," University of Toronto Quarterly, 49 (Summer 1980), 326–27.

[39] "Gossip Transfigured into Art," rev. of A Fairly Good Time, Book World [Chicago Tribune], 31 May 1970, p. 5.

[40] Layton, p. C3.

[41] Rev. of From the Fifteenth District, Canadian Fiction Magazine, Nos. 34–35 (1980), pp. 172–74.

[42] Rev. of From the Fifteenth District, West Coast Review, 15, No. 1 (June 1980), 34–37.

[43] See, for example, Wayne Grady, "The Other Canada," rev. of Home Truths, Books in Canada, Oct. 1981, pp. 18–19; and Anne Michaels, rev. of

Home Truths, *Quarry*, 32, No. 2 (Spring 1983), 69–72.

⁴⁴ Rev. of *Home Truths*, *Canadian Fiction Magazine*, No. 43 (1982), pp. 125–29.

⁴⁵ Judith Skelton Grant, rev. of *Home Truths*, *World Literature Written in English*, 21 (Autumn 1982), 619–25.

⁴⁶ For discussions of the play's dramatic limitations, see Gina Mallet, "'What Is to Be Done?' a Treat at Tarragon," *The Toronto Star*, 12 Nov. 1982, p. D1; Carole Corbeil, "Stage Director Captures Gallant Style," *The Globe and Mail*, 27 Nov. 1982, p. E5; and Richard Plant, "Dramatic Readings," rev. of *What Is to Be Done?* by Mavis Gallant, and thirteen other books, *Books in Canada*, April 1984, pp. 13–17.

⁴⁷ "The Novels of Mavis Gallant," *Canadian Fiction Magazine*, No. 28 (1978) [*A Special Issue on Mavis Gallant*], pp. 68–73.

⁴⁸ "Memory, Imagination, Artifice: The Late Short Fiction of Mavis Gallant," *Canadian Fiction Magazine*, No. 28 (1978) [*A Special Issue on Mavis Gallant*], pp. 74–91.

⁴⁹ "'Orphans' Progress,' Reader's Progress: Le 'on dit' et le 'non-dit' chez Mavis Gallant," *RANAM* (*Recherches Anglaises et Américaines*, Université des sciences humaines, Strasbourg, France), No. 16 (1983), pp. 57–67; rpt. "'Orphans' Progress,' Reader's Progress: Voice and Understatement in Mavis Gallant's Stories," trans. Eva Schacherl and Michel Fabre, in *Gaining Ground: European Critics on Canadian Literature*, ed. Robert Kroetsch and Reingard M. Nischik, Western Canadian Literary Documents, No. 6 (Edmonton: NeWest, 1985), pp. 150–60. Another article on the same story, Ursula Jantz's "'Orphans' Progress' in Its Canadian and Universal Context," in *Essays in Honour of Erwin Stürzl on His Sixtieth Birthday*, ed. James Hogg (Salzburg: Institut für Englische Sprache und Literatur, Universität Salzburg, 1980), I, 302–09, is clumsily written and ill thought out.

⁵⁰ "Perils of Compassion," *Canadian Literature*, No. 56 (Spring 1973), pp. 61–70.

⁵¹ "Exiles in Time: Gallant's *My Heart Is Broken*," *Canadian Literature*, No. 93 (Summer 1982), pp. 106–07.

⁵² "The Three Stages of Mavis Gallant's Short Fiction," *Canadian Fiction Magazine*, No. 28 (1978) [*A Special Issue on Mavis Gallant*], pp. 92–114. See also Ronald Hatch, "Mavis Gallant: Returning Home," *Atlantis* [Acadia Univ.], 4, No. 1 (Autumn 1978), 95–102, which puts the same argument more briefly.

⁵³ "Mavis Gallant and the Expatriate Character," in *Zeitschrift der Gesellschaft für Kanada-Studien*, I (Jan. 1981), 142.

[54] See above, note 28.

[55] "Strange Fashions of Forsaking: Criticism and the Fiction of Mavis Gallant," *Dalhousie Review*, 64 (Winter 1984–85), 722. Keefer's article appeared after the present study of Gallant had been submitted. We reached similar conclusions about some of the criticism on Gallant's work.

[56] "Mavis Gallant and the Angel of History," *University of Toronto Quarterly*, 55 (Spring 1986), 282–301.

[57] See Grant and Malcolm, C52–C66.

[58] Under the title "Things Overlooked Before," this essay was included in *The Affair of Gabrielle Russier*, by Gabrielle Russier, trans. Ghislaine Boulanger (New York: Knopf, 1971), pp. 1–72. The book was widely and enthusiastically reviewed, though perhaps "reviewed" is the wrong word since most reviewers simply abbreviated and repeated Gallant's points about this celebrated French scandal.

[59] Gallant quoted in Carole Corbeil, "Home Truths with a Touch of Gallant Wit," *The Globe and Mail*, 7 Nov. 1981, p. E1.

[60] Mavis Gallant, ts. of "Address to Glendon College Convocation, June 16, 1984," Mavis Gallant Collection, Thomas Fisher Rare Book Library, Univ. of Toronto, p. 2.

[61] "The Statues Taken Down," *The New Yorker*, 9 Oct. 1965, p. 56.

[62] For "riddle" see *A Fairly Good Time*, p. 17; for "clues" see "From Cloud to Cloud," *The New Yorker*, 8 July 1985, p. 25.

[63] The first opinion is Malcolm's in the story "Malcolm and Bea" (1968; *EW*, p. 109). The second is Shirley Perrigny's in *A Fairly Good Time*, p. 17. When Graeme Gibson introduced this quotation from *A Fairly Good Time* during his interview with Gallant, she concurred with her character's view.

[64] Mavis Gallant, "The Chosen Husband," *The New Yorker*, 15 April 1985, p. 42.

[65] Mavis Gallant, "Questions and Answers," *The New Yorker*, 28 May 1966, p. 38.

[66] In her interview with Beattie, Gallant talks about seeing three people dining in Venice as the inspiration for the central characters in *Green Water, Green Sky*. See also Hancock, pp. 50, 58, where she talks about the originals of characters in *A Fairly Good Time*.

[67] Beattie.

[68] Unless otherwise specified, all information about Gallant's involvement in, or abstention from, the shaping of her story collections is drawn from my interview with her.

[69] Gallant appears to use the terms *short novel* and *novella* interchangeably. She told me that "Its Image on the Mirror" is "a real novella, an

authentic novella, my only attempt to write that form" (Grant), yet "Its Image on the Mirror" is listed on the contents page of *My Heart Is Broken* as "Its Image on the Mirror — A Short Novel." It is possible, however, that her publisher supplied the phrase "A Short Novel."

[70] Mavis Gallant, ts. note concerning "The Latehomecomer," n.d., Mavis Gallant Collection, Thomas Fisher Rare Book Library, Univ. of Toronto.

[71] The information in this paragraph is drawn from a telephone interview with Robert Weaver, 30 Oct. 1985.

[72] The information in this paragraph, except where otherwise indicated, is based on a telephone interview with Douglas M. Gibson, 7 Jan. 1986, and on my interview with Gallant.

[73] Mavis Gallant, ts. note concerning the Montreal stories, Sept. 1980, Mavis Gallant Collection, Thomas Fisher Rare Book Library, Univ. of Toronto.

[74] Gallant, ts. note, Sept. 1980.

[75] They were unable to use Gallant's typescripts as a basis for the text of "Thank You for the Lovely Tea" (1956; *HT*, pp. 2–16), "Jorinda and Jorindel" (1959; *HT*, pp. 17–28), "The Prodigal Parent" (1969; *EW*, pp. 120–25), "In the Tunnel" (1971; *EW*, pp. 142–67), and "With a Capital T" (1978; *HT*, pp. 317–30) since the Thomas Fisher Rare Book Library does not have them.

[76] The information concerning the assembling of *Overhead in a Balloon* is based on my interview with Gibson, 7 Jan. 1986.

[77] David Williamson, "Gallant's Short Stories Are Brilliant Gems," rev. of *Home Truths*, *Winnipeg Free Press*, 28 Nov. 1981, Sec. Leisure, p. 5.

SELECTED BIBLIOGRAPHY

Primary Sources

Manuscripts

Mavis Gallant Collection. Thomas Fisher Rare Book Library, Univ. of Toronto. Toronto, Ont.

Books

Gallant, Mavis. *The Other Paris: Stories.* Boston: Houghton Mifflin, 1956.
——. *Green Water, Green Sky.* Boston: Houghton Mifflin, 1959.
——. *My Heart Is Broken: Eight Stories and a Short Novel.* New York: Random House, 1964.
——. *A Fairly Good Time.* New York: Random House, 1970.
——. *The Pegnitz Junction: A Novella and Five Short Stories.* New York: Random House, 1973.
——. *The End of the World and Other Stories.* Introd. Robert Weaver. New Canadian Library, No. 91. Toronto: McClelland and Stewart, 1974.
——. *From the Fifteenth District: A Novella and Eight Short Stories.* New York: Random House, 1979.
——. *Home Truths: Selected Canadian Stories.* Introd. Mavis Gallant. Toronto: Macmillan, 1981.
——. *What Is to Be Done?* Dunvegan, Ont.: Quadrant, 1983.
——. *Overhead in a Balloon: Stories of Paris.* Toronto: Macmillan, 1985.
——. *Paris Notebooks: Essays and Reviews.* Toronto: Macmillan, 1986.

Contributions to Books and Periodicals

Gallant, Mavis. "By the Sea." *The New Yorker,* 17 July 1954, pp. 27–30.
——. "Thieves and Rascals." *Esquire,* July 1956, pp. 82, 85–86.
——. "A Short Love Story." *The Montrealer,* June 1957, pp. 48–60, 62.
——. "The Old Place." *Texas Quarterly,* 1, No. 2 (Spring 1958), 66–80.
——. "Rose." *The New Yorker,* 17 Dec. 1960, pp. 34–37.

——. "Two Questions." *The New Yorker*, 10 June 1961, pp. 30–36.

——. "Night and Day." *The New Yorker*, 17 March 1962, pp. 48–50.

——. "One Aspect of a Rainy Day." *The New Yorker*, 14 April 1962, pp. 38–39.

——. "Willi." *The New Yorker*, 5 Jan. 1963, pp. 29–31.

——. "Careless Talk." *The New Yorker*, 28 Sept. 1963, pp. 41–47.

——. "The Statues Taken Down." *The New Yorker*, 9 Oct. 1965, pp. 53–56.

——. "Questions and Answers." *The New Yorker*, 28 May 1966, pp. 33–38.

——. "A Report." *The New Yorker*, 3 Dec. 1966, pp. 62–65.

——. "The Sunday after Christmas." *The New Yorker*, 30 Dec. 1967, pp. 35–36.

——. "The Captive Niece." *The New Yorker*, 4 Jan. 1969, pp. 28–32.

——. "Good Deed." *The New Yorker*, 22 Feb. 1969, pp. 35–41.

——. "The Rejection." *The New Yorker*, 12 April 1969, pp. 42–44.

——. "Profile — Mavis Gallant." In *Writers and Writing*. Toronto: Ontario Educational Communications Authority, 1981, pp. 61–67.

——. "What Did Sartre Do during the Occupation?" Rev. of *The Left Bank: Writers, Artists and Politics from the Popular Front to the Cold War*, by Herbert R. Lottman. *The New York Times Book Review*, 4 April 1982, pp. 3, 26–27.

——. "The Chosen Husband." *The New Yorker*, 15 April 1985, pp. 40–49.

——. "From Cloud to Cloud." *The New Yorker*, 8 July 1985, pp. 22–25.

——. "Florida." *The New Yorker*, 26 Aug. 1985, pp. 24–27.

——. "Paris Truths: On the Street Where She Lives." *Destinations*, 1, No. 4 (Winter 1986), 42, 44, 46, 48.

Secondary Sources

Auchincloss, Eve. Rev. of *My Heart Is Broken*, by Mavis Gallant, *The Keepers of the House*, by Shirley Ann Grau, and *Extreme Magic*, by Hortense Calisher. *The New York Review of Books*, 25 June 1964, pp. 17–18.

Beattie, Earl. "Interview with Mavis Gallant." *Anthology*, CBC, 24 May 1969.

Besner, Neil Kalman. "Mavis Gallant's Short Fiction: History and Memory in the Light of Imagination." Diss. British Columbia 1983.

Bieler, Zoe. "Visiting Writer Finds Montreal Changed in the Past Five Years." *The Montreal Star*, 30 Aug. 1955, p. 26.

Bilan, R. P. Rev. of *From the Fifteenth District*. In "Letters in Canada 1979: Fiction 2." *University of Toronto Quarterly*, 49 (Summer 1980), 326–27.

Broyard, Anatole. "Books of the Times." Rev. of *From the Fifteenth District*. *The New York Times*, 2 Oct. 1979, p. c9.

Campbell, Francean. "Meet Mavis Gallant, Maybe." *The Montreal Star*, 26 Sept. 1970, p. 17.

Cassill, R. V. "Gossip Transfigured into Art." Rev. of *A Fairly Good Time*, *Book World* [*Chicago Tribune*], 31 May 1970, p. 5.

Charney, Diane Joy. Rev. of *From the Fifteenth District*. *Library Journal*, Aug. 1979, p. 1587.

Corbeil, Carole. "Home Truths with a Touch of Gallant Wit." *The Globe and Mail*, 7 Nov. 1981, p. E1.

——. "Stage Director Captures Gallant Style." *The Globe and Mail*, 27 Nov. 1982, p. E5.

Crook, Maxine. "Interview with Mavis Gallant." *Morningside*, CBC, 8 Dec. 1976.

Davies, Robertson. "The Novels of Mavis Gallant." *Canadian Fiction Magazine*, No. 28 (1978) [*A Special Issue on Mavis Gallant*], pp. 68–73.

Dobbs, Kildare. "Train Trip Becomes a Journey of Life." Rev. of *The Pegnitz Junction*. *The Toronto Star*, 2 June 1973, p. 73.

Elson, Brigid. Rev. of *From the Fifteenth District*, by Mavis Gallant, and *79 Best Canadian Stories*, ed. Clark Blaise and John Metcalf. *Queen's Quarterly*, 87 (Spring 1980), 160–61.

Engel, Howard. "Interview with Mavis Gallant." *Stereo Morning*, CBC, 28–29 Oct. 1981.

Fabre, Michel. "'Orphans' Progress,' Reader's Progress: Le 'on dit' et le 'non-dit' chez Mavis Gallant." *RANAM* (*Recherches Anglaises et Américaines*, Université des sciences humaines, Strasbourg, France), No. 16 (1983), pp. 57–67. Rpt. "'Orphans' Progress,' Reader's Progress: Voice and Understatement in Mavis Gallant's Stories." Trans. Eva Schacherl and Michel Fabre. In *Gaining Ground: European Critics on Canadian Literature*. Ed. Robert Kroetsch and Reingard M. Nischik. Western Canadian Literary Documents, No. 6. Edmonton: NeWest, 1985, pp. 150–60.

Ferguson, Suzanne C. "Defining the Short Story: Impressionism and Form." *Modern Fiction Studies*, 28 (Spring 1982), 13–24.

Foote, Timothy. "Coin's Edge." Rev. of *From the Fifteenth District*, *Time* [Canadian ed.], 26 Nov. 1979, pp. 75–76.

French, William. "Rewards at Home End the Era of the Literary Exile." *The Globe and Mail*, 1 June 1982, p. 13.

Fulford, Robert. "On Mavis Gallant's Best Fiction Yet: The Memoirs of a WASP in Wartime Montreal." Rev. of *My Heart Is Broken*. *Maclean's*, 5 Sept. 1964, p. 45.

Gibson, Graeme. "Interview with Mavis Gallant." *Anthology*, CBC, 31 Aug. 1974.

Girard, Anne-Marie, and Claude Pamela Valette. "Entretien avec Mavis Gallant." *Les Cahiers de la Nouvelle: Journal of the Short Story in English*, No. 2 (Jan. 1984), pp. 79–94.

Grady, Wayne. "The Other Canada." Rev. of *Home Truths*. *Books in Canada*, Oct. 1981, pp. 18–19.

Grant, Judith Skelton. Rev. of *Home Truths*. *World Literature Written in English*, 21 (Autumn 1982), 619–25.

———. Personal interview with Mavis Gallant. 26 Jan. 1984.

———, and Douglas Malcolm. "Mavis Gallant: An Annotated Bibliography." In *The Annotated Bibliography of Canada's Major Authors*. Ed. Robert Lecker and Jack David. Vol. 5. Downsview, Ont.: ECW, 1984, 179–230.

———. Telephone interview with Robert Weaver. 30 Oct. 1985.

———. Telephone interview with Douglas M. Gibson. 7 Jan. 1986.

Hancock, Geoff. "An Interview with Mavis Gallant." *Canadian Fiction Magazine*, No. 28 (1978) [*A Special Issue on Mavis Gallant*], pp. 18–67.

———, ed. *Canadian Fiction Magazine*, No. 28 (1978) [*A Special Issue on Mavis Gallant*].

———. "Mavis Tries Harder." *Books in Canada*, June–July 1978, pp. 4–8.

Hatch, Ronald. "Mavis Gallant: Returning Home." *Atlantis* [Acadia Univ.], 4, No. 1 (Autumn 1978), 95–102.

———. "The Three Stages of Mavis Gallant's Short Fiction." *Canadian Fiction Magazine*, No. 28 (1978) [*A Special Issue on Mavis Gallant*], pp. 92–114.

———. Rev. of *From the Fifteenth District*. *Canadian Fiction Magazine*, Nos. 34–35 (1980), pp. 172–74.

———. "Mavis Gallant and the Expatriate Character." *Zeitschrift der Gesellschaft für Kanada-Studien*, 1 (Jan. 1981), 133–43.

———. Rev. of *Home Truths*. *Canadian Fiction Magazine*, No. 43 (1982), pp. 125–29.

Janeway, Elizabeth. "We Exit Wondering." Rev. of *My Heart Is Broken*. *Saturday Review*, 18 April 1964, pp. 45–46.

———. Rev. of *A Fairly Good Time*. *The New York Times Book Review*, 7 June 1970, pp. 5, 34.

Jantz, Ursula. "'Orphans' Progress' in Its Canadian and Universal Context." In *Essays in Honour of Erwin Stürzl on His Sixtieth Birthday.* Ed. James Hogg. Salzburg: Institut für Englische Sprache und Literatur, Universität Salzburg, 1980. Vol. 1, 302–09.

Keefer, Janice Kulyk. "Strange Fashions of Forsaking: Criticism and the Fiction of Mavis Gallant." *Dalhousie Review,* 64 (Winter 1984–85), 721–35.

——. "Mavis Gallant and the Angel of History." *University of Toronto Quarterly,* 55 (Spring 1986), 282–301.

Lawrence, Karen. "From the Other Paris: Interview with Mavis Gallant." *Branching Out,* Feb.–March 1976, pp. 18–19.

Layton, Aviva. "Missed Connections." Rev. of *The Pegnitz Junction. The Montreal Star,* 9 June 1973, p. C3.

Lehmann-Haupt, Christopher. "Books of the Times: Vanishing Creams." Rev. of *A Fairly Good Time,* by Mavis Gallant, and *One or Another,* by Rosalyn Drexler. *The New York Times,* 5 June 1970, p. 33.

Malcolm, Douglas. "An Annotated Bibliography of Works by and about Mavis Gallant." *Essays on Canadian Writing,* No. 6 (Spring 1977), pp. 32–52.

Mallet, Gina. "'What Is to Be Done?' a Treat at Tarragon." *The Toronto Star,* 12 Nov. 1982, p. D1.

Markle, Fletcher. "Interview with Mavis Gallant." *Telescope,* CBC, 22 Jan. 1965.

——. "Interview with Mavis Gallant." *Telescope,* CBC, 29 Jan. 1965.

Martens, Debra. "An Interview with Mavis Gallant." *Rubicon,* No. 4 (Winter 1984–85), pp. 150–82.

McDonald, Marci. "Exile in Her Own Write." *Maclean's,* 19 Nov. 1979, pp. 6, 9–10, 12.

Merler, Grazia. *Mavis Gallant: Narrative Patterns and Devices.* Ottawa: Tecumseh, 1978.

——. Rev. of *From the Fifteenth District. West Coast Review,* 15, No. 1 (June 1980), 34–37.

Metcalf, John. "The Curate's Egg." *Essays on Canadian Writing,* No. 30 (Winter 1984–85), pp. 35–59.

Michaels, Anne. Rev. of *Home Truths. Quarry,* 32, No. 2 (Spring 1983), 69–72.

New, W. H. "The Art of Haunting Ghosts." Rev. of *From the Fifteenth District. Canadian Literature,* No. 85 (Summer 1980), pp. 153–55.

O'Rourke, David. "Exiles in Time: Gallant's *My Heart Is Broken.*" *Canadian Literature,* No. 93 (Summer 1982), pp. 98–107.

Pendergast, Constance. "Love's Grim Remains." Rev. of *Green Water, Green Sky. Saturday Review*, 17 Oct. 1959, p. 19.

Philpott, Joanne. "The Writing Comes First." *The Globe and Mail*, 26 July 1984, p. L6.

Plant, Richard. "Dramatic Readings." Rev. of *What Is to Be Done?* by Mavis Gallant, and thirteen other books, *Books in Canada*, April 1984, pp. 13–17.

Pritchard, William H. Rev. of *The Pegnitz Junction. The New York Times Book Review*, 24 June 1973, p. 4.

Pritchett, V. S. "Shredded Novels." Rev. of *From the Fifteenth District*, by Mavis Gallant, and *In Between the Sheets and Other Stories*, by Ian McEwan. *The New York Review of Books*, 24 Jan. 1980, pp. 31–32.

Rascoe, Judith. "This Side of Happy." Rev. of *A Fairly Good Time. The Christian Science Monitor*, 4 June 1970, p. 7.

Royer, Jean. "Mavis Gallant: 'La vie n'est pas un roman.'" *Le Devoir* [Montréal], 21 May 1983, pp. 19, 36.

Stevens, Peter. "Perils of Compassion." *Canadian Literature*, No. 56 (Spring 1973), pp. 61–70.

Summers, Merna. "An Attempt to Find the Origin of the Worm." Rev. of *From the Fifteenth District. The Edmonton Journal*, 27 Oct. 1979, p. 14.

Weaver, Robert, introd. *The End of the World and Other Stories*. New Canadian Library, No. 91. Toronto: McClelland and Stewart, 1974, pp. 7–13.

Williamson, David. "Gallant's Short Stories Are Brilliant Gems." Rev. of *Home Truths. Winnipeg Free Press*, 28 Nov. 1981, Sec. Leisure, p. 5.

Woodcock, George. "Memory, Imagination, Artifice: The Late Short Fiction of Mavis Gallant." *Canadian Fiction Magazine*, No. 28 (1978) [*A Special Issue on Mavis Gallant*], pp. 74–91.

*Norman Levine
and His Works*

Norman Levine (1923–   )

LAWRENCE MATHEWS

Biography

ALBERT NORMAN LEVINE was born in Ottawa on 22 October 1923, the son of Moses Mordecai and Annie (Gurevich) Levine, Jews who had emigrated from Poland. The family was part of the small Jewish community in Ottawa's mainly French Lower Town. Moses Levine was a fruit pedlar.

Norman Levine's first language was Yiddish. He spoke no English until the age of five, when he began to attend York Street Public School. Later he studied at the High School of Commerce but left at sixteen to become an office boy at the Department of National Defence. He joined the Royal Canadian Air Force in 1942 and became a flying officer, piloting Lancaster bombers with the 429th Squadron, based in Leeming, Yorkshire.

After the war, Levine attended McGill University, taking a B.A. (first-class honours in English) in 1948 and an M.A. in 1949, with a thesis titled "Ezra Pound and the Sense of the Past." He also edited *Forge*, the university literary magazine, and wrote poetry, some of which was collected in *Myssium*, a 1948 Ryerson Press chapbook. Under the informal supervision of Professor H. G. Files, he began the first draft of a novel, *The Angled Road*.

In June 1949 Levine returned to England, his home for the next thirty-one years. He had won a Beaver Club fellowship to go to King's College, London, but had already decided to become a writer rather than an academic. He never started his dissertation on Hardy, Lawrence, and Eliot (to be titled "The Decay of Absolute Values in Modern Society"). Instead he moved to St. Ives, Cornwall, where he lived for most of his years in England, and began to write full time. He has done so ever since, except for a one-year term as head of the English Department at Barnstaple Boys' Grammar School in Barnstaple, Devon (1953–54).

Two books appeared during the early years in St. Ives. *The Tight-*

Rope Walker, a slim volume of poetry, was published by Totem Press of London in 1950.[1] *The Angled Road* was published by Werner Laurie in Great Britain in the fall of 1952 and by McClelland and Stewart in Canada in the spring of 1953. Levine was also beginning to publish stories, poems, travel articles, and reviews, at first in obscure periodicals like *The Norseman,* later in more prestigious ones such as *Harper's Bazaar, Vogue,* and *Encounter.*

In 1952 he married Margaret Emily Payne, an Englishwoman, who was born in Blackheath, London. They were to have three daughters.

St. Ives was a leading centre of British painting from just after World War II until the mid-1960s, so it is not surprising that many of Levine's friends have been painters: Francis Bacon, Peter Lanyon, Alan Lowndes, Patrick Heron, Terry Frost, Bryan Wynter. He has never considered himself part of any literary group or movement; writers who have been his friends include Charles Causley, Philip Oakes, and Mordecai Richler.

In 1956 Levine returned to Canada for three months, making a cross-country journey which furnished the material for his next book, *Canada Made Me* (1958) — part autobiography and part observations of contemporary Canadian life. Much of this work is harshly critical of his native land. Putnam was the British publisher, but there was no simultaneous Canadian edition, although McClelland and Stewart distributed five hundred copies in Canada. Jack McClelland thought the book gave "a misleading picture of the country"[2] and did not want his name associated with it. Levine found himself at the centre of a national controversy. At the same time, *Canada Made Me* established his reputation as a mature literary artist.

His next three books were first published in the United Kingdom, with a Canadian firm subsequently taking copies of the British edition: *One Way Ticket* (1961), a collection of stories; *From a Seaside Town* (1970; republished in 1975 as *She'll Only Drag You Down*), a novel; and a second volume of stories, *I Don't Want to Know Anyone Too Well* (1971). During this time, Levine's growing artistic stature was recognized in various ways: he received three Canada Council grants (a fellowship in 1959, arts awards in 1969 and 1971); he was appointed writer-in-residence at the University of New Brunswick (1965–66); he edited an anthology of Canadian fiction (*Canadian Winter's Tales* [1968]); and he was the first writer commissioned by the CBC to write a short story for the radio series *Anthology* (1971).

More recently, Levine has published *Selected Stories* (1975), one of which, "In Lower Town," was published together with photographs by Johanne McDuff as a separate book in 1977. *I Walk by the Harbour* (1976) is a very slim volume of poetry; most of its contents were written, according to Levine's prefatory note, in 1949 and 1959. *Thin Ice* (1979) is a collection of stories, published by Deneau & Greenberg in Canada and by Wildwood House in the United Kingdom. The Canadian firm — now called simply Deneau — has also brought out paperback editions of *Canada Made Me* (1979; the first Canadian edition), *From a Seaside Town* (1980), *Thin Ice* (1982), and *I Don't Want to Know Anyone Too Well* (1982). In 1984 Deneau published *Why Do you Live So Far Away?* and Penguin published *Champagne Barn*, collections consisting almost entirely of previously published work.

A remarkable feature of Levine's career has been his popularity in Europe. His work has been translated into many languages. He is especially well known in Germany, partly because his West German translators are Heinrich Böll and Anne-Marie Böll. But collections of his stories have appeared in East Germany in editions of thirty thousand and twenty thousand. By contrast, *Thin Ice* was published in Canada in an edition of five thousand.

Levine's first wife died in 1978. He returned to Canada in 1980 and in 1983 married Anne Sarginson in Toronto. He now lives there but still has his residence in St. Ives, to which he returns from time to time. He continues to write.

Tradition and Milieu

The notion of "placing" a writer in a Canadian context is one that Levine has himself had sardonic fun with. In *From a Seaside Town*, the travel writer Joseph Grand is interviewed by an academic:

In the hunt for Canadian literature even travel writers are collected, made a bit of a fuss of. I was going to meet a lecturer in English in the lounge of the Chateau Laurier. . . . He was going to write an article about my work for a little magazine. I already knew the pretentious phrases. The way the piece would be slanted. A Canadian in England would become "an expatriate" and linked to the American expatriates of the 1920s. . . . He was very neat, very correct. I suddenly felt a little envious of him. He was a Canadian of three generations. He was older than the country. We didn't have much in common. "Mr. Grand. Do you come for a renewal of roots?" He was, he looked, firmly rooted here. But at the same time it produced this shallow looking individual, provincial, innocent. "Why do so many of our writers live out of Canada," he asked. "I don't know," I said. "People leave for personal reasons."[3]

Grand's interviewer is eager to find connections, patterns, "roots." He is of the academic generation that has produced (for example) Margaret Atwood's *Survival: A Thematic Guide to Canadian Literature*, D. G. Jones's *Butterfly on Rock: A Study of Themes and Images in Canadian Literature*, John Moss's books on the Canadian novel, and Frank Davey's *From There to Here: A Guide to English-Canadian Literature since 1960* — surveys which fail to mention Levine's work, even in passing. A critical industry preoccupied with devising overviews of the national literary psyche will have no patience with Joseph Grand's "personal reasons."

Nor does North American Jewishness provide a convenient category for discussion of Levine's work. In a 1976 interview for *Queen's Quarterly*, he was asked about this, and his reply deals with the issue of Canadianness, as well:

I don't have strong feelings about being a Jew. I don't have strong feelings about being a Canadian, except that I am a Jew and I am a Canadian. . . . I think you're a writer first, and you're a Jew, a Protestant, a Catholic, a Canadian afterwards. These are added things. I feel continuity with other writers.[4]

This suggests that Levine's work might best be considered in the context of the broader international tradition he has chosen for himself.

The early novel *The Angled Road* (1952) demonstrates his desire to find a place in this tradition. It was, he has said, influenced by "all the people I was reading at the time that I liked. . . . It's got

Hemingway, it's got Faulkner, it's got Proust — the whole reading list" (McDonald, p. 220). By the time his next book, *Canada Made Me* (1958), was published, he had rejected some of the earlier influences and embraced a new one:

> ... when I first went to England the man I hadn't read before was Graham Greene. And although he was writing about the England of the '30s and '40s, the thing I liked about Greene was that he was describing the England I could see around me. Here was the visible world. I've always liked two things in writers: I want them to make me see ... and also I like things to be clear.[5]

The title of *Canada Made Me* is his homage to Greene. In a 1970 interview for *Canadian Literature*, he mentions some of the other writers who have been important for him:

> ... if you look around this room you can see on the desk a book by Orwell, another by Hemingway, Babel, but mostly Chekhov and Graham Greene. And Joyce — I like the Joyce of *The Dead*, not *Ulysses*.[6]

In the *Queen's Quarterly* interview, Levine's shortlist of "major influences" consists of Greene, Chekhov, and the painter Francis Bacon (McDonald, p. 229).

There are obvious similarities among these figures. In speaking of his personal experience, Levine has perhaps provided an implicit definition of their tradition as he understands it:

> One of the things a writer finds out is that you don't lie. I don't know about the truth, whatever the truth is, but you don't lie. Telling a lie, to me, smacks too much of death. Although life and death are very much interlocked, and I'm aware just how vulnerable we are as human beings, I try not to lie when I write. (McDonald, p. 225)

The reference to the connection between lies and death implies that the Conrad of *Heart of Darkness* should be added to the list. Trying not to lie has led Levine to this odd kind of truth:

> ... I found that about most human affairs there's always something awkward, something incomplete. This tells me a

great deal more about human life, this awkward incompleteness, than anything that's laid down. This is the thing that I
value. (McDonald, p. 228)

By itself, this passage may give an inaccurate impression of Levine's
work; it needs to be supplemented by a remark he makes elsewhere
in the interview: "I try in my own kind of way, I suppose, to give a
certain dignity to people who get pushed around" (McDonald,
p. 222). Awkward incompleteness paradoxically linked with dignity: the affinities with Greene and Chekhov hardly need to be
laboured.

The question of whether his writing will become a living part of
their tradition must of course remain open for the time being.
Levine has commented that ". . . the nice thing about writing is that
no writer knows if he's any good or not. It takes up to 50 years for
time to do its work" (Grady, p. 24). It is, however, fairly easy to
make a prediction about his place in Canadian literature. As Canadian criticism matures, his work will become increasingly visible on
its maps. Many Canadian reviewers have of course praised Levine's
writing, as I will demonstrate in the next section of this essay. But it
is fair to say that he has not achieved the status of a "major" figure
on the Canadian scene — an ironic fact, considering that he has
said that one of his reasons for leaving Canada in 1949 was that "I
didn't think that the [Canadian] critics had the standards that I
wanted" (Grady, p. 24). The provincialism of Joseph Grand's interviewer is, for the moment, triumphant. But when the interviewer's
day has passed, Levine's books will still be around to present themselves to the scrutiny of other standards. Only then will Levine's
true "place" in Canadian tradition become apparent.

Critical Overview and Context

"Levine criticism" is in an embryonic state. There have been no
books about his work and no theses — very little of anything except
reviews. The reaction to all of Levine's books has, in a sense, been
mixed. In the case of the mature fiction, however, the favourable
reviews far outnumber the others and have on the whole been the
more thoughtful. And the best of these have laid the groundwork
for the more thorough critical discussion that is certain to come.

Some which deserve to be singled out are Alan Heuser's brilliant discussion of *From a Seaside Town*;[7] Barry Cameron's analysis of *Selected Stories*, which is less a review than a detailed explanation and defence of Levine's method;[8] D. G. Stephens' discussion of the same volume;[9] and Bernard Levin's piece on *Thin Ice*.[10]

Reviewers of the early poetry found it promising but tended to hedge their bets. E. K. Brown liked *Myssium* for its "sharpness of perception" and "vigour of intelligence" but was not so impressed with its "style and structure."[11] Northrop Frye thought that *The Tight-Rope Walker* displayed a "high level of competence in what is so far a rather restricted range."[12] The reviewer for *The Times Literary Supplement* disliked the poems written from what he called Levine's "detached observation-point" but approved of those in which the poet "accepts the sensibility of a human being."[13]

The Angled Road attracted much more attention and inspired a much broader range of response. At one extreme, Nancy Spain in the *Daily Express* [London] predicted that ". . . 200 years from now [Levine's] name will be written nice and big in the literary history of the 20th Century";[14] at the other, Marghanita Laski in the *Spectator* dismissed *The Angled Road* as "a very self-concentrated, very adolescent book."[15] But most reviewers, on both sides of the Atlantic, found both something to praise (usually the prose) and something to condemn (usually the character of David Wrixon, the protagonist). The reviewer for *The Times Literary Supplement* liked the "good, freshly written account" of Wrixon's childhood but commented that "the author seems also oddly unaware that the behaviour of his central character is often exceedingly unpleasant."[16] In Canada, Claude T. Bissell compared the novel to "an interesting but not genuinely distinguished diary,"[17] while Alice Eedy in *The Canadian Forum* called Levine "a writer of . . . fine perception" but found that the book degenerates into "flat autobiograph[y]" towards the end.[18]

Because of its subject matter, *Canada Made Me* has been the most controversial of Levine's books. The charge that he was unfair to Canada so dominates the reviews that it is easy to overlook the fact that nearly all include praise for his technical skill. Paul West's judgement in his *New Statesman* review that *Canada Made Me* is "a passionate and brilliantly rendered bigotry" is representative.[19] (One of Levine's publishers was later to shorten this, for purposes of jacket copy, to "passionate and brilliantly rendered.") The reviewer for *The Times Literary Supplement* sniffed at Levine's "attraction to the morally diseased and the deformed" but then called him "a writer of considerable power."[20] Nigel Gander, in *The Daily Telegraph* [London], complained that "Mr. Levine is not always fair . . ." but liked his "sharp eye for detail."[21] In Canada, the reaction was much harsher. The headline of Terrence Dorrien's review in *The Globe and Mail* — "Ex-Canadian Blasts Us"[22] — shows how personally Canadian reviewers took Levine's evaluation of the country. They could be personal in return. Patricia Owen suggested that Levine was "blinded by old fears and frustrations."[23] J. M. S. Careless was disappointed that Levine, "a skilled and sensitive author," for some reason "felt an evident necessity to repudiate this country decisively."[24]

Since *Canada Made Me*, Levine has published seven books of fiction. In the reviews, certain critical attitudes appear again and again. There is virtually unanimous agreement, for example, that Levine's prose is clear, simple, intense. Most reviewers think that he excels at description. But many, having acknowledged these points, find serious deficiencies: in the characters, especially the narrator-protagonist, who is dull and uncommunicative; in the plot, or lack of it; in the subject matter, which is monotonous and too obviously autobiographical; in the impression which the book leaves on the reader ("depressing"); and in the theme (Levine has "little to say"). Some of the reviews of *One Way Ticket* illustrate this tendency. In the *Spectator*, Patricia Hodgart praised Levine for his skill in "recording impressions and experience" but found the characters "less satisfying."[25] F. W. Watt noted Levine's "ability to record apt details of appearance and behaviour" but concluded that it is "on the whole a depressing book to read"; in particular, Watt complained that in story after story the narrator, "arriving in search of something, finds nothing."[26]

But these judgements do not represent a consensus. Other critics believe that objections like those of Hodgart and Watt are usually wrongheaded and that careful, sympathetic reading will reveal the unobtrusive excellence of Levine's work. Donald Stephens in *Canadian Literature* thought *One Way Ticket* "a wonderfully rich and varied picture of ordinary people,"[27] and Desmond Pacey praised it without reservation in his *Canadian Forum* review.[28] A very high percentage of the British reviews of Levine's mature fiction display this sort of attitude. In Canada the response has been more varied.

The major British reviews of *From a Seaside Town*, for example, were all favourable. Clive Jordan in *New Statesman* liked its "simple and direct" style and its "attractive economy"; he found the book "oddly affecting."[29] The reviewer for *The Times Literary Supplement* thought Joseph Grand, the protagonist, to be "disarmingly honest, thus likeable."[30] Maurice Capitanchik in the *Spectator* reported that ". . . there is a rare honesty and genuine simplicity about this sad, funny, and economically written novel."[31] In Canada, opinion was divided. Alan Heuser's *Montreal Star* review was the most perceptive and enthusiastic. After demonstrating something of the book's subtlety and complexity, he concluded that "Levine has struck a universal chord. . . . The book deserves to be read again and again" (Heuser, p. 16). Heuser called the novel "tragicomic" (p. 16), but other reviewers who liked it had difficulty finding a comic element. Alden Nowlan drew attention to Levine's "artistic courage and honesty" but concluded that *From a Seaside Town* is "a very sad book" about "spiritual paralysis."[32] George Woodcock decided that ". . . it stirs one's empathies and quietly saddens one"; he compared it to "a lesser painting by Monet."[33] Reviewers who disliked the book found the sense of paralysis and sadness overwhelming. Phyllis Grosskurth thought the protagonist "laconic, ineffectual, and utterly boring in his paralyzed inertia."[34]

This pattern is repeated in the reviews of *I Don't Want to Know Anyone Too Well*. In England, William Cooper remarked on the "completely unforced" quality of the stories and said that while they "are pervaded by the ineffable sadness of life, they shape themselves beautifully and leave one's spirits raised."[35] The reviewer for *The Times Literary Supplement* commented on the success of Levine's effort "to instil in events modestly stated a real sense of depth" and noted the "gentle humour" and "atmosphere of sympathetic concern."[36] In Canada, Morris Wolfe liked "the mood created by [Levine's] gentle, tragic view of life and spare, understated prose,"[37] and Donald Stephens asserted that Levine "has caught the measure of his time with great subtlety."[38] But Donald Cameron reported that Levine "stopped growing long ago,"[39] and John Metcalf, while paying tribute to Levine's ability to write stories that are "moving" and "haunting," argued that "one is always aware of Hemingway's looming bulk and sadly aware that such stories in 1971 are a cliché."[40]

Selected Stories, published only in Canada, inspired two of the best reviews of Levine's work. Using different but complementary methods of assessing his achievement, Barry Cameron and Donald Stephens arrived at similar conclusions. For Cameron, Levine is "one of the most talented and painstaking craftsmen" of the short story.[41] For Stephens, Levine has "with care, with grace, and with elegance . . . astringently given to short fiction a new nuance."[42] But E. L. Bishop, while acknowledging the "high degree of craftsmanship," found an "emotional flatness," a hero who is "not sufficiently engaging," and undeveloped minor characters,[43] and R. H. Ramsey called the book "basically an undistinguished collection" whose prose "remains flat and lifeless" and whose characters are "stereotyped people in stereotypical situations."[44]

The most important review of *Thin Ice* is Bernard Levin's in *The Sunday Times* [London]. He argues that Levine's work transcends its autobiographical basis — we do not wonder whether Levine's life is like that of his narrator — and that his vision is neither tragic nor pessimistic; further, Levine's sort of optimism is based not on "a romantic view of an imaginary human nature" but rather on observation of "the lives most of us actually lead, and the people we actually meet."[45] Jonathan Steffen in *New Statesman* pronounced the stories "starkly elegant,"[46] but Victoria Glendinning in *The Times Literary Supplement* thought the book inferior to *Canada Made Me*: "The writing [in *Thin Ice*] is sad, spare, a thinned-out version of the autobiographical record."[47] In Canada, Cary Fagan declared that *Thin Ice* contained "some near masterpieces" and emphasized the compassion in Levine's writing, his concern for "the lonely, the unhappy, the outsiders" in a world that is "beautiful, sad, finite."[48] William French wrote that the book possesses "a surprising organic unity that lifts the collection above Levine's previous volumes of short stories."[49] The most uncompromisingly negative review was Terry Goldie's. Taking exception to the jacket copy, which refers to Levine as "one of Canada's major writers," Goldie touches some familiar bases — Levine's style is "pure," but his sensibility is "as limited as a cage" and his stories leave the reviewer with "a tremendous depression" — before concluding that ". . . the major writer must have major things to say. Levine does not."[50]

Reviews of *Why Do You Live So Far Away?* and *Champagne Barn* conform to the pattern described above. Clearly there is considerable disagreement about Levine's merit. It seems that there are at least two ways to approach his work, two conflicting sets of assumptions which readers bring to it. Perusal of the reviews reveals that there has been virtually no dialogue between the two groups of critics. In what follows, I will attempt to deal seriously with some of the characteristic complaints about Levine's work, while arguing that his achievement has been of considerable value.

Levine's Works

Norman Levine is a writer of confessions. Virtually everything he has published is autobiographical in some fairly straightforward sense. Christopher Lasch has provided a succinct account of what this sort of writer hopes to accomplish:

> . . . the best work in this vein attempts, . . . through self-disclosure, to achieve a critical distance from the self and to gain insight into the historical forces, reproduced in psychological form, that have made the very concept of selfhood increasingly problematic.[51]

For Levine, the "concept of selfhood" has always been "problematic"; it is this that, according to his own testimony, moved him in the direction of what he calls "thin, thin autobiographical things":

> Most young writers find it very difficult to be that personal, to get down to the personal life, so they have to use masks: call the narrator a dentist or a doctor or a tramp or what-have-you, rarely a writer. And I thought, "Why go through all this little thingamagig of pretending you're somebody else?" I think this is one of the things I learned from growing up in a community of mostly French Canadians and European Jewish immigrants in Ottawa — there was all this pressure to change from whatever past came through your parents to the present. The change involved not only changing your name and your attitudes, but telling little lies about yourself as a way of getting through this process. One of the things a writer finds out is that you don't lie. (McDonald, p. 225)

But Levine's work does not fit comfortably on Lasch's list of examples of "the confessional mode": "[Norman] Mailer's *Advertisements for Myself*, Norman Podhoretz's *Making It*, Philip Roth's

93

Portnoy's Complaint, Paul Zweig's *Three Journeys*, Frederick Exley's *A Fan's Notes*" (Lasch, p. 50). Lasch points out that what flaws these works is the sense that at times their authors, always conscious of their need to ingratiate themselves with an audience, sacrifice truth in order to perform more successfully:

> Today, the convention of a fictionalized narrator has been abandoned in most experimental writing. The author now speaks in his own voice but warns the reader that his version of the truth is not to be trusted.
>
> . . . .
>
> In recording his "inner" experiences, he seeks not to provide an objective account of a representative piece of reality but to seduce others into giving him their attention, acclaim, or sympathy and thus to shore up his faltering sense of self. (Lasch, pp. 53–55)

Levine, by contrast, never tries to charm. He is uncompromisingly old-fashioned in his assumption that the writer's province is, in some essential way, "truth." Speaking in his own voice, he asks us to trust him.

This explains much about his laconic style, which has often been compared to Hemingway's. But consider a passage taken at random from *Selected Stories*:

> She fussed over me, giving me things to eat. And as soon as I finished something on a plate she quickly took the plate away and I could hear her washing it up in the kitchen. Her whole flat was spotless, everything in place. After a while, all this neatness was getting me down. Until I went to look in the drawer of a dresser in the living room for the old photographs. And saw, to my relief, that the neatness, everything in its place, was only on the surface. That in the drawers, in the dresser, things were still jumbled up.[52]

True, the diction is extremely simple, and the sentences are short and often fragmentary. But would anyone confuse the speaker of this passage with the Hemingway "Tough Talker" of Walker Gibson's celebrated analysis?[53] Is Levine's persona, like Frederic Henry in *A Farewell to Arms*, "a hard man who has been around in a violent world"?[54] Frederic Henry would not use words like "fussed" or "spotless" or "jumbled." And if he were to describe his emotional state, it would hardly be in terms as mild as "getting me down" or "to my relief." Hemingway used Henry's "hardness" to undercut one kind of false romanticism, but at the cost of endorsing another kind: the myth of the hard-boiled. Levine transforms that style. His persona is placed, not in some extreme situation in which it is easy to perceive what is good and clean and true, but rather in the banality of quotidian existence where the romantic gesture of adopting an antiromantic stance is pointless. The voice we hear makes no attempt to ingratiate itself with us, but neither does it seek to impress us by being so curt and reticent. It is, in fact, close to being disinterested; unlike Frederic Henry's, it has nothing to protect. It is therefore ideally suited to the confessional writer's aim of achieving "a critical distance from the self" (Lasch, p. 48).

Levine accomplished this, fully and triumphantly, in his 1970 novel *From a Seaside Town*. An examination of his early works — the poetry, *The Angled Road*, *Canada Made Me* — reveals a young writer developing strengths and eliminating weaknesses, trying out various conventional forms but moving steadily in his own direc-tion. The first stories representative of his artistic maturity appeared in *One Way Ticket* (1961); his experiments with persona in this volume prepared the way for both *From a Seaside Town* and his later collections *I Don't Want to Know Anyone Too Well* and *Thin Ice*. These volumes exhibit most of the same "confessional" characteristics as the novel, but in my discussion of them, I will concentrate on showing the injustice of the often-repeated charges that Levine's fiction is "depressing" and that he does not have "major things to say."

Levine's preoccupation with style may in part be explained by the fact that he began as a poet — although his published output of poetry has been small. *Myssium* (1948) collects nine poems; *The Tight-Rope Walker* (1950) has eighteen, three of them reprinted from *Myssium*; *I Walk by the Harbour* (1976) has eleven, two of them reprinted (with minor alterations) from *The Tight-Rope Walker*. Much of the early work is painfully imitative. T. S. Eliot's presence dominates one page, Dylan Thomas' the next. Occasion-ally Levine is able to move beyond pastiche:

On the flat dark tongue of coated roads
Ugly short men held fat butter hands

And small girls raised thin legs
And clapped hands to the rhythm of a bouncing ball
And swallow breasts nervously chewed gum[55]

There are too many adjectives here, but the underlying principle of the passage, that poetry can be discovered in precise observation of the ordinary, was to become centrally important in his later writing.

St. Ives encouraged Levine to depend less on literary influences and more on the external world. In a prefatory note to *I Walk by the Harbour*, most of whose poems were written in 1949 and 1959, Levine comments that ". . . it was a reaction to the physical presence of this particular place (the harbour, the moors, going out fishing) which produced most of the poems."[56] In the best poems in both that volume and *The Tight-Rope Walker*, Levine's delight in figurative language is married to his desire to record his experience accurately. For example, in "St. Ives Cornwall" the energy of the metaphors is used to convey a precise visual sense of the harbour: "Cradled sea-horse, bent gnarled finger, blue-eyes / At the end of a fish-hook, hooking the filth."[57] Sometimes rhetoric overwhelms subject matter in these poems. But at their most successful — in "Crabbing,"[58] for example — they show Levine making sophisticated use of poetic techniques to bring the texture of an experience to life.

The Angled Road (1952) is an oddity: a *Bildungsroman* whose protagonist never reaches maturity. There is something both courageous and naïve about Levine's approach. The material is autobiographical in obvious ways, and it is apparent that he wants to tell the truth, no matter what the cost. But this attitude leads to problems with structure. Levine appears unwilling or unable to subordinate his raw material to aesthetic ends. The equation of honesty with artistic merit is no doubt common enough among first novelists, and the result is predictable.

David Wrixon grows up on Dorset Street in a Canadian slum which Levine coyly avoids identifying as Ottawa's Lower Town. (Wrixon is, strangely, not Jewish; Levine has written that at this time he was "running away from being a Jew" and so "cut out the fact that my characters were Jewish."[59]) The dominant figure in Wrixon's life is his mother — "his first love, and his longest."[60] His father, a pedlar, is weak and ineffectual, although David feels affection for him. Mrs. Wrixon desperately wants her son to escape from Dorset Street to a world of cultured respectability; throughout his adolescence, she lives vicariously through him. Then he joins the RCAF and becomes a bomber pilot stationed in England. He has two affairs, with Valerie, an aspiring actress, and with Pat, a university student. The first ends when Valerie becomes pregnant and, at his insistence, has an abortion; the second, when he decides that he is not ready for marriage. When the war is over, he returns to Dorset Street. Several months later, he leaves again, this time for university. The break with his parents' world is to be final.

What Levine is attempting to do with Wrixon's character is suggested in the Emily Dickinson poem he uses as an epigraph: man is compelled "to choose himself / His pre-appointed pain" (p. 6). The choices Wrixon makes as an adult are in a sense determined by his background, but they tend to cause more pain to others than to himself. He acts with a ruthlessness towards his women that mirrors his mother's manipulation of his father. He is understandably fearful of sinking back into his parents' poverty, but there is nothing likeable about him. At one point he considers committing suicide by flying his bomber straight out to sea. He conducts a stagy internal dialogue — four pages of self-pitying analysis of his personal situation — before acknowledging that the members of his crew do not deserve to die and that this may be an argument for turning back. Levine's third-person narrator (point of view shifts constantly between first and third) makes a harsh and accurate judgement on Wrixon: "The making of the man was there. But he was shallow" (pp. 127–28). At the end of the novel he is still, in most respects, an adolescent. From his mother he has gained a sense of the importance of his life, but he has no corresponding sense of the importance of others. He is very much in love with his own ego.

Treated ironically, a character like Wrixon might have been an amusing focus for satire, but Levine asks us to *care* about him and thereby assures the failure of the novel. This is not to say that *The Angled Road* is completely without merit. Its strongest section describes David's childhood. There we are conscious of him less as a "character" than as a perceiving intelligence, collecting vivid fragments of the world around him: his father's helper, for example, ashamed of his bread-and-jam lunch, trying to conceal his food as he eats. In the section set in England, directness is too often replaced by self-conscious image-mongering, as when Valerie's face "appeared to be written by the rain" (p. 60). But some of the set-piece descriptive passages — of flying, of London, of Cornwall — are effective. As in his poetry of this period, Levine was cultivating in his prose a style which could capture individual slices of life with clarity and vigour. But he had not found a way to clothe this material with any depth of human significance.

In *Canada Made Me* (1958) Levine attempted to analyze the character of a nation instead of an individual. The Canada he describes in meticulous detail is at least as unattractive as David Wrixon. But this time there is a sense of distance between author and subject that was not there in the novel. *Canada Made Me* is to a much greater extent a finished, professional performance. His subject allows him to make full use of his skill in describing people and places, and he has many cogent things to say about Canadian society. But the book is flawed in important ways: it is long-winded, Levine's implicit argument does not have the clarity and force that it needs, and his handling of his own persona is inept.

Canada Made Me records Levine's 1956 voyage from England to Canada on an emigrant ship and his subsequent journey across the country and back, with stopovers in most major cities and in many out-of-the-way places. He visits friends from childhood and from university, businessmen who have "made it," journalists, academics; but he also spends time with the losers, the people who struggle without hope or who have given up, the denizens of beer parlours and bush camps and cheap rooming houses. His motive, he has said, was to inspire reform:

> . . . a lot of *Canada Made Me* is an attempt to alter Canadian society the way I wanted it to be altered. What I found was a thin veneer on top of life that money and machinery provides, but underneath it — and this is the part that I was exploring — is a large seedy underbelly where people are just ordinary people. . . . I wanted people to be a little more sophisticated. (McDonald, p. 222)

It is not surprising that Levine's motive was misinterpreted. Comparison with Graham Greene is instructive. The book's title proclaims the influence, and *Canada Made Me* seems to be modelled on *The Lawless Roads*, one of the books Levine brings to Canada with him. In it, Greene describes his journey through Mexico, especially the states of Tabasco and Chiapas in 1938, when the

98

Roman Catholic church was being persecuted by a totalitarian regime. Greene of course writes as a committed Catholic, and that commitment gives his perceptions and judgements a coherence that makes it relatively easy for a reader to respond to the book. By contrast, it is not always easy to see what, if anything, Levine is committed to. At one point he admits that this is a problem:

> How I envied Graham Greene's characters. They rebelled, they were on the run, anarchistic, but they were lucky. They all had behind them an established order of values.
>
> One still clung to a morality but without the faith that ruled it. One was like a chicken running around without its head. All that was left was the personal.[61]

Greene's attitudes are Catholic; Levine's attitudes are . . . Levine's. Why should a reader take them seriously, especially if they convey messages that he does not particularly wish to hear? Levine does not appear to have asked himself this question.

If he had, he might have gone to some lengths to make his persona more sympathetic. The Levine who speaks to us in *Canada Made Me* is the stereotypical Angry Young Man. He complains constantly about his poor health and lack of money. He shows little feeling for others — one always wonders whether he ever actually liked the people he refers to as friends. He has a sense of humour but invariably takes himself very seriously. Surely the reviewers were right to be suspicious of Levine's good faith, as he stalks the country like an overage Holden Caulfield, relentlessly cataloguing examples of phoniness and squalor. After a single visit to an Indian reservation, he is able to conclude that "of course the white man did not like something he could not understand, so he tried to destroy it" (p. 180). It is the "of course" that grates here, with its implicit moral complacency. The judgement may well be *right*, but the rhetoric is distracting. When reviewers wrote about Levine's "bigotry," they were only giving him what he asked for.

This is unfortunate, because his indictment of Canadian society deserves serious thought. His thesis is that the country does offer material prosperity, but in order to achieve it, the individual must make himself over in the image which society requires. He feels this most powerfully in the case of the Lower Town of his childhood. He does not idealize this community: life was hard for his parents' generation; people were not uniformly happy. But for Levine the point is that it *was* a community. The next generation, his, has been taught to identify itself with "the outside":

> I can still remember those afternoons when we had to go up to the front of the class, in turn, and pretend we were selling something: a car, a washing machine, a house, while our teacher criticized our technique. To "get on" meant turning one's back on Lower Town and the values it represented. (pp. 47–48)

Now they are confronted by a new problem:

> ... they have to reconcile what they are told is the envy of the world with the emptiness, dullness, and the boredom of their own lives. ... For all the comfort: the fine homes, deep freeze, the gadgets, they were resentful; they felt they were being cheated, though of what they didn't quite know. (pp. 60–61)

Levine devotes much of the book to documenting this emptiness, dullness, and boredom. A depressing portrait gallery of "successful" Canadians takes shape, their sameness being perhaps their most depressing characteristic. Levine's acquaintance "L": "Behind that exterior of charm and friendliness, there was nothing, only indifference" (p. 58); academics in Winnipeg: "They all had 'solid respectability' advertised in their entire bearing and with it a passiveness and deadness" (p. 98); "Mrs. M.," a pillar of Saskatoon society: "A mask that one looks at and is fascinated, but there was nothing coming out behind it" (p. 129). There are many other examples.

But Levine writes more interestingly about "the failures, ... the seedy, . . . the newcomers who could not fit in" (p. 225). He approves of failure, because to fail is to have retained one's integrity, to have refused at some level to wear the bland masks that signal respectability. There is an implied sympathy in his portraits of such down-and-outers as Henry, the Vancouver remittance man, a failed actor become alcoholic cab driver. Levine is careful to avoid sentimentality — in fact, he notes Henry's own tendency to self-pity — and he avoids pronouncing the sort of overt judgement he makes of "L" and "Mrs. M.," but a sense of Henry's essential though damaged dignity somehow emerges. Similarly, a description of a day in court in Vancouver (a procession of confused and inarticulate people being hustled through an incomprehensible ritual) ends, not with a diatribe against the legal system, but with ironic understatement: "The judge was a professional. The policeman was a professional. Only the victim, if he was poor, was the amateur" (p. 182). Such passages work well because Levine simply presents his evidence and trusts the reader to respond appropriately.

The book's other major problem, structure, was perhaps insoluble, assuming that Levine was committed to writing about the whole country. He says everything essential in the first hundred or so pages, in the chapters describing the voyage from England, the return to Ottawa, the trip to the mine in the bush of northern Ontario. It is not that the quality of the writing diminishes after that point, but rather that the same kind of experience continues to be reported and analysed. Edmonton and Winnipeg are as desolate as the cities of the East, and the beer parlours of the West are no more civilized than those of Sault Ste. Marie. Levine's characteristic method of description in this book — to overwhelm the reader with detail — becomes gradually more oppressive, too, especially since so much of it is negative. There is a disquieting sense that he wanted to use everything recorded in his notebook. In the case of *Canada Made Me*, less would have been more.

Levine's own judgement of the book, about twenty years after the fact, is interesting: "There's a nice immediacy about sections of it and I'm glad I've got that part of Canadian life down in certain pages" (McDonald, p. 223). This, I think, is how most readers will respond now to the book: as a series of discrete units, many of which are extremely successful on their own terms.

All but one of the stories in *One Way Ticket* (1961) were written between 1956 and 1960, that is, during and after the writing of *Canada Made Me*. The collection consists of eight short stories and one longer one. In the best of them, Levine solves brilliantly the problems with which he was wrestling in *Canada Made Me*.

"A Small Piece of Blue"[62] provides a useful focus for discussion, because much of it is taken verbatim from the section of *Canada Made Me* in which Levine returns to the Algoma Ore mine in northern Ontario where he had worked one summer during his university days. But much has been changed, too. In *Canada Made Me*, it is of course "Levine himself" who speaks to us. He is quite explicit about the conclusion he wants us to draw about life in the bush — "the boredom, the isolation, and the continual defeat of any form of human relationship" (*Canada Made Me*, p. 93). In "A Small Piece of Blue," Levine eliminates the editorializing, a conventional enough decision. But we might also expect a reworking of the narrator's character so that we are led to make this sort of judgement for ourselves, either because we trust his responses as compatible with ours or because he is presented in a clearly ironic way. Both of these approaches would require Levine to give us a much more complete picture of the narrator's character than we get of his own persona in *Canada Made Me*. But Levine chose to do something radically different: to create a narrator about whose character, responses, and judgements we know virtually nothing. This makes for a sort of fiction which demands a great deal from the reader, who is used to getting more guidance about what he should think and feel.

The narrator of "A Small Piece of Blue" is called Tree. All that we know about him is that he has just graduated from university and thinks that working at the mine will be an antidote to the intellectual life. There is no plot. Tree describes a series of experiences he has before beginning work at the mine. He makes travel arrangements with an unpleasantly salesmanlike company man in the Algoma Ore office in Sault Ste. Marie. Then he rents a room for the night from a landlady whose face Tree finds "startling" because ". . . where her nose should have been there was a flat surface of scarred flesh with two small holes" (p. 89). Like Levine's *Canada Made Me* persona, Tree prefers the sight of the deformity itself to the false nose he later sees her wearing. This is Tree's only value judgement. In the morning he takes the company train to the mine. The girl in the office there is coarse-featured and unsmiling. The man in charge of the dormitory is old, unshaven, toothless; his room "stank of old age" (p. 96). At his first meal, Tree sits opposite a worker suffering from various deformities: "Stubbles for fingers on a wrist which was raw. . . . He used [a] handkerchief to hold his jaw together" (p. 97). The next morning he is sent to have a medical examination. The doctor is an alcoholic named Crepeau who, like Tree, is from McGill. They begin to drink, and Crepeau amuses himself by shooting at a candle flame with an air rifle. He claims to have chosen to become a failure, to repudiate what the university has given him: "a fake smartness like a car on the assembly line" (p. 101). The sources of his personal bitterness remain obscure, but his attitudes are clear: "I don't want any of that kind of civilization. . . . I drink, and I write poetry" (p. 103). Finally he suggests that they walk by the lake, which, Crepeau says, seems to him to be shaped like a heart.

Tree never tells us what he thinks of all this. There is potential in Crepeau to be either a comic drunk or a dangerous psychopath, but Tree is neither amused nor afraid, as far as we know. The Levine of *Canada Made Me* would agree with much of what Crepeau says about Canadian society, but the doctor hardly qualifies for the role of author's mouthpiece. The same problem arises with respect to the narrative as a whole. Tree does not say what the experience "means" to him. His determinedly neutral tone of voice is not much help. We need to pay attention to the coherence of the images.

This is not difficult in the case of "A Small Piece of Blue," since virtually everything in the story speaks of suffering, frustration, bitterness, despair. While we can admire some of the characters — the landlady, for example, who is able to speak of her deformity "without sadness or humour" (p. 89) — we are appalled at the barrenness of their lives as Tree perceives them. Even the warmth of ordinary human contact seems beyond their reach, let alone any potential for fulfilment or joy. Desolation reigns. That Tree does not call our attention to this fact makes it all the more moving. His final description of the lake as "a small piece of blue locked in the surrounding earth" (p. 105) crystallizes our sense of the personal isolation which the characters experience.

But the image remains open-ended. Is the story about working conditions or the human condition? Levine does not ask us to choose between Brecht's perspective and Beckett's. Instead he forces us to look at the characters without the comforting safety goggles of "a perspective," forces us to contemplate their pain, not as illustration of a theory, but as naked fact of human experience.

The two other stories in *One Way Ticket* that are as successful as "A Small Piece of Blue" also use its methods: "The Cocks Are Crowing" (pp. 107–22), about a plutocrat dying of Parkinson's disease, and "Feast Days and Others" (pp. 159–71). In the latter, Levine departs, but only very slightly, from the practice of making the narrator in some fairly obvious way a surrogate for himself. "Feast Days and Others" is told by a young girl modeled on one of his daughters. The family lives in a semidetached cottage in the English countryside; the father writes book reviews for a London

paper. Again the story is plotless. The girl describes a series of random events — catching mice, a freak August storm that knocks out
the electricity in the village, a Christmas Day visit from her grandparents, the arrival by mail two weeks later of a Christmas goose
which has to be buried immediately because of the smell. The various elements of the story cohere into a pattern similar to that
formed by the images in a lyric poem. The pattern suggests that the
grounds for celebration can be found in almost any unremarkable
happening or minor disaster. The August storm generates "a
strange excitement, almost of gaiety" among the villagers (p. 164).
Grandad is incontinent on the way to the railway station, but he
makes a joke of it, and Gran treats him with understanding and
affection. The scene describing the burial of the goose ends with the
baby chasing a sunbeam. The ironic message of the title is that there
need be no "Others"; every day would be a "Feast Day" if we
could share the narrator's perceptions. Not that her emotions are
used to manipulate us: her account is as objective as Tree's.

The longer story, "The Playground" (pp. 11–75), is not as good
as these three. It does succeed brilliantly in creating a sense of place:
St. Ives, Cornwall. But it has no intensity. Most of the characters
are members of the local bohemian community, and there is a kind
of *Great Gatsby* feel to the narrative — one paragraph begins
"These were the people Bill Stringer met at the round of parties in
the summer of 1959" (p. 24) — but the scale is smaller, and there is
no Gatsby to provide shape and focus. Instead there is a meticulous
examination of the surface of lives that are essentially trivial and
selfish. The one exception to this is Carl Darch, the painter — pat-
terned after Levine's friend Francis Bacon[63] — who appears for
only a few pages and does not interact with the other characters.
His seriousness about his art distinguishes him from the others, but
Levine does not try to develop this contrast in dramatic terms.

There are five other stories in *One Way Ticket*. "A Sabbath
Walk" (pp. 123–39), written in 1950, is sentimental: an old man is
beaten up by a gang of youths and then finds that his only friend
has moved away. "The Lesson" (pp. 141–46) is very slight but well
executed: a young man's attempt to seduce a woman he meets on a
bus is foiled by her husband's not-necessarily expected presence at
the depot. "Ringa Ringa Rosie" (pp. 77–85) has a setting virtually
identical to that of "Feast Days and Others" but is not so subtle and
suffers by comparison. "The Dilettantes" (pp. 147–57), set on the

fringes of London's literary world, is the only story in the volume to feature Levine's underrated talent for humour. "A Memory of Ottawa," like "A Small Piece of Blue," derives directly from *Canada Made Me* but is fairly conventional in its method, although it does vividly evoke Lower Town. With the exception of "A Sabbath Walk," these five stories all display a high level of competence, but they lack the originality of the best work in the volume.

From a Seaside Town (1970) benefits from the experimentation with persona evidenced in *One Way Ticket*. But while the stories in that volume record the narrator's perceptions of the world outside himself, *From a Seaside Town* turns the focus inward. The novel makes use of familiar autobiographical material. Joseph Grand, its narrator, lives in the resort town of Carnbray, Cornwall. He is a Canadian Jew married to an Englishwoman; they have three daughters. Grand makes his living as a travel writer, but the magazine he depends on folds. In "desperation" he begins to write the book we are reading: a book of "confessions" (p. 37).

Nothing much happens. Grand visits friends in London. A London friend visits Grand in Carnbray. Then his sister and brother-in-law arrive unexpectedly. He almost has an affair with an actress. Eventually he is commissioned to write a couple of articles about Canada, goes to Montreal and Ottawa, sees his parents, returns to England. His father dies. Various minor characters drift in and out of his life. Time passes unobtrusively.

This, I suspect, confused many reviewers. Alden Nowlan, for example, observed that Grand "shows us his world, but he can't seem to help us make sense of it" (Nowlan, p. 63), and Peter Buitenhuis commented that "on the last page but one, Levine writes in a kind of despair: 'Life seems to be a series of brief encounters.'"[64] The force of "seems" was apparently lost on Buitenhuis. Neither Grand nor Levine writes in despair.

The difficulty is that Levine demands a great deal of his reader, as he does in the best work in *One Way Ticket*. It may seem odd to say that Levine uses essentially the same method as he does in "A Small Piece of Blue." In a confessional novel, after all, the narrator's personality must be the main focus of interest. Joseph Grand does in fact make value judgements and reveal his emotional responses in a way that the narrators of the stories do not. But what Grand does *not* express overtly remains more important. What he tells us needs to be read carefully for implication, for nuance, for poetry.

Consider, for example, the passage in which Grand describes a visit to his senile father:

> At the nursing home. Father was alone in the room with the large plate glass window. He was watching broken hunks of ice being carried by the river. I stood by his chair and watched the grey-white chunks of ice go quietly by. We didn't speak, just watched, as a large chunk appeared then moved by very slowly and disappeared. I have always been touched by the silent breaking up of winter. There's something inevitable and majestic as these large hunks of ice move slowly along on the flat water. The minutes passed. The ice passed. We said nothing. A sadness in the room. I told my father I was going back to England. (pp. 165–66)

In a sense, Grand does reveal his emotion directly. But "touched" and "sadness" are generic terms which do nothing to communicate the precise quality of the experience. Perfunctory reading may suggest that the breaking up of the ice provides an annoyingly neat metaphor for what is happening to his father, whose life is about to "disappear" like the large chunk of ice. But not all of the details are appropriate. The father's death is "inevitable" but not "majestic." The passing of the ice implies the coming of spring, for which there will be no counterpart in his father's experience. The inappropriateness intensifies the emotion. First Grand notices what is similar (the father's fate will be to disappear like the chunk of ice) and then what is different (the father's death will not be majestic — but it should be; the father's winter should turn to spring — but it won't). What occurs in nature has its own consolation; what is happening to Grand's father has none. If Grand had spelled all this out, of course, the evocativeness of the passage would have been dissipated. But the subtlety is there.

What is true of a given passage applies to the novel as a whole. Levine is more concerned to make us understand what it is like to be Joseph Grand than to have Grand tell us what his life means. But this does not imply that Grand's life is without meaning.

Levine's own comment on the novel suggests an approach ignored by the reviewers. In the *Queen's Quarterly* interview, he states that "love within a marriage" is what the book is "essentially about" (McDonald, p. 229). Critics like Nowlan and Buitenhuis comment on the marriage only to complain about the "mechanical" quality of Grand's sex life (Nowlan, p. 63), and even Alan Heuser, in what is otherwise an excellent review, comments that Grand's wife, Emily, is "a mere convenience of bed, kitchen, and children" (Heuser, p. 16). To make this sort of judgement is, I think, to have missed the complexity beneath the surface of the marriage.

In the first place, the sexual dimension of the relationship is not as monotonous as the reviewers indicate. Sometimes, it is true, sex *is* mechanical for the Grands: "She undresses. And there's no fooling about. It's over in ten minutes" (p. 217). But on other occasions, it assumes a solemn, symbolic value, as it does after the death of Grand's father: "That night, in bed, it seemed important to emphasize that we were alive" (p. 195). A more characteristic episode is the one described in the first chapter:

> After twelve years of married life we knew our positions in bed as we did around the kitchen table.
>
> I slipped out of her.
>
> "Where's the towel?" she said.
>
> I reached over and got the towel. She wiped her groin. Then she gave me the towel. I tried to wipe the wet part of the sheet. In the end we pulled the sheet so neither of us would have the wet part.
>
> "That was good," she said.
>
> She lay against my side, her head on my arm. Then it became uncomfortable.
>
> "Shall I turn?" she asked.
>
> She turned on her side, away from me, and I came close behind her so that we lay like a pair of stacked chairs.
>
> "Goodnight love," she said. (pp. 9–10)

Grand's description seems to aim at clinical objectivity, an approach which would proclaim the banality of the encounter. But as with the description of the ice in the river, not all of the elements in the passage support this interpretation. The reference to the kitchen table (a world of shared commitment outside the bed), the comedy of the wet sheet, the affectionate gestures of communication, the homeliness and humour of the image of the "stacked chairs" all indicate that what Grand is telling us about is far from "mechanical." It is as if he is letting us know in an undertone that

banality has somehow been conquered, the moment redeemed.
There is no reason to believe that Emily is lying — she never does —
when she says that it was good.

Scenes like this one reveal the nature of the marriage. The texture
of routine never quite obliterates the possibility of experience that is
fresher, more authentic. At one point, Grand recalls that when he
first met Emily, he felt that he had to lie about his background:
"Only later was I to know that I didn't have to, that I could have
played it straight with her all along" (p. 47). Emily enables Grand
to "play it straight"; her presence prevents him from sinking into
the morass of bad faith that engulfs so many of the secondary characters in *From a Seaside Town*. She is consistently identified with an
uncompromising honesty. One of the first things we learn about her
is that ". . . she had no small talk and came out with truthful but
embarrassing things" (p. 8). At one point, Grand chides her for telling a neighbour about their financial problems. She retorts that he
can "put it all in a story" (p. 216), as though that were not essentially the same thing. He thinks about this:

> What could I say. I saw nothing wrong in writing about it
> because I saw writing as something different than living. I
> mean I tell the truth in writing. But in life I live it in different
> ways, with different people, full of evasions. (p. 216)

The book of "confessions" is Grand's paradoxical attempt to tran-
scend his evasiveness by revealing it "in writing" for all the world,
but especially Emily — and himself — to see. The book is full of
"truthful but embarrassing things" about Grand himself, including
an extended account of his futile attempt to be unfaithful to Emily.
The reviewers who emphasized the boredom, pettiness, and sadness missed the way in which the revelation of truths which are
boring, petty, and sad itself becomes the occasion for quiet celebration in a world characterized by game-playing and the wearing of
masks. Grand's marriage is to *From a Seaside Town* what Lower
Town is to *Canada Made Me* — imperfect, but the touchstone of a
human reality whose existence is ignored or denied by the
"outside" world.

The only character outside the marriage who is able to live without a mask is Charles Crater, a painter who, like Carl Darch in
"The Playground" (*One Way Ticket*, pp. 11–75), is clearly a
fictionalized version of Francis Bacon.[65] For Crater, art is enough.

He is immensely successful, earning thousands of pounds for a single painting, but he lives very simply. Although his homosexuality is a burden to him, he is somehow able to transmute personal pain into art of the highest order. A sad man, he is courageous in a way that Grand does not need to be, and perhaps could not be.

The other important secondary characters are trapped in tedium and dishonesty by the roles they have chosen to play. Jimmy Middleton, the philandering Christian, is an incarnation of the *Playboy* philosophy; he may also be a compulsive liar. Grand's London friend Albert "has a thing about being a Jew" (p. 12); he convinces himself that he is a Nazi-hunter and fantasizes that he is followed by spies, in the meantime doing nothing with his life. Anna Likely, the actress who leads Grand on, is more interested in exploiting the melodramatic possibilities of the situation than she is in seducing Grand; all the world, obviously, is her stage.

Grand's life is located somewhere midway between theirs and Crater's. He wants to be his own man, but the world is always ready to supply him with a prefabricated identity: as writer, as husband, as Canadian, and as Jew, to name only the most prominent. Grand's struggle has a comic dimension that Crater's does not, but it is serious nonetheless: "Part of me wants the conventional and some other part wants to be outside society. Yet I cannot take one without longing for the other" (p. 162).

The problem of Jewishness is central. "I thought I put the Jewish business behind me by marrying an English girl," he says at one point (p. 44). His children celebrate Christmas but not Chanukah. On such issues it is easy for him to keep his emotional distance from his friend Albert and from his sister and brother-in-law. But when his father dies, and Grand is unable to afford the airfare to go to Canada for the funeral, he visits the old Jewish cemetery in Penzance. The caretaker accompanies him. Once they are inside the walled cemetery, some mischievous boys bolt the door, locking them in. They are trapped for three hours. Alan Heuser comments on the significance of this experience:

> The episode epitomizes Grand's dilemma. He is unwittingly and necessarily imprisoned within a defunct identity he denies, and in denying he affirms it as something hauntingly present. It is an existential paradox, if you will, and the episode is very funny and very moving. . . . (Heuser, p. 16)

So the conventional keeps asserting itself even as Grand attempts to reject it. Apparently there can never be a final reconciliation between its claims and those of the iconoclast within himself. All he can do is to be aware of the conflict and not to lose sight of the truth. That way sanity lies; and in *From a Seaside Town*, sanity is Emily, who combines conventionality *par excellence* in her roles as wife and mother with an honesty as radical as any Grand can envison for his art.

Looking banality in the eye, Grand finds something to celebrate in the most unexpected places. After a night of lovemaking with Emily, for example:

> Next morning when I went to the toilet, a satisfied exhausted feeling, the skin of the cock is smooth because of last night, the falling urine sparkled as the sun caught it, and the smell reminded me of French Canadian pea soup. (p. 167)

Precise observation of unpromising fact grows into a delicate and humorous poetry. Almost despite himself, Grand finds something to affirm. And Levine, in writing about Grand, makes his own affirmation.

I Don't Want to Know Anyone Too Well (1971) shares with *From a Seaside Town* this sense of near-paradoxical affirmation. It collects fifteen stories, three of them reprinted from *One Way Ticket* — "A Small Piece of Blue," "Feast Days and Others," and "By the Richelieu" (called "The Cocks Are Crowing" in the earlier volume). The twelve new pieces have for the most part familiar settings — Ottawa, Montreal, London, Cornwall — and the familiar Levine protagonist — air-force officer in 1944, university student in 1947, writer in England in the 1950s and 1960s. The events recorded tend to be in themselves trivial and often sad. But the critic who would use these stories as evidence that Levine's work is "depressing" has not looked deeply enough, as William Cooper suggests in his review when he comments that, although they are "pervaded by the ineffable sadness of life," somehow they "leave one's spirits raised."

"A True Story"[66] is a case in point. As usual, the plot is minimal. The narrator teaches school in a small Canadian town. By chance he meets a young woman — ". . . there was an awkwardness about her, something incomplete" (pp. 45–46) — who has coffee with him but rejects his advances. Weeks later he learns that she has died. He attends the funeral. The fundamentalist congregation is cheerful, certain of her salvation. Returning to school, he meets a colleague and the story ends:

> "Isn't it a glorious day," he said.
> "It is," I said.
> The sun was shining. The snow on the ground and on the trees glistened. We could see our breath in the cold still air. (p. 48)

So far, so sad. But the narrator tells us not only about his encounter with the girl, Marie, but also about his English classes and about ex-Colonel and Mrs. Brown, in whose farmhouse he rents living space. The first-year high-school students have been taught to write an archaic, stilted prose. The narrator tells them to simply write down what they see in the course of a walk. They begin to perceive what is really there in the world around them; their writing becomes clear and direct. The Browns are Anglo-Irish. Socially they are out of place, their farming technique is poor, they suffer many setbacks. But they persevere, although they often seem ridiculous — Mrs. Brown skips rope like a young girl; Mr. Brown tries to fix farm machinery by kicking it.

These facts, casually woven into the narrative, affect the reader's response to Marie. Like the Browns, she is awkward and out of place; like the students, she is able to tell the narrator the truth about herself, as she perceives it: "I don't seem to know how to behave with other people. . . . I don't have friends . . . I don't seem able to give enough . . ." (p. 46). She risks rejection by revealing herself in this way, but the narrator, who has intended to seduce her, now tries to comfort her. Perhaps she will now be encouraged to persevere like the Browns. Perhaps her life will change as dramatically as the students' writing.

Then she dies. It seems that the "ineffable sadness" of life has triumphed. Although at the funeral the believers have no sense of loss, the narrator distances himself from their attitude; he sits with the small group who wear black and mourn openly. On the other hand, he says nothing about his own feelings. This prepares us for the passage that ends the story.

Almost the only fact we know about the other teacher is that he believes in reincarnation. When he speaks, we are reminded of the religious connotations of the word "glory." The narrator's response seems ambiguous enough, especially since he says nothing about his tone of voice. But the last paragraph provides a pertinent gloss. He expresses no religious views. Like his students, he reports what he perceives: sunshine, snow, trees, their own breath, cold air — an environment which has its own literal kind of "glory" but which seems essentially hostile or at best indifferent to humanity. But human beings make themselves at home there, and this is the glory that the narrator is affirming: the simple presence of human breath, in all its vulnerability. The world drives us to extreme and apparently absurd gestures: living like the Browns, believing in reincarnation or the Bible, reaching out naïvely to others as Marie has done. But these gestures declare our humanity. The story invites us to contemplate not only the sadness of life but also the odd dignity-in-absurdity of our existence. In so doing, it can leave the reader's spirits raised.

Many of the stories in *I Don't Want to Know Anyone Too Well* possess this quality. In "In Quebec City" (pp. 7–22), Frieda Rubin's experience parallels Marie's. She is much older than the narrator, an RCAF pilot in training, but confides to him that she feels "trapped" by life (p. 14). Her husband, Mendel, is genial but insensitive. Her eighteen-year-old daughter, Constance, is silly. Frieda reads Colette, grows orchids, and plays Chopin. Jimmy Ross, the narrator, is uncomprehending but fascinated. He regards Constance's invitation to her bed as a rather poor consolation prize. Then he leaves for overseas. Twenty years after the war he returns to Quebec City by chance. Frieda has died, Mendel has remarried, and Constance has her own family in Detroit. There is sadness in all of this, but the effect created is more complex than recitation of the facts suggests. The moral is not that the crass shall inherit the earth: Mendel and Constance are both amiable enough. In fact it is not clear that there is a moral. Frieda's life has been unfulfilled, but her struggle to maintain her identity is worth celebrating. And she has touched Ross in a way that she could never touch her husband or daughter, a valuable moment for both of them. Ross does not spell this out, but Levine allows us to infer it.

Three of the other of the most successful stories work in the same way. "A Father" (pp. 147–53) describes a young officer's farewell to his family. The father's legendary ineptitude at cards has made him an object of contempt among his friends, and he has known a deeper humiliation in his metamorphosis from man about town in Warsaw to fruit pedlar in Ottawa. The moment of leave-taking is tense; the mother is deeply distressed. The father defuses the crisis by telling a series of absurd jokes. The son feels that he has, for the first time, seen what is most powerfully alive in him. In "The English Girl" (pp. 69–76), the narrator remembers, in affectionate, meticulous detail, his affair at McGill with a girl whose name we never learn; in fact he tells us little about her personality, either. The emphasis is on the evocation, at a distance of fifteen years, of the lost world which they shared. In "I Like Chekhov" (pp. 77–83), Chester Conn Bell, who has taught for a year at a Yorkshire secondary school, goes to a pub with two of his colleagues on the last day of the school year. Bell, a writer, is moving on. The others, referred to only as the Latin Master and the Geography Master, are obviously stuck permanently in the small town, as is the barmaid, the "handsome but vulnerable" Sophie Jewtree (p. 80). On a pretext, she invites Bell into a back room; they kiss, "not gently" (p. 82) — but nothing comes of it. Bell's self-confidence and optimism (bordering on naïveté) are set against the other characters' resignation to lives that are routine, if not quietly desperate. In all three stories, the sadness of parting or loss coexists with a sense of affirmation that seems stronger.

Two others achieve their level of excellence. "My Karsh Picture" (pp. 49–54), the funniest story Levine has written, describes the taking of the portrait of a nineteen-year-old officer about to go to war — not by Karsh, but by Karsh's "toucher-upper" (p. 50) and his helper, a tailor's assistant. "South of Montreal" (pp. 154–59) describes the narrator's summer of 1947 at Ile aux Noix on the Richelieu, tutoring three teenaged boys (a French Canadian and two Guatemalans) in English. Reviewers have misread the story as a study of French-English relations,[67] but in fact it deals with the theme of the precariousness of "civilization."

"The Man with the Notebook" (pp. 120–31) is a story in which sadness predominates. An old man makes his living writing sketches about people he has observed. At a certain point, he begins to notice that one by one his subjects die soon after he has written about them. He stops writing and eventually dies himself from hunger and cold. The story is eerily effective until the last paragraph, when Levine uncharacteristically presents a reductive moral: ". . . it is hard to write — or live for that matter — without hurting someone" (p. 131). The other stories are all well crafted but not so distinctive. "I Don't Want to Know Anyone Too Well" (pp. 132–46), "English for Foreigners" (pp. 107–10), "My Wife Has Left Me" (pp. 84–94), and "A Canadian Upbringing" (pp. 111–19) depend more or less heavily on their eccentric characters. Their style marks them as Levine's, but they lack the subtlety and intensity of his best work. Eleven of the fifteen stories in this collection (including the three reprinted from *One Way Ticket*) present Levine at his characteristic best, squeezing the blood of poetry from the stone of bland and trivial fact.

Selected Stories (1975) may be placed in a sort of parenthesis in any discussion of the books of Levine's artistic maturity. It comprises eight previously published stories (two of which appeared as chapters in *From a Seaside Town*) and one new one ("In Lower Town," pp. 107–16), arranged in such a way as to present a sort of biography of the Levine persona, although his name and various other details change from story to story. The book begins with "A Father" (pp. 5–11), in which the son, on his way to war, glimpses his father's essential humanity in an unexpected way. It ends with "In Lower Town," in which the son, now a successful writer, makes a return visit. The neighbourhood is being torn down and replaced by new buildings, but the community is alive in the narrator's memory, just as his father, much earlier, had cherished the image of himself as a sophisticated European long after coming to Canada. The protagonist, too, keeps his personal past alive.

Perhaps *Selected Stories* occupies the place of the *Bildungsroman* which *The Angled Road* failed to be. Even though the protagonist is in his forties in some of the stories, flashbacks emphasize the subtle and pervasive influence of the past in forming his mature personality. Like David Wrixon, he is tested in various ways — by love ("The English Girl" [pp. 28–35]), by poverty ("Ringa Ringa Rosie" [pp. 53–60], and "I'll Bring You Back Something Nice" [pp. 61–81]), and by a more general sense of being "trapped by life" ("Why Do You Live So Far Away?" [pp. 82–106]). He has a sense of irony about himself that Wrixon did not, but the irony is not corrosive; it helps him to cope with adversity. He is also more sympathetic with those engaged in their own difficult struggles (Frieda Rubin of "In Quebec City" [pp. 12–27], Madame de Wyssmann of

"South of Montreal" [pp. 36–41], and the Brennans of "My Wife Has Left Me" [pp. 42–52]). Still, the book is unsatisfying. It breaks no new ground, and the stories are not Levine's nine best or anything close to it. There may have been sound practical reasons for publishing *Selected Stories*, but there is little artistic justification.

In *Thin Ice* (1979), Levine continues to mine the confessional vein of *From a Seaside Town* and *I Don't Want to Know Anyone Too Well*. I wish to concentrate my discussion, however, on *Thin Ice*'s thematic dimension, in the hope of refuting the canard that Levine does not have "major things to say." *Thin Ice* consists of twelve stories, only one of which ("In Lower Town") has been previously collected. Six are set in Canada, six in England. They describe the protagonist's brief encounters with women, his return to Lower Town, his family life in Cornwall, his sense of himself as a writer. In six of the stories, the narrator is essentially an observer of others. In six, he is like Joseph Grand, observing himself. But *Thin Ice* has a deeper unity. The ideas of freedom, bondage, and commitment recur in story after story — "Chains and freedom, I thought. Chains and freedom"[68] — in a way that suggests we are being given a dozen glimpses of a single vision.

The six stories in which the emphasis is on the narrator's observation of others divide up neatly into three pairs: two describe characters who are not free, two deal with the theme of freedom misused, and two embody the notion that freedom is properly exercised in the context of commitment. This makes Levine sound uncharacteristically didactic, but there is no preachiness. The texture of these stories is as engaging as in the best work in his previous books.

Of the two stories in which the main character is "trapped by life," one is among the weakest in the volume and one among the best. "To Blisland" (pp. 73–79) describes the visit of the narrator and his wife to their eighteen-year-old daughter, Carol, in a mental institution. The story hovers on the brink of sentimentality, as Levine exploits the obvious potential for pathos. "Hello, Mrs. Newman" (pp. 80–88) is more complex and interesting. Mrs. Newman is trapped in a social role that is partly thrust upon her and partly of her own devising. A native of St. Ives, she has been the wife of a colonial administrator. When they return there to retire, she will not admit to her origins, although the townspeople know about her past in intimate detail. After her husband dies, her social isolation is almost complete. Still she maintains an almost perfect façade of superiority, although the narrator is sometimes able to see, for a moment, the suffering behind it. Eventually she dies, apparently by suicide. The thematic territory here is clearly borrowed from *From a Seaside Town*. Unlike Joseph Grand, Mrs. Newman is unable to separate personal and social identity, but there is something impressive about her futile struggle to live out the role she has chosen.

Other characters in *Thin Ice* do have freedom but fail to make constructive use of it. In "Champagne Barn" (pp. 60–72), the narrator, in one of four stories about his return to Ottawa, visits his spinster cousin Esther and his boyhood friend Harvey. Life has passed Esther by — her doctor, she says, "said it was the first time he had seen an intact hymen in someone of my age" (p. 63) — and she expresses her frustration by arguing with her television and having restaurant meals sent back. Harvey has given his life to the making of money, driven by his fear of the poverty he experienced in childhood. Although he is likable, there is a sense that he has devoted his immense energy to unworthy ends. The narrator is staying with his mother, in a senior citizens' apartment building; death is everywhere, and it is sad that people are unable to make more of their lives in the time that they have. But being alive at all is cause for rejoicing. The complexity of the mood is epitomized by the narrator's last image of Lower Town: five butchers cutting meat — "Hack, hack, hack. While the birds sang. The black squirrels moved quickly and stopped on the grass" (p. 72). Life and death are seamlessly interwoven. We should cherish our freedom while we have it.

"Grace and Faigel" (pp. 89–105) is not so ambitious thematically but hits its seriocomic target. The narrator, chronically faithful to his wife in England, almost has two affairs while he is in Ottawa to give a reading. Grace, about to be divorced, likes sex because of "the power it gives [her] over a man" (p. 96). She leads the narrator on — he is well aware that he is making a fool of himself — and finally escapes. Faigel is married, but her husband is out of town during the week. She speaks matter-of-factly about experiences that shock the narrator — "Shop-lifting, cocaine, three in a bed" (p. 102) — and alienates him by checking her engagement book before suggesting an "appointment" for the following week. Though he is attracted strongly to both women, he is taken aback by the cold-bloodedly experimental way both seem to approach their relationships with men. Sexual freedom has led to emotional detachment and trivialization.

Of the two stories dealing with the importance of commitment, "The Girl Next Door" (pp. 106–13) is much the simpler. A girl named Lynn, who has left her boyfriend, moves into a rented room next to the narrator's. Her freedom is in a sense absolute, but she becomes depressed and finally suicidal. The narrator, committed to his own writing project, feels unable to give her the attention she needs. Eventually she returns to her boyfriend, and a month later the narrator sees her laughing with a group of young people.

"By a Frozen River" (pp. 1–12) is set in a northern Ontario town where the narrator has, as usual, gone in order to write. He meets two couples, the Labelles — an alcoholic photographer and his Jewish wife, who is, at fifty-eight, seventeen years her husband's senior — and the Bischofswerders, the only permanent Jewish residents. The Labelles quarrel constantly but stay together; Mr. Bischofswerder conducts services at the *shul* even though he (and, temporarily, the narrator) comprise the entire congregation. What the Labelles and Mr. Bischofswerder have in common is their apparently irrational dedication to a cause which, practically speaking, might just as well be abandoned. But they gain a strange dignity by reaffirming their choice to continue. Their moral stature would diminish if they chose to renounce the commitments on which they have centred their lives.

Of the six stories which deal with the narrator's own sense of himself, five are directly about problems peculiar to writers. The exception is "A Visit" (pp. 48–59), in which his mother, sister, and retarded nephew come to Cornwall. He resents being part of the family; he counts the days until it is time for them to leave. His wife sees the situation differently: "I don't belong to anything. There's your mother, your sister, and yourself — you all belong to something. Even if you have run away from it" (p. 57). Her notion that it is enviable to "belong" surprises him. His mother and sister (like the characters in "By a Frozen River") seem quietly heroic in their dedication to the retarded nephew. The story affirms the value of this sort of commitment, despite the narrator's understandable impatience at having it forced upon him.

There is no sacrifice of universality in the stories which examine the protagonist's professional concerns as a writer. In "Thin Ice" (pp. 114–24), for example, a writer-in-residence at an unnamed Maritimes university is stranded in a small town because of a snowstorm. With almost no money, he is reduced to crashing a wedding reception in order to eat and to selling a copy of his own book at a secondhand store. He learns how fragile his (or anyone's) material well-being is, how easily freedom of action may be snatched away.

In two stories, the notion of total freedom is played off against a more limited but somehow worthier or more productive kind, involving commitment. In "We All Begin in a Little Magazine" (pp. 38–47), the narrator contrasts his present life — "Writing has become my living" — with the excitement of the early days "when you wrote when you felt like it" (p. 43). He and his family have rented a house whose owner edits a little magazine. People associated with it keep calling and turning up unannounced, but the narrator knows that he is no longer one of them. To be "a writer" is to sacrifice the naïve enthusiasm of the amateur. In "Class of 1949" (pp. 13–29), the protagonist is visited in Cornwall by Victor (the friend with whom he had come to St. Ives in 1949) and Abdullah, Victor's Moroccan lover. Independently wealthy, Victor is free in a sense that the narrator is not — free, among other things, to repudiate the past; he has forgotten almost everything about the life they had shared. After Victor has gone, the narrator returns to his study: "Why am I chained to this desk, I asked myself. What's so important about writing? Victor was living a much freer life" (p. 29). But this feeling soon fades. Although Victor is not overtly condemned for having done nothing constructive with his life, his lack of commitment to anything is contrasted implicitly with the narrator's dedication. The writer's chains are in a sense his freedom. The past provides his material. Writing is the act by which he gives meaning to his life.

The other two stories concerning the narrator's own sense of himself deal with the importance of becoming reconciled to one's personal past. Again, a naïve notion of freedom (that it can be equated with denial of, or escape from, one's origins) is juxtaposed with a more sophisticated one (that it involves acknowledging the past and allowing it to nourish the present). In "In Lower Town" (pp. 30–37), the narrator remembers the odd freedom that his father and other Jews enjoyed: they could speak Yiddish and not be understood by anyone outside their community. As a boy, he had to struggle to keep a straight face as he sold vegetables to a woman

while ". . . my father went on in Yiddish about her likely performance in bed" (p. 32). The narrator's generation no longer have to be
outsiders. His friend Reinhardt tells him about "going to these
group [sex] things" with "very high-class people" (p. 35). The narrator, however, prefers to remain an outsider in many respects. He
finds that Lower Town is "like a magnet" to him (p. 34), and he
continues, despite his mother's objections, to write about the old
days. Although his language is not Yiddish, he is able, in his
writing, to refuse assimilation, to assert his own freedom by recalling what binds him to the past.

This point is made even more explicitly in "A Writer's Story"
(pp. 125–37), set in Cornwall in 1952. The narrator remembers
suffering from writer's block: "I thought at first that, at twenty-
seven, I had run out of material. But as the weeks went by I realized
it wasn't that at all. I didn't know what my material was" (p. 128).
He has been trying to deny his past. He learns how to solve this
problem by listening to two local old-timers, who are saturated
with their own personal pasts and ply him with endless anecdotes.
By the end of the story, he has begun to learn the lesson, as he starts
to make lists of people he grew up with in Ottawa, popular songs
he had known in school, and so on — the "personal" material he
will need in order to keep writing. What he had first seen as something limiting, a "chain" (to borrow the rhetoric of another story),
is what will finally allow him the freedom to practise his art.

Why Do You Live So Far Away? and *Champagne Barn*, both
published in 1984, add little new material to Levine's canon. The
former collects seven stories, two of them previously unpublished in
book form; the latter collects twenty-three, all of them published in
one or more of Levine's earlier books. The two "new" works in *Why
Do You Live So Far Away?* are "Boiled Chicken,"[69] which, like
"Ringa Ringa Rosie" (*One Way Ticket*, pp. 77–85), deals with the
domestic life of the impoverished writer, and dates from the 1950s;
and "Continuity" (pp. 107–19), a story originally intended for inclu-
sion in *Thin Ice*, according to Levine, but excluded from that volume
on the grounds that ". . . it didn't fit into the sequence" ("Author's
Note," n. pag.). It does, however, fit the theme of *Thin Ice*, as the
narrator confronts his personal and cultural past and accepts the
burden (and gift) of insecurity, something common to his identity as
writer and as Jew, and something which, paradoxically, provides
him with the sense of "continuity" referred to by the title.

There is "continuity" in Levine's art, as well, but it, too, is not as simple as may at first appear. "Altogether the stories form a kind of autobiography," Levine writes in his Introduction to *Champagne Barn*, but he goes on to warn that ". . . it is autobiography written as fiction."[70] The narrator of Levine's stories is like the speaker of a lyric poem: he tells us about "himself," but, in one sense, that information is the least important dimension of what he tells us. Levine is a Jew and a Canadian and was an expatriate, but to read his work to find out what he has to say about these subjects is to be disappointed. His artistic goal is a deeper and more traditional one: in the face of transience, loss, uncertainty — in our age, uncertainty even about one's own identity — to find in daily experience the enduring sources of consolation.

NOTES

[1] Mr. Levine informed me, in a letter of 23 December 1981, that the title should be *The Tightrope Walker* but that the printer made a mistake. (The printer was Guido Morris, one of the most distinguished in Britain; he printed the book by hand at his Latin Press in St. Ives.)

[2] Quoted in "One Man's Canada," rev. of *Canada Made Me*, *Time* [Canadian ed.], 19 Jan. 1959, p. 9.

[3] *From a Seaside Town* (London: Macmillan, 1970), p. 146. All further references to this work are indicated in parentheses.

[4] David McDonald, "Simplicity and Sophistication: A Conversation with 'Norman Levine," *Queen's Quarterly*, 83 (Summer 1976), 228. All further references to this work (McDonald) appear in the text.

[5] Wayne Grady, "Interview," *Books in Canada*, Feb. 1980, p. 24. All further references to this work (Grady) appear in the text.

[6] John D. Cox, "Norman Levine: An Interview," *Canadian Literature*, No. 45 (Summer 1970), p. 66.

[7] Alan Heuser, rev. of *From a Seaside Town*, *The Montreal Star*, 26 Sept. 1970, p. 16. All further references to this work (Heuser) appear in the text.

[8] Barry Cameron, rev. of *Selected Stories*, *Queen's Quarterly*, 83 (Winter 1976), 690–92.

[9] Donald Stephens, "Looking Homeward," rev. of *Selected Stories*, *Canadian Literature*, No. 70 (Autumn 1976), pp. 93–96.

[10] Bernard Levin, "The Writer and His Double," rev. of *Thin Ice*, *The Sunday Times* [London], 23 March 1980, p. 42.

[11] Rev. of *Myssium*, in "Letters in Canada 1948: Poetry," *University of Toronto Quarterly*, 18 (April 1949), 262.

[12] Rev. of *The Tight-Rope Walker*, in "Letters in Canada 1950: Poetry," *University of Toronto Quarterly*, 20 (April 1951), 259.

[13] "Varieties of Experience," rev. of *The Tight-Rope Walker*, by Norman Levine, and *Reservations*, by Valentin Iremonger, *The Times Literary Supplement*, 6 April 1951, p. 211.

[14] "I Want to Place a Bet for A.D. 2152," rev. of *The Angled Road*, *Daily Express* [London], 20 Nov. 1952.

[15] "Fiction," rev. of *The Angled Road*, by Norman Levine, *Rack*, by Iris Morley, *Man Alone*, by Paul Pilotaz, and *Dr. Ischenasch*, by D. M. Dowley, *Spectator*, 19 Dec. 1952, p. 854.

[16] "Drama and Melodrama," rev. of *The Angled Road*, by Norman Levine, *The Chalice and the Sword*, by Ernest Raymond, *Away Went Polly*, by Caryl Brahms, and *The Hidden Hand*, by Eden Phillpotts, *The Times Literary Supplement*, 12 Dec. 1952, p. 813.

[17] Rev. of *The Angled Road*, in "Letters in Canada 1953: Fiction," *University of Toronto Quarterly*, 23 (April 1954), 265.

[18] Rev. of *The Angled Road*, *The Canadian Forum*, Oct. 1953, p. 163.

[19] "One Man's Canada," rev. of *Canada Made Me*, *New Statesman*, 27 Dec. 1958, p. 915.

[20] "The Seamy Side," rev. of *Canada Made Me*, *The Times Literary Supplement*, 12 Dec. 1958, p. 724.

[21] "Canada Attacked," rev. of *Canada Made Me*, *The Daily Telegraph* [London], 6 Feb. 1959.

[22] "Ex-Canadian Blasts Us," rev. of *Canada Made Me*, *The Globe and Mail*, 13 Dec. 1958, p. 17.

[23] Rev. of *Canada Made Me*, *The Tamarack Review*, No. 10 (Winter 1959), p. 107.

[24] Rev. of *Canada Made Me*, in "Letters in Canada 1958: Social Studies II," *University of Toronto Quarterly*, 28 (July 1959), 430, 431.

[25] "Egos and Otherness," rev. of *One Way Ticket*, by Norman Levine, *When My Girl Comes Home*, by V. S. Pritchett, and *New Authors: Short Story One*, *Spectator*, 1 Dec. 1961, p. 831.

[26] Rev. of *One Way Ticket*, in "Letters in Canada 1961: Fiction," *University of Toronto Quarterly*, 31 (July 1962), 472.

[27] "Ordinary People," rev. of *One Way Ticket*, *Canadian Literature*, No. 12 (Spring 1962), p. 71.

[28] Desmond Pacey, rev. of *One Way Ticket*, by Norman Levine, and *Mrs. Golightly and Other Stories*, by Ethel Wilson, *The Canadian Forum*,

March 1962, p. 285.

[29] "Bearing Witness," rev. of *From a Seaside Town*, by Norman Levine, and four other books, *New Statesman*, 24 July 1970, p. 96.

[30] "Turned In," rev. of *From a Seaside Town*, *The Times Literary Supplement*, 28 Aug. 1970, p. 941.

[31] "Balls and Chains," rev. of *From a Seaside Town*, by Norman Levine, and four other books, *Spectator*, 25 July 1970, p. 77.

[32] Alden Nowlan, "From My Notebook: A Study in Spiritual Paralysis," rev. of *From a Seaside Town*, *The Atlantic Advocate*, Oct. 1970, pp. 62, 63. All further references to this work (Nowlan) appear in the text.

[33] "A Saddening Novel of Exile by a Canadian Expatriate," rev. of *From a Seaside Town*, *Toronto Daily Star*, 12 Sept. 1970, p. 67.

[34] "Paralized Inertia [sic]," rev. of *From a Seaside Town*, *Saturday Night*, Dec. 1970, p. 37.

[35] "Recent Fiction," rev. of *I Don't Want to Know Anyone Too Well*, and four other books, *The Daily Telegraph* [London], 23 Dec. 1971.

[36] "Small but Significant," rev. of *I Don't Want to Know Anyone Too Well*, by Norman Levine, *The Smell of It*, by Sonallah Ibrihim, *The Innocent and the Guilty*, by Sylvia Townsend Warner, and *City Life*, by Donald Barthelme, *The Times Literary Supplement*, 3 Dec. 1971, p. 1497.

[37] "It's Dangerous to Get to Know People Too Well," rev. of *I Don't Want to Know Anyone Too Well*, *Saturday Night*, Feb. 1972, p. 36.

[38] "The Bright New Day," rev. of *I Don't Want to Know Anyone Too Well*, by Norman Levine, and five other books, *Canadian Literature*, No. 54 (Autumn 1972), p. 85.

[39] "Quick Reads, Bitter Barbs and an Inside Story," rev. of *I Don't Want to Know Anyone Too Well*, by Norman Levine, and six other books, *Maclean's*, April 1972, p. 108.

[40] Rev. of *I Don't Want to Know Anyone Too Well*, *The Canadian Forum*, June 1972, p. 39. Metcalf has since repudiated this assessment of Levine, whom he now considers one of Canada's "major story writers" (*Kicking Against the Pricks* [Downsview, Ont.: ECW, 1982], p. 169).

[41] Barry Cameron, pp. 690–91.

[42] Stephens, "Looking Homeward," p. 94.

[43] Rev. of *Selected Stories*, *Quarry*, 25, No. 2 (Spring 1976), 74.

[44] R. H. Ramsey, "Flatlands," rev. of *Selected Stories*, *The Canadian Forum*, March 1976, pp. 37, 38.

[45] Levin, p. 42.

[46] "Too Late," rev. of *Thin Ice*, by Norman Levine, *The Long-Haired Boy*, by Christopher Matthew, *The Good Morrow*, by Dawn Lowe-

Watson, and *Alexandra*, by Valerie Martin, *New Statesman*, 15 Feb. 1980, p. 250.

[47] "Peddling the Provinces," rev. of *Thin Ice* and *Canada Made Me*, *The Times Literary Supplement*, 14 March 1980, p. 289.

[48] "The Writer as Subject," rev. of *Thin Ice, Brick: A Journal of Reviews*, No. 9 (Spring 1980), pp. 47, 48.

[49] "Norman Levine, a Literary Amoeba, Continues to Reproduce Himself in His Stories," rev. of *Thin Ice, The Globe and Mail*, 10 Nov. 1979, p. E12.

[50] Rev. of *Thin Ice*, in *Canadian Book Review Annual 1979*, ed. Dean Tudor, Nancy Tudor, and Kathy Vanderlinden (Toronto: Peter Martin, 1980), pp. 166, 167.

[51] Christopher Lasch, *The Culture of Narcissism: American Life in an Age of Diminishing Expectations* (1978; rpt. New York: Warner, 1979), p. 48. All further references to this work (Lasch) appear in the text.

[52] "In Lower Town," in *Selected Stories* (Ottawa: Oberon, 1975), p. 115. All further references to this work appear in the text.

[53] Walker Gibson, "Tough Talk: The Rhetoric of Frederic Henry," in *Tough, Sweet and Stuffy: An Essay on Modern American Prose Styles* (Bloomington: Indiana Univ. Press, 1966), pp. 28–42.

[54] Gibson, p. 40.

[55] "The Green Was a Fresh Yellow Green," in *Myssium*, Ryerson Poetry Chap-Book, No. 131 (Toronto: Ryerson, 1948), p. 5.

[56] *I Walk by the Harbour*, Fiddlehead Poetry Book, No. 190 (Fredericton: Fiddlehead Poetry Books, 1976), p. 3.

[57] In *The Tight-Rope Walker* (London: Totem, 1950), p. 12.

[58] In *I Walk by the Harbour*, p. 6.

[59] "The Girl in the Drugstore," in *The Sixties: Writers and Writing of the Decade*, ed. George Woodcock (Vancouver: Univ. of British Columbia Press, 1969), p. 52.

[60] *The Angled Road* (London: Werner Laurie, 1952), p. 127. All further references to this work appear in the text.

[61] *Canada Made Me* (London: Putnam, 1958), p. 105. All further references to this work appear in the text.

[62] In *One Way Ticket* (London: Secker & Warburg, 1961), pp. 87–105. All further references to this work are indicated in parentheses.

[63] Compare the description of Darch's studio and paintings (p. 61) with almost any account of Bacon's life and work — for example, John Russell, *Francis Bacon* (London: Thames and Hudson, 1971).

[64] "A Novelist in Suspension," rev. of *From a Seaside Town*, *The Globe*

Magazine [*The Globe and Mail*], 3 Oct. 1970, p. 20. Buitenhuis misquotes the line from the novel; it should read: "Life seems to be a series of unconnected brief encounters" (*From a Seaside Town*, p. 219).

⁶⁵ Compare the personal reminiscences in Levine's essay "Francis Bacon," *The Atlantic Advocate*, Sept. 1964, pp. 51–54, with Grand's visit to Charles in Chapter iii of *From a Seaside Town* (pp. 19–26).

⁶⁶ In *I Don't Want to Know Anyone Too Well* (London: Macmillan, 1971), pp. 40–48. All further references to this work appear in the text.

⁶⁷ See Ramsey, p. 38; and Arnold Keller, "The Small Frustrations of Norman Levine," rev. of *Selected Stories, Matrix*, 1, No. 2 (Fall 1975), 7.

⁶⁸ "Class of 1949," in *Thin Ice* (Ottawa: Deneau & Greenberg, 1979), p. 29. All further references to this work appear in the text.

⁶⁹ In *Why Do You Live So Far Away?* (Ottawa: Deneau, 1984), pp. 50–54. All further references to this work appear in the text.

⁷⁰ Introd., *Champagne Barn* (Toronto: Penguin, 1984), p. xv.

SELECTED BIBLIOGRAPHY

Primary Sources

Levine, Norman. *Myssium.* Ryerson Poetry Chap-Book, No. 131. Toronto: Ryerson, 1948.

——. *The Tight-Rope Walker.* London: Totem, 1950.

——. *The Angled Road.* London: Werner Laurie, 1952.

——. *Canada Made Me.* London: Putnam, 1958.

——. *One Way Ticket.* London: Secker & Warburg, 1961.

——. "Francis Bacon." *The Atlantic Advocate,* Sept. 1964, pp. 51–54.

——, ed. *Canadian Winter's Tales.* Toronto: Macmillan, 1968.

——. "The Girl in the Drugstore." In *The Sixties: Writers and Writing of the Decade.* Ed. George Woodcock. Vancouver: Univ. of British Columbia Press, 1969, pp. 49–52.

——. *From a Seaside Town.* London: Macmillan, 1970.

——. *I Don't Want to Know Anyone Too Well.* London: Macmillan, 1971.

——. *Selected Stories.* Ottawa: Oberon, 1975.

——. *I Walk by the Harbour.* Fiddlehead Poetry Book, No. 190. Fredericton: Fiddlehead Poetry Books, 1976.

——. *In Lower Town.* Ottawa: Commoners' Publishing Society, 1977.

——. *Thin Ice.* Ottawa: Deneau & Greenberg, 1979.

——. *Champagne Barn.* Toronto: Penguin, 1984.

——. *Why Do You Live So Far Away?* Ottawa: Deneau, 1984.

Secondary Sources

Bishop, E. L. Rev. of *Selected Stories. Quarry,* 25, No. 2 (Spring 1976), 73–74.

Bissell, Claude T. Rev. of *The Angled Road.* In "Letters in Canada 1953: Fiction." *University of Toronto Quarterly,* 23 (April 1954), 265.

Brown, E. K. Rev. of *Myssium.* In "Letters in Canada 1948: Poetry." *University of Toronto Quarterly,* 18 (April 1949), 262.

Buitenhuis, Peter. "A Novelist in Suspension." Rev. of *From a Seaside Town*. *The Globe Magazine* [*The Globe and Mail*], 3 Oct. 1970, p. 20.

Cameron, Barry. Rev. of *Selected Stories*. *Queen's Quarterly*, 83 (Winter 1976), 690–92.

Cameron, Donald. "Quick Reads, Bitter Barbs and an Inside Story." Rev. of *I Don't Want to Know Anyone Too Well*, by Norman Levine, and six other books. *Maclean's*, April 1972, p. 108.

Capitanchik, Maurice. "Balls and Chains." Rev. of *From a Seaside Town*, by Norman Levine, and four other books. *Spectator*, 25 July 1970, pp. 76–77.

——. "Canadian in Cornwall." *Books and Bookmen*, Sept. 1972, pp. 32–33.

Careless, J. M. S. Rev. of *Canada Made Me*. In "Letters in Canada 1958: Social Studies ii." *University of Toronto Quarterly*, 28 (July 1959), 430–31.

Cooper, William. "Recent Fiction." Rev. of *I Don't Want to Know Anyone Too Well*, and four other books. *The Daily Telegraph* [London], 23 Dec. 1971.

Cox, John D. "Norman Levine: An Interview." *Canadian Literature*, No. 45 (Summer 1970), pp. 61–67.

Dorrien, Terrence. "Ex-Canadian Blasts Us." Rev. of *Canada Made Me*. *The Globe and Mail*, 13 Dec. 1958, p. 17.

"Drama and Melodrama." Rev. of *The Angled Road*, by Norman Levine, *The Chalice and the Sword*, by Ernest Raymond, *Away Went Polly*, by Caryl Brahms, and *The Hidden Hand*, by Eden Phillpotts. *The Times Literary Supplement*, 12 Dec. 1952, p. 813.

Eedy, Alice. Rev. of *The Angled Road*. *The Canadian Forum*, Oct. 1953, p. 163.

Fagan, Cary. "The Writer as Subject." Rev. of *Thin Ice*. *Brick: A Journal of Reviews*, No. 9 (Spring 1980), pp. 47–48.

——. "The Visible World: An Interview with Norman Levine." *Descant*, No. 40 (Spring 1983), pp. 75–84.

French, William. "Norman Levine, a Literary Amoeba, Continues to Reproduce Himself in His Stories." Rev. of *Thin Ice*. *The Globe and Mail*, 10 Nov. 1979, p. E12.

Frye, Northrop. Rev. of *The Tight-Rope Walker*. In "Letters in Canada 1950: Poetry." *University of Toronto Quarterly*, 20 (April 1951), 259.

Gander, Nigel. "Canada Attacked." Rev. of *Canada Made Me*. *The Daily Telegraph* [London], 6 Feb. 1959.

Glendinning, Victoria. "Peddling the Provinces." Rev. of *Thin Ice* and

Canada Made Me. The Times Literary Supplement, 14 March 1980, p. 289.

Goldie, Terry. Rev. of *Thin Ice*. In *Canadian Book Review Annual 1979*. Ed. Dean Tudor, Nancy Tudor, and Kathy Vanderlinden. Toronto: Peter Martin, 1980, pp. 166–67.

Grady, Wayne. "Interview." *Books in Canada*, Feb. 1980, pp. 24–25.

Grosskurth, Phyllis. "Paralized Inertia [sic]." Rev. of *From a Seaside Town*. *Saturday Night*, Dec. 1970, pp. 36–37.

Heuser, Alan. Rev. of *From a Seaside Town*. *The Montreal Star*, 26 Sept. 1970, p. 16.

Hodgart, Patricia. "Egos and Otherness." Rev. of *One Way Ticket*, by Norman Levine, *When My Girl Comes Home*, by V. S. Pritchett, and *New Authors: Short Story One*. *Spectator*, 1 Dec. 1961, pp. 830–31.

Jordan, Clive. "Bearing Witness." Rev. of *From a Seaside Town*, by Norman Levine, and four other books. *New Statesman*, 24 July 1970, pp. 95–96.

Keller, Arnold. "The Small Frustrations of Norman Levine." Rev. of *Selected Stories*. *Matrix*, 1, No. 2 (Fall 1975), 6–7.

Lasch, Christopher. *The Culture of Narcissism: American Life in an Age of Diminishing Expectations*. 1978; rpt. New York: Warner, 1979.

Laski, Marghanita. "Fiction." Rev. of *The Angled Road*, by Norman Levine, *Rack*, by Iris Morley, *Man Alone*, by Paul Pilotaz, and *Dr. Ischenasch*, by D. M. Dowley. *Spectator*, 19 Dec. 1952, p. 854.

Levin, Bernard. "The Writer and His Double." Rev. of *Thin Ice*. *The Sunday Times* [London], 23 March 1980, p. 42.

McDonald, David. "Simplicity and Sophistication: A Conversation with Norman Levine." *Queen's Quarterly*, 83 (Summer 1976), 217–30.

Metcalf, John. Rev. of *I Don't Want to Know Anyone Too Well*. *The Canadian Forum*, June 1972, p. 39.

———. *Kicking Against the Pricks*. Downsview, Ont.: ECW, 1982.

Nadel, Ira Bruce. "'Canada Made Me' and Autobiography." *Canadian Literature*, No. 101 (Summer 1984), pp. 69–81.

Nowlan, Alden. "From My Notebook: A Study in Spiritual Paralysis." Rev. of *From a Seaside Town*. *The Atlantic Advocate*, Oct. 1970, pp. 62–63.

"One Man's Canada." Rev. of *Canada Made Me. Time* [Canadian ed.], 19 Jan. 1959, p. 9.

Owen, Patricia. Rev. of *Canada Made Me. The Tamarack Review*, No. 10 (Winter 1959), p. 107.

Pacey, Desmond. Rev. of *One Way Ticket*, by Norman Levine, and *Mrs. Golightly and Other Stories*, by Ethel Wilson. *The Canadian*

Forum, March 1962, p. 285.

Ramsey, R. H. "Flatlands." Rev. of *Selected Stories*. *The Canadian Forum*, March 1976, pp. 37–38.

"The Seamy Side." Rev. of *Canada Made Me*. *The Times Literary Supplement*, 12 Dec. 1958, p. 724.

"Small but Significant." Rev. of *I Don't Want to Know Anyone Too Well*, by Norman Levine, *The Smell of It*, by Sonallah Ibrihim, *The Innocent and the Guilty*, by Sylvia Townsend Warner, and *City Life*, by Donald Barthelme. *The Times Literary Supplement*, 3 Dec. 1971, p. 1497.

Spain, Nancy. "I Want to Place a Bet for A.D. 2152." Rev. of *The Angled Road*. *Daily Express* [London], 20 Nov. 1952.

Steffen, Jonathan. "Too Late." Rev. of *Thin Ice*, by Norman Levine, *The Long-Haired Boy*, by Christopher Matthew, *The Good Morrow*, by Dawn Lowe-Watson, and *Alexandra*, by Valerie Martin. *New Statesman*, 15 Feb. 1980, pp. 250–51.

Stephens, Donald. "Ordinary People." Rev. of *One Way Ticket*. *Canadian Literature*, No. 12 (Spring 1962), pp. 70–71.

———. "The Bright New Day." Rev. of *I Don't Want to Know Anyone Too Well*, by Norman Levine, and five other books. *Canadian Literature*, No. 54 (Autumn 1972), pp. 84–86.

———. "Looking Homeward." Rev. of *Selected Stories*. *Canadian Literature*, No. 70 (Autumn 1976), pp. 93–96.

"Turned In." Rev. of *From a Seaside Town*. *The Times Literary Supplement*, 28 Aug. 1970, p. 941.

"Varieties of Experience." Rev. of *The Tight-Rope Walker*, by Norman Levine, and *Reservations*, by Valentin Iremonger. *The Times Literary Supplement*, 6 April 1951, p. 211.

Watt, F. W. Rev. of *One Way Ticket*. In "Letters in Canada 1961: Fiction." *University of Toronto Quarterly*, 31 (July 1962), 472–73.

West, Paul. "One Man's Canada." Rev. of *Canada Made Me*. *New Statesman*, 27 Dec. 1958, p. 915.

Wolfe, Morris. "It's Dangerous to Get to Know People Too Well." Rev. of *I Don't Want to Know Anyone Too Well*. *Saturday Night*, Feb. 1972, p. 36.

Woodcock, George. "A Saddening Novel of Exile by a Canadian Expatriate." Rev. of *From a Seaside Town*. *Toronto Daily Star*, 12 Sept. 1970, p. 67.

*Leon Rooke
and His Works*

Leon Rooke (1934–   )

KEITH GAREBIAN

Biography

BORN 11 SEPTEMBER 1934 in Roanoke Rapids, North Carolina, Leon Rooke is yet another expatriate writer of the first rank now living and working in Canada. The third and final child of Louise Gray, a farmer's daughter, and Jesse Lofton Rooke, a farmer's son, he has dim childhood memories of his parents, largely because he was separated from them in 1940, when he went with his brother and sister to live on his grandparents' farm outside Garysburg, N.C. Where birth was life's first mystery, the role of woman in an agrarian society was life's second. Poverty was less of a mystery, but it provided an education of sorts, as did Rooke's encounters with black playmates. This farm life lasted for six years, after which young Rooke moved back to town. Too shy for his own good, he nevertheless excelled in baseball, became sports editor of his school newspaper, and began writing poems and stories about 1948.

His graduation from Roanoke Rapids High School in 1952 was marred by an incident with a teacher who insulted him by implying that, owing to his father's low-income level, Rooke would never achieve much in life. Rooke reacted by working for a year in a bank and trust company in Charlotte, N.C., so that he could pay his way through college. He has said of the school incident: "The possibility of going to college had not occurred to me. But I was mortally offended by this remark and said to myself, 'By God I *will* go to college.'"[1] From 1953 to 1955 he attended Mars Hill College, wrote and directed his first play, and won the Betty Smith Award, a state drama festival prize. In 1955 he entered the University of North Carolina at Chapel Hill to study journalism. However, in his senior year he switched to drama and won the Frederick H. Koch Play-writing Award. It was at this time that his interest in fiction acquired a serious dimension, as he pounded away at short stories on a secondhand typewriter. Nevertheless, he did not abandon his drama writing, and he worked two summer sessions as technician and actor in *Unto These Hills*, an outdoor drama, staged at Cherokee, N.C.

Army service pulled him away from university in 1957, and when he returned after his compulsory stint to the University of North Carolina in 1960, it was to study screenwriting at graduate school on the basis of a Screen Gems Graduate Writing Fellowship. Academic life did not carry much appeal for him, and Rooke did not complete his degree, dropping out after the first term and working as a writer for the University News Bureau. Writing was a preoccupation. He produced several stage and radio plays (of which only *Evening Meeting of the Club of Suicide* [1972], *Krokodile* [1973], *Sword/Play* [1974], and "Cakewalk" [1980] were published, later in his career). "My first writings were aimed at the stage," he has said. "And when some of those first plays were produced and I heard actors returning the words it probably had the effect of making me listen more atten- tively to how the voices sounded on the page."[2] Despite his evident dramatic talent, he was haunted by the literary ghost of fiction.

Rooke can remember thinking, his first evening on campus as thick fog swirled around old lampposts: "God, this is a dream, something is going to happen to me here!"[3] The great literary ghost at Chapel Hill was Thomas Wolfe, whom Rooke read and loved. The South was populated by writers destined to be great names of the century: William Faulkner and Eudora Welty in Mississippi; Carson McCullers and Flannery O'Connor in Georgia; Tennessee Williams and Truman Capote of New Orleans; William Styron in Virginia; and Shirley Ann Grau in Louisiana. All this did something to Rooke's sense of loyalty to the region, although he dissociates him- self from regionalism as a writer, claiming in a biographical note that "place (locale) in fiction" is "a vastly over-rated virtue."[4]

His Uncle Donald Gray, a chronic knockabout who detested living in a small town and had travelled across the United States, exerted a special influence on him. Rooke, identifying with his uncle's spirit of rebellion and adventure, decided to become a traveller himself and visited Alaska, San Francisco, New Orleans, and Virginia between 1957 and 1964. Yet his were not really leisurely adventures. Alaska met his life when he was drafted into the army in 1958 and had to serve for eighteen months with an infantry battalion in Anchorage — perhaps the source for his novella "Brush Fire."[5] New Orleans entered his life when he went there to work a third summer on *Unto These Hills*.

From 1963 to 1965 he was engaged by The North Carolina Fund for a pilot project to combat poverty, although he himself was not exactly affluent. His luck increased when he was appointed writer-in-residence at the University of North Carolina. A short sojourn in Fancy Gap, Virginia, was followed by journalistic and editorial work on *The North Carolina Anvil* [Durham, N.C.], a weekly newspaper of politics and the arts, and then by romance with Constance Merriam Raymond, whom he married in 1969.

The new partnership arrived in Victoria, B.C., soon after the wedding because Constance had a position teaching English at the University of Victoria. Rooke attained a certain amount of respect through his own writing and teaching, although he was regarded by many critics as being a "grim, unbalanced, keyhole guy — too obsessed with evil, death, weirdness, etc."[6] for his works such as *Last One Home Sleeps in the Yellow Bed* (1968), *Vault: A Story in Three Parts* (1973), *The Broad Back of the Angel* (1977), *The Love Parlour* (1977), and *Cry Evil* (1980). Rooke was too strange, too idiosyncratic a virtuoso for many Canadian critics. Nevertheless, their critical attitudes modulated into cautious admiration for *Fat Woman* (1980), Rooke's first full-length novel, which was nominated for both the *Books in Canada* First Novel Award and, more importantly, the Governor-General's Award. Although Rooke did not win either, he did win the Periodical Distributors of Canada Award for the best paperback novel and, in the following year, the $20,000 Canada-Australia Literary Award, given on the basis of overall literary contribution instead of a single work. The award, which included a trip to Australia, came the same year in which he brought out *Death Suite*, his sixth collection of short fiction, and *The Magician in Love*, a fabulistic and satiric novella. A special issue of *Canadian Fiction Magazine* (No. 38) was devoted exclusively to his work, and it seemed that his reputation was in high gear. In 1982 Rooke published *The Birth Control King of the Upper Volta*, a short-story collection about people who meet their joys and misfortunes head-on. His second novel, *Shakespeare's Dog* (1983), won the Governor-General's Award for fiction. In 1984 Rooke produced two more short-story collections, *A Bolt of White Cloth* and *Sing Me No Long Songs I'll Say You No Prayers*, the latter a volume of selected stories that contained ten hitherto unpublished ones.

Tradition and Milieu

Most of the best American and Canadian fiction has been regional, perhaps because, as Flannery O'Connor once asserted, "The writer operates at a peculiar crossroads where time and place and eternity somehow meet."[7] But in Leon Rooke's case, the regional is not of primary concern. Although his fiction is strongly developed in character voice and idiom, obviously drawn from a social fabric, Rooke is able to show something meaningful about the mystery of personality by imaginative leaps above the narrower reaches of regional realism. Surfaces are important to Rooke, but only as something to penetrate, to pass through into an experience of what usually does not meet the external senses or our conventional apprehension of social or geographical reality. All fiction writers are fundamentally seekers and describers of the real in particular contexts, but the vision of each writer depends on his view of the ultimate reaches of reality. In Rooke's case, there is an interest in characters who, somewhat like O'Connor's figures, are forced to meet evil and grace, and who act on a trust beyond themselves — whether they know very clearly what they act upon or not.

This produces distortion — images that connect the concrete and the invisible — and yields what some would call the grotesque, where there are strange gaps in coherence, and unusual experiences which we are not accustomed to observing either in our own lives or in most fiction. Yet these distortions or grotesque elements are means of renewal, for Rooke's peculiar vision and form are not in the service of an obvious ideology. Although his subjects and events are often ordinary or mundane, his penetration into the secret life of an individual is against the bourgeois mode of discreet silence or evasion. Consuming passions and wild conflagrations that occur deep within the soul are revealed with intensity and perverse fantasy that push excessively at times towards a derangement of the senses. The spirits in "Hanging Out with the Magi,"[8] for instance, are a case of the bourgeois melting in a desperate desire for the impossible, where events in a daily human existence are lived as symbols, where the real is displaced by the imaginary.

Rooke eliminates the usual distinctions between conscious and unconscious life, dream and banal reality. Subjectivity is vital; yet this subjectivity is dissolved in a mode of surrealism or, perhaps, figurative expressionism — a reaction that any modernist or post-modernist would have to the realist's certitude of life, ethics, and epistemology. The world is exposed as a radical contradiction, and the writing multiplies exaggeration and fantasy until the images of the external world seem unstable and transitory. Yet this is not self-destructive art. It does not push towards nothingness. Although Rooke depicts the violence of irrational forces in many of his stories — especially in the Gothic tales — the banal is theatricalized, altered, and crystallized as a fluttering of contradictions. In the tradition of modernism and post-modernism that began in European painting, Rooke suggests that what earlier generations have taken for the world is only the world seen through the eyes of habit. The world, he appears to say, is not "given" but depends on the kinds of assumptions we bring to it, and it is best not to bring too many.

In terms of cultural tradition, Rooke is clearly post-modernist in sensibility. The outlines of his fiction frequently blur, for language reveals itself as process rather than as coherent meaning. One reason for the blurring might well be Rooke's multitude of voices and identities. Paradoxically, though he is a contemporary writer, he holds the old-fashioned notion that one of the writer's jobs is to project many identities, and not simply to write of the self: "To write of the self only is the power of a few, the disgrace of many, someone said. The voices in my fiction I regard as authentic; mine I see as a thing made up from day to day. Shapeless. Mass without form" (Hancock, p. 108). So that while we marvel at Rooke's ventriloquial virtuosity, we cannot really find the "fixed" man behind the voices.

The Houdini of the short story, ever concocting new schemes of literary entrapment for himself to overcome, he loves surprises in writing, which accounts for his idea of form as "a thing apart from structure," which includes "not only the pattern with which lines are formed and which guides the eye along a page — how a work falls on the page — but also as the overall shape which holds the work. The mould. But a mould that isn't fixed, varying, as it does, with any given work" (Hancock, p. 109). Rooke scraps "the old vice about beginning, middle, and end" and instead sees them as "a stretch of shifting coordinates that relate in ways unpredictable" (Hancock, p. 110).

Plot, "which was always the least important element for everything except Agatha Christie mysteries and Dime Westerns, takes an unlamented back seat" (Hancock, p. 110). Language and "a liberated approach to point of view and delineation of character" take the front seat (Hancock, p. 110). Rooke tries not to be dated by the dictates of traditional fiction, yet he is also very traditional at times. This paradox is, perhaps, not very mysterious after all, because, as Rooke says, "If a work is successful then it is no longer 'experimental.' It is the state where narrative development, where craft, has naturally got itself. It is the New Traditional" (Hancock, p. 111).

One thing which keeps Rooke in the traditional camp — despite his rhetorical strategies — is his unwillingness to relinquish character. It is important to him — just as it was to the nineteenth-century realists — to see characters in fiction as living human beings, and he extends this belief to include even the extremes. "Hanging Out with the Magi" has several "spirits," but Rooke believes in them, and the air of credibility he creates enriches the strange angles of real life.

Although he came out of the Deep South and its strong literary tradition, Rooke feels quite apart from that rich and complex tradition. The politics of the 1960s changed his sense of loyalty to the South and took away some of the power of his Southern literary "ghosts." But he learned from Max Steele and John Ehle, and when he read the Welsh writer Dylan Thomas, he discovered that ". . . prose could sing in the same way poetry could" (Hancock, pp. 120–21). Certain Southern writers showed him something about mood, youth, and innocence. The Southern tradition did give him the sense of storytelling, and with this fair start, Rooke had to go on to learn language and the dimensions of form.

From the start of his writing career, he gravitated towards strong stylists, such as Wright Morris, for instance, and discovered that "if the style is strong then the content usually is as well" (Hancock, p. 122). Style, to Rooke, is "the unique imprint of the single writer" — "like a woman walking in high heels. The way they know how. And one never exactly the same as another" (Hancock, p. 122). Stylistically, Rooke is closer to Donald Barthelme, Italo Calvino, and John Barth than he is to other writers. Often, like these coevals, he makes fictive worlds where the making and the language are self-consciously shared by author and reader. It is a knotty collaboration, characteristic of modern metafiction which has been described at length in Linda Hutcheon's study of contemporary self-reflexive novels *Narcissistic Narrative: The Metafictional Paradox.* The self-reflexiveness of Rooke's writing is implicit: that is to say, it is internalized within the text. Rooke's fiction illustrates three of the main recurring structural models articulated by Hutcheon: (1) The detective story (as in "Fromm Investigations"⁹ and the tripartite "Murder Mystery (The Strip)" [*DS*, pp. 129–36]), based on the general pattern of the puzzle or enigma. The literary form, as Hutcheon observes, "is itself a very self-conscious one: in fact, the reader of a murder mystery comes to *expect* the presence of a detective-story writer within the story itself . . . . The incriminating evidence is within the text; some details might seem in the end irrelevant to the plot, but they are all functional, even if only in leading the reader astray."¹⁰ (2) Fantasy (as in "Hanging Out with the Magi" or the Magician tales in *The Broad Back of the Angel* and *The Magician in Love*), which compels the reader to "create a fictive imaginative world separate from the empirical one in which he lives." It is a "compromise between the empirically real and the totally imaginary."¹¹ (3) The Erotic (especially in "Sixteen-Year-Old Susan March Confesses to the Innocent Murder of All the Devious Strangers Who Would Drag Her Down" [*DS*, pp. 59–72]), which tantalizes the reader. There is sometimes a fourth model, Games (as in "Biographical Notes" [*CE*, pp. 97–131] or "Dinner with the Swardians"¹²), and a fifth model (as in *Shakespeare's Dog*), which is an overtly linguistic type that directs the reader's attention to language at play, while also being a narrative with covert purpose.

Rooke's narrative models put him ahead of most Canadian writers. The ones he is closest to are Alice Munro, for emotional bondage to time and place, and John Metcalf, for witty satire. But he is very much outside the Canadian mainstream, a position which is, after all, most appropriate for someone who believes that the short story deals with "characters who are somewhat apart from the times" (Hancock, p. 114). However, while socially a loner or a fringe citizen in his elevated Victoria home above a ravine and bay, he crosses the boundary between isolation and communion by his fiction. His "performing self," as Geoff Hancock shrewdly observes, is "the binding agent": "In his ventriloquism, he makes us aware of the plight of his characters. No matter how high-performance his devices, his fiction is as close to us as that."¹³

Critical Overview and Context

In the first official bibliography of Leon Rooke,[14] compiled by J. R. (Tim) Struthers, there are only two references to critical writing about the author. These citations are to a book review by Stephen Scobie and the special issue on Rooke of *Canadian Fiction Magazine*, edited by Geoff Hancock. So far, Rooke remains a literary magician loved wisely and well, but who has not received his due share of critical analysis.

Were Rooke's first volume of short stories not reissued in 1981, it would not have been heard of at all, except by academics; I was able to review it, however, and praise its "extraordinary sensitivity to emotional inflections."[15] In *Last One Home Sleeps in the Yellow Bed*, which first appeared in 1968 in the United States, Rooke shows a deep empathy even for those characters who are ludicrous, desperate, or galling. There are stories of young lovers in an icehouse one summer, a married man's bleak reflections on his own insecurity, a woman destined for a violent fate, and a daughter from the Vieux Carré who makes a hard-won peace for herself. Yet none of these interesting pieces comes up to the beautifully textured, reflective prose-poetry of "When Swimmers on the Beach Have All Gone Home" (*LOH*, pp. 10–35), or to the cumulative tension of the powerful novella "Brush Fire" (*LOH*, pp. 95–178), with its soul-curdling epiphany and conclusion. Although a beginner's book, this collection is remarkably advanced in style — which is not to imply, however, that it is devoid of substance. Rooke dazzles even in engaging minor pieces, and for the most part, he writes of passions recollected at high or middle pitch. Nostalgia is sometimes heightened by provocative sensuality or abrupt shock, and the form is often that of a dramatic monologue by a narrator bent on revealing life by its dark underside.

One reason, perhaps, why it is not possible to find critical writing on Rooke's early works is because the works themselves are often unavailable. *Vault* (1973), for instance, can be located in precious few libraries, and so is the case with *The Broad Back of the Angel* (1977). Both of these volumes were from Rooke's pioneer stage of development, when he was a new exotic experimentalist.

Rooke's reputation with Canadian critics really began with *The Love Parlour* (1977), *Cry Evil* (1980), and *Fat Woman* (1980). Yet critics, such as Struthers, continued to perceive "an unmistakably

Southern quality in Rooke's usual cadence and his prevailing concern with languor, decadence, and dejection."[16] Rooke's attention to morbidity also continued to attract comment. *Cry Evil* was judged by Jerry Wasserman to be "stocked with characters who, if they aren't mad or paranoid or perverse, are victims of the madness, paranoia, or perversity of others."[17] *Fat Woman*, a not altogether successful comic novel, was often criticized because its frustrated, obese protagonist chooses to struggle against life's calumnies. Cary Fagan found that the book suffered from the same afflictions as Ella Mae herself, "a poverty of ideas and spirit, and a tediousness that derives from time moving 'so slow you'd swear it was tied down.'"[18] Yet the novel was a runner-up to W. D. Valgardson's *Gentle Sinners* for the *Books in Canada* First Novel Award and later lost the Governor-General's Award to George Bowering's *Burning Water*. Readers were divided in their responses to Ella Mae, who either caught their sympathy or disgusted them by her woes. John Richardson found her to be "a character you want to hug but, like an eccentric relative who visited you as a child, the novelty of both encounters wears off after a very short time."[19] Unable to come to terms with Rooke's form, some found *Fat Woman* "more like a fleshed-out short story" or "a novel that never gets off the ground."[20] A prominent dissenter from this body of objectors was writer Robert Kroetsch, who called the novel "a beaded moccasin, a triumph of hand and eye."[21]

Rooke feels that Canadian critics have failed to note that he writes chiefly of victories achieved by characters rather than of defeats suffered, but the peculiarity of his vision and the compressed intensity of his form do contribute to popular misconceptions of his craft. *Death Suite* (1981) and *The Magician in Love* (1981) were completely off the beaten track. The abnormality of some of the characters and situations obscured for several critics the subtleties of the works. Although, on one hand, *Death Suite* was praised by Debra Martens for its "imagination and insight," its "surreal quality" complemented by an "understanding of human nature,"[22] it was regarded by B. Derek Johnson, on the other hand, as "a series of musical passages in the same minor key." Johnson felt that "some tales are told with such a weird accent, or from such an oblique point of view, that the narrator can be as much of a puzzle as the characters."[23]

Death Suite, however, produced the first truly perceptive and coherent reading of Rooke's work. In his review, Stephen Scobie suggested that Rooke's form *is* his content: ". . . the wildness, the exuberance, the grotesqueness, and the sudden tonal shifts from fantasy to the catching and placing of realistic detail in the context of humdrum existence, are all as relevant thematically as they are dazzling technically.''[24] Scobie pointed out that one key to unlocking some of Rooke's mystery is his insistence on voice. At last there was recognition for Rooke's black humour and for his clever narrative techniques. Writing of *The Magician in Love* in the same review, Scobie asserted that

> Rooke's art is one of performance, of impersonation, and the virtuoso brilliance of his writing (which may appear suspect in the drab world of many Canadian novels and critics) is again thematically essential, not merely entertaining and decorative, in two ways. First, he must depend upon the inventiveness and energy of the writing in order to enter . . . "fully realized world[s] of appetite and speech"; his characters are themselves virtuosos of illusion and self-deception, and he must match their technique in order to portray them. But second, by playing the role of impersonator, or ventriloquist, for so many *different* voices, Rooke draws attention to his own "performing self . . . ." Rooke's performance also contains an edge of irony; implicit in the tone is the awareness that holds back from these realized worlds that makes us see how hollow and desperate they are. (Scobie, p. 9)

In his article "The Hi-Tech World of Leon Rooke," Geoff Hancock added his support to Scobie's analysis by contending that Rooke's art "is one of high performance; he travels in the fast lane of short fiction. His stories are power equipped. The latest in fabulation and metafiction. Meaning layered as high as a carpark" (p. 135). Cutting through the gaudy, glitzy hype of some of Hancock's jazzy, colloquial prose, we find some valuable insights:

> Leon Rooke reinforces the *fiction* of his fiction. Not only is he interested in writing, he is also interested in its parallel companion, reading . . . . Leon reminds us that the telling of a story is part of the story. An essential part of Leon's method is calling attention to the artifice and fabrication of his short stories. (p. 136)

Hancock locates Rooke in "the self-conscious tradition of post-modernism" (p. 138) — a tradition that calls attention to itself and challenges its readers to deconstruct their attitudes towards form. So, in essence, Hancock's comments reveal our need to find, not necessarily a new critical language for Rooke, but a new openness to his forms. Rooke, in his own view, is a New Traditionalist — a writer whose position isn't fixed by conventions, yet who uses the conventions sometimes traditionally, often experimentally, so that real life seems to come at us from new angles. His craft, therefore, needs critics who can approach it from new angles.

However, even with his second novel, *Shakespeare's Dog* (1983), and his short-story collections *The Birth Control King of the Upper Volta* (1982), *A Bolt of White Cloth* (1984), and *Sing Me No Love Songs I'll Say You No Prayers* (1984), his critics did not seem to respond to his imaginative challenges with adequate skill. The usual hackneyed epithets were trotted out — "strange, hidden worlds, off-centred, comic";[25] "verbal exhilaration";[26] "haunting, off-beat, and provocative"[27] — and everybody appeared to agree that Rooke was a linguistic magician, although some dissenters found the mannerist style objectionable. "Rooke can be a challenging, delightful stylist. But at some points [in *The Birth Control King of the Upper Volta*], he seems to be writing himself to a dead end,"[28] claimed James Stewart Reaney. B. Derek Johnson objected that ". . . Rooke ultimately seems bent on exposing his own characters, as if they were never more than holograms, inventions that existed only to enhance the cleverness of his narrative."[29]

Once again lost in all these objections was the point that in Rooke, form is content — a subtlety that Scobie had argued back in 1981: "Whooping and hollering, cajoling or complaining, Rooke's characters meet the world at an interface of language; their perception *is* their rhetoric" (Scobie, p. 8).

The performing voice, the virtuoso ventriloquism, the diverse forms of rhetoric where perception is speech and speech is perception — all these distinguishing features of Rooke's writing make for texts that require decoding, not for an explicative purpose, but for an interpretive one. Readers would do well to keep in mind Paul Ricoeur's analogy of a musical score which represents reading as "the realization, the enactment, of the semantic possibilities of the text."[30] Rooke does not make statements; he invents situations and characters. Then he allows them their own speech, perception, and interaction, without imposing a resolution. Consequently, Rooke's stories require that readers do some work of their own. As

Hancock puts it in "The Hi-Tech World of Leon Rooke": "The reader may have to change attitudes towards fiction to accommodate Leon's stories" (p. 138).

Rooke's Works

Disregarding the more obvious elements of gamesmanship in Rooke's use of parody, fragments, and drawings, and his own comments on certain recurring patterns — characters being reborn in various stories; duplication of the "life and death swirl" (Hancock, p. 115) from story to story — we are, nevertheless, faced with extraordinary narrative qualities that are sensitive to the temporal dimension and the values of form. Rooke evidently believes — along with Shakespeare, who lives in one particular story through the voice of his dog, Hooker — that the greatest struggle of man is against time. Rooke does agree to a point with the dog's "Two Foot" master that this is "a stinking maggoty world in some regard," but their great convergence of attitude is in the belief that "the true war" is "one with time."[31] In the bawdy comedy of *Shakespeare's Dog* — where Rooke develops a brilliant mimicry of Elizabethan language and life — sex becomes a way of filling the void in existence. Hooker, the canine voice, runs his paces through archetypal roles: "Dog, the hunter. Dog, the creator. Dog, the rib-layer. Dog, the heart-warmer. Dog, the great howler. Dog's is the vigil eternal. So sayeth the muse. So blows Hooker" (p. 130). There is pathos along with the robustness, and the ideology of survival of the fittest is given a virtuoso turn. Hooker's story is a rich, bustling period piece that extends beyond a mimicry of Elizabethan speech and sensibility to reach a crucial concern, shared not only by Shakespeare but by all writers as universal artists.

Shakespeare's Dog is a mannerist *tour de force*. It does not so much provide a scrupulously accurate view of life in Shakespeare's England, as much as it constructs an Elizabethan dog's cosmos. Consequently, it becomes a world in itself, revealing its energy through a performative voice, which repudiates "content" while stressing its own formal virtuosity. There is, of course, a strong referential code in the novel, in that Hooker alludes to personalities, customs, and beliefs in Elizabethan England. We hear of the queen, the Regarders (enforcers of the antipoaching statutes), Shakespeare's parents, grandparents, wife, children, and literary peers, witchcraft hysteria, superstition about ghosts, medical quackeries, public executions, and cruel sport with animals. Moreover, although Shakespeare is a mere twenty-one years of age and is only about to leave Stratford for London at the end of the book, we hear echoes from some of his famous works: a quotation from "Venus and Adonis" (p. 22), and paraphrases or borrowings from *Troilus and Cressida* (p. 34), *As You Like It* (p. 71), and *Hamlet* (pp. 28, 58, 80, 101, 111, 141).

However, the special feature is Hooker's talking voice, which, unlike the invented voices in Anthony Burgess' *A Clockwork Orange* or William Burroughs' *Naked Lunch*, is not an extreme case of a dialect antithetical to a particular society's norm. Rather, it is a voice that gives us a different vocabulary only in certain areas: onomatopoeic "woof-woof," "arf-arf," "blech and blah" (p. 3), or coinings such as "my dogger" (p. 129), "my dogly vinegar" (p. 5), "glom" (p. 11), and "potch" (p. 15). Hooker delights in wordplay, even to the extent of bawdry (". . . he'd pizzled my bloodmate . . ." [p. 4]), aural jests ("My peat, my pet" [p. 7]), compounds ("tongue-wag" [p. 8]; "stinkpodge" [p. 13]), abusive vilification ("Word-blower! Thou shitted stool!" [p. 15]; "Excrete, keck, titubate, and aroint thyself!" [p. 96]), and, in a parody of Elizabethan orthographic licence, variations on Shakespeare's name: Shagsbier (p. 9), Shakspere (p. 25), Shaxpoot (p. 32), Shakespiers (p. 33), Shagspeer (p. 71), Shakeshitter (p. 95), Shacklespeares (p. 99), and Shakesfeed (p. 112). In some of these instances, there are new words substituted for old, but the real significance of the wordplay is the author's freedom from traditional contours of language. Hooker's singular voice is evidence of energy and uniqueness of imagination. Although there is an unresolved question of audience (Just whom is Hooker addressing? Other talking dogs as articulate as he is, or sympathetic humans?), the language and speech patterns (particularly in the dialogue of man and man, or man and dog) are harmonious with the social context, rather than antagonistic to it. In other words, Hooker follows the grammatical and linguistic conventions of Elizabethan society and, so, is not *substantially* deviant. However, the fact that he is a talking dog is an aberration from realist conventions. Rooke proves once again to be a New Traditionalist, grounding his jest or game in our cultural knowledge (which is expected to include a sophisticated back-ground in Elizabethan diction and rhetoric) and controlling the process of decoding by a deployment of three aspects of text struc-ture, termed *cohesion, progression*, and *localization* by Roger Fowler.[32]

As an example of Rooke's ingenuity, let us examine the opening paragraph of the novel, where I have numbered each sentence:

(1) That spongy, water-licking Wolfsleach was down on the grass doing sport with Marr, and when he saw me romping toward him with choppers flaring, he whirled in gummy panic and gave Marr a great kick in her hind parts that sent her spinning over on all fours, whimpering her sorrows at pleasure abated and leaking drool from her yellow mouth. (2) Agh, you wench, I thought, you thrush-throated, humping dog; oh, the Devil take you. (3) So I tagged her one on the fly, a quick bite that tozed gristle and fur, and kept on going. (4) Blech and blah, woof and roar — oh, you mangy huffers with pig's feet for brains, here humping away to heart's content — and in *my* yard! (5) There goes dignity, as the barrel-eyed Two Foots would say. (6) Well, you'll taste the poison of my fangs, you'll get Hooker's come-upperance and what-for. (7) You'll have my claw studs where dogger was. (8) Woof-woof and art-arf, damn you all. (p. 3)

The clear sentence-linkage, conventional clausal arrangements, and coherent syntactical frames all point to a cohesive dimension. The alliterative patterns (water, Wolfsleach, was, with, when, toward, with, whirled, whimpering, wench, woof, with, away, well, what-for, where, was, Woof-woof; grass, gummy, gave, great, gristle, going, goes, get; he, him, he, her, hind, her, her, her, humping, her huffers, here, humping, heart's, Hooker's, have), participial phrases ("romping toward him," "spinning over," "whimpering her sorrows," "leaking drool," "humping away"), vernacular ("come-upperance and what-for"), and onomatopoeia ("romping," "whimpering," "agh," "blech and blah, woof and roar," "woof-woof and arf-arf") reveal a superficial symmetry even in subparts of sentences. This shows that the passage, which seems highly idiosyncratic at first, hangs together even as it introduces some of the principal characters already in conflict. This is decidedly a dog's view of things, for man (Two Foot) is relegated to the periphery of action. The cohesion contributes to the impression of the singularity of the narrative voice, and to the consistency of Rooke's style.

The second dimension in the text is a progressive one, one that leads the reader onward, projecting him forward from one segment to another. Here the sequence of tenses and time adverbs enter importantly into play, as do the logical and temporal connectives. The introductory indicative adjective *that* has a briskness and emphasis that raises suspense, in that the reader wishes to know more about Wolfsleach, especially as "that" dog is already indicated to be one of Hooker's antagonists. The verbs in the active voice ("was . . . doing sport," "saw," "whirled," "gave . . . a great kick," "sent her spinning," "tagged her one"), the use of emphatics ("you'll taste," "you'll get," "you'll have"), and the sequential connectives ("and when," "and gave," "that sent," "and leaking," "so I tagged her," "and kept on going," "and in," "as . . . would say") are all features that control the reader's experience of narrative time and action. There is a density of semantically strong predicates that makes the train of action distinctly forceful and progressive. The paragraph is suspenseful in the sense that the described action is incomplete, and the surface symmetry opens up new expectations of rhetoric, characterization, and event.

Yet, there is a subtle undertow in the text that is called localization. For instance, the long compound-complex sentence in the opening is immediately followed by a second, much shorter sentence that is an interiorization ("Agh, you wench, I thought . . .") marked by caesurae. The fifth sentence breaks the alliterative patterns set by the first four. Also, the first sentence, which has syllabic prominence in a branching rhythm (through coordinate and subordinate clauses), is quite unlike the last four sentences. Indeed, from the sixth sentence on, there is a shift to pseudo transitives ("you'll taste," "you'll get," "you'll have") that adds to the dramatic tone. Normally such breaks in pattern would be disruptive to the narrative, but here the subtle modulations of rhythm, grammar, and diction show which character and what voice are dominant, without interrupting or impeding the progression. Hooker's language is, fundamentally, the cosmos of the novel, and it is pure performance. Without Rooke's control, the language could have run amok, ruined by its own verbal energy and invention. The parody of the real world is ventriloquism of a high order, for it gives us an inner nature for the dog. Although Shakespeare's own story remains sketchy, his dog dances superbly with language.

Even where his concerns are more thematic, Rooke proves to be a formalist rather than a suasive maker of statements or messages. One of his chief subjects is man's emotional bondage to time, but the theme is handled with delicate craft. An early piece, "The Ice House Gang" (*LOH*, pp. 3–9), addresses this subject by melting time, yet compelling us to be aware of it. Rooke recreates a young man's summer idyll with a sensual girl. The colloquial idiom ("... some pip-squeak of a girl is rah-rahing . . ." [*LOH*, p. 4]) and imprecise chronology ("how long before who knows" [*LOH*, p. 4]) give the narrative a spontaneity, but Rooke skilfully builds up the romantic sensuality by the girl's free and easy nature, provocative gestures and laughter, and testing seductiveness. She is obviously a young temptress who is playing an erotic game with the boy, as she undresses him in the icehouse. Her disarmingly fresh candour becomes increasingly sensual as her body lunges at his and they crush themselves into each other "not with laughter this time but silently, seriously, with much dexterity on that ice" (*LOH*, p. 7)

Rooke's technique rescues his fiction from the charge of naïve emotionality. "Field Service Four Hundred Forty-Nine from the Five Hundred Field Songs of the Daughters of the Vieux Carré" (*LOH*, pp. 72–94) demonstrates this vividly. The eccentric, even enigmatic, title suits this first-person memoir of a woman still infatuated by the memory of a lover called Code Young. The narrative is an outpouring of memories and feelings. Sentences run on breathlessly, passages have a raw and boozy vitality, and the monologue has a sensual undercurrent that pulls everything else with it. Letti, the narrator, recollects the boys and men in her past, but everything centres on the great subject of her passion — Codey. Although she can be brutally punishing with men who attempt to be aggressive with her, Letti remembers with seething yearning the times she had her Codey. Even with a baby daughter as her responsibility, she had kept the largest part of her being for her lover. She is frankly carnal ("I enjoyed myself, oh it was good standing there in the open in the nude exhilarated by the approaching morning, the cool wind, the silent murmurings of the Quarter which I loved" [*LOH*, p. 92]), and she still sighs for a man whose absence she has now had to make peace with. The affair is over in a purely physical sense, yet we know by the manner of her lyrical recollection of it that it is far from over in a spiritual sense.

Equally strong in passion, but stronger still in content, is "When Swimmers on the Beach Have All Gone Home" (*LOH*, pp. 10–35), a confession by a beach lifeguard. It opens in pumping, exclamatory or ejaculatory fashion ("This city — God, this city — I love it!" [*LOH*, p. 10]), which is quite appropriate to the recreation of an incident where a girl, on crazy impulse, jumps off a bridge in a suicide attempt. The narrator, a lifeguard for nine years, retraces the immediate past surrounding the incident, and his dramatic recounting — especially an earlier attempt to rescue a twelve-year-old girl desperately and bitterly bent on suicide at sea — has an intensely poetic texture.

There is something classical or mythological in the narrator's identity as swimmer and lifeguard. He is different from John Cheever's famous swimmer, Neddy Merrill, in that he does not carry an air of superiority about him, or look on water as "a clemency, a beneficence."[33] Rather than being "a pilgrim, an explorer,"[34] he follows the archetype of rescuer or thaumaturge ("... my life-saving never ends" [*LOH*, p. 26]), but he is, moreover, a water-creature who knows and explores the mysterious elemental power of the sea. He has a strange feeling about his identity and role, for he finds that "... when you save a person's life that life has a way of attaching itself to you" (*LOH*, p. 30). He is bemused by the aftereffects of his rescue missions:

> Passing through town, someone will telephone, will remind me of their gratitude, will hope that I am getting alone fine [sic], will insist that he or she drop by for a moment to chat, will invite me to visit with them. I am touched, their kindness pleases me, but I sense behind these pleasantries something that is more remote, harder to specify, impossible to analyze or compute in any matter meaningful to me. It is as if death has touched them and now I for them exist in that form, am always here as a reminder that will not let go of them. Like the taste of the sea which those who have come close to drowning say never leaves them. (*LOH*, p. 30)

The irony of death lingering as a phantom aura around the lifeguard is compounded by the realization that for all his skills, the lifeguard can never save the would-be victims from "what they were before that sinking in the sea" (*LOH*, p. 31).

There are some wryly comic moments in this story, especially in the black humour generated by the girl's clumsy attempt at suicide off the bridge ("The little waves slapped at her, the mud clung to her, she tried to crawl out of the water but the root she grabbed gave way and she slid down the bank and back into the water" [*LOH*, p. 18]); but the predominantly introspective or reflective tone is carried through by a fugal rhythm that has none of the dramatic percussions of sound found in Cheever's "The Swimmer." Water is the largest symbol in the story — which is more a mental confession than a linear narrative — and the flow and power of the prose is like the building surge of a sea wave. An example can be had in the following passage:

But if those who fell into that danger by accident and whose rescue was a blessing on earth, the others who got there by intent and who did not like it at all that I had in mind saving them, those are worse. Their life since that day, they say, has changed, they don't know now how they could even have thought of doing such a thing to themselves; they are constantly coming to me as if they think I can give them some key to an understanding of why they did so, of what they were like then, or they want to show me how much indeed they have changed from what they were, I would not recognize them, they say, and the one time that I had courage enough to say to the lady who said it to me, yes you are right you certainly are I certainly would not have recognized you, she wept and could not stop, she would kill herself *again*, she said, and all the while she spoke she pulled at my clothes and beat on me as if I were some lover who had jilted her. (*LOH*, p. 31)

The passage billows with piled-up clauses — especially coordinate main clauses and noun clauses linked together. The opening conjunction is obviously a rhetorical device to suggest a follow-up by contrast to a preceding idea. The theme is rushed along and made tumid by the swell of examples. And once again, Rooke's technique serves content admirably and dramatically.

Rooke minimizes emotion only when a story demands distanced writing, as in "Last One Home Sleeps in the Yellow Bed" (*LOH*, pp. 57–71), which is deliberately imprecise, cold, and compressed because its point of view is that of a man who has no answer for simple questions in life. The very opening strikes a hesitant, uncertain note in the vagueness about time and about an existential danger to the protagonist:

> Once upon a time, but which time he could not recall, he had been hit somewhere, hard to define the exact spot or how, by what he thought of now only as a betrayal; something there was, once upon a time and even yet, in a deliberate itch to pull him under, strip him naked, pin his limbs to a table. (*LOH*, p. 57)

The conventional, familiar introductory phrase "once upon a time" — which becomes a nostalgic time frame in "Field Service Four Hundred Forty-Nine" ("*Once upon a time / Codey / that first night remember*" [*LOH*, p. 72]) — is more than simply a narrative device for beginning a tale. Here its vagueness is a symptom of the modernist writer's problem with epistemology in fiction. Rooke's story has a loose temporal cast because it is not easy to give the protagonist's history a definitive shape. The vagueness appears suited to a man who urges a return to nature "to find the truth" (*LOH*, p. 58) — a postulate that is no more helpful and certainly no less problematic than Rousseau's naturalism or Hume's empiricism. This protagonist is insecure, and this insecurity wrestles with him as he wonders: "What makes a man become a man, when does a man become himself?" (*LOH*, p. 59). Unfortunately, he finds nothing to provide a base for his identity, and although in the habit of "writing notes, thoughts, phrases, compilation of a book called 'definitions and responses,' which would contain reminiscences on the questions most troublesome to him during his life," he feels time running out and begins to brood, going into retreat, "thinking that solitude might be creative" (*LOH*, p. 66). All this retreat achieves is to make him lonelier. He then rehearses suicide in a wryly poignant but comic fashion ("He counted off those who might be concerned but the figure he kept retreating to was himself" [*LOH*, p. 68]), and when the question of suicide bores and fatigues him, he postpones answering any of his soul-disturbing questions. This is his ultimate self-betrayal, but it does alleviate his anxiety by a moment of domestic comedy. The ending melts away the dry, clinical tone which had turned him into a specimen for examination, and although the story still suffers from overcompression, the wry humour and irony give it special grace notes.

Problems of the soul concern Rooke, the "stoop-shouldered moralist" (Hancock, p. 114), and sometimes flare into wild conflagrations. Rooke's grappling with form then becomes a special problem, particularly when the form starts to move towards allegory. "Iron Woman,"[35] for instance, begins realistically with the birth of a girl to a father who already presages her ruin. Rooke encapsulates her unhappy adolescence and signals the major theme, transformation, very early. This is obviously going to be a tale about a young woman who will struggle to liberate herself from rejection. Locked between bed and broom, Rebecca transmogrifies the banal and sordid realities of her life by glorious fantasies. Her clumsy lover is transformed into an object from which she can "peel away the stingy facade and go for the core, find the beautiful language of love!" (BB, p. 148).

The story is a compendium of sublimated desires. Rebecca's marriage quickly sours, and, resentful of her husband's brutal character ("He thinks he's man, beast, and king, that he has the divine right to murder me!" [BB, p. 149]), she acquires a psychosis that is semierotic and semimurderous. She divorces her husband, gains weight in her unhappiness, drifts into nebulous relationships, and advertises her death so that she can free herself of an old personality. She gives up sex, except for masturbation, and hallucinates that there is another person alive within her.

Now into allegory, Rooke lards his story of transformation with religious and scientific parody. As Rebecca's inner voice gives a clinical description of her inner change into an iron woman, Rooke's metaphor becomes grotesquely comic. Rebecca becomes an avenging figure in full armour, and the story's epigraph from mediaeval romance ("she rode vpon them with full iron" [BB, p. 144]) proves particularly apt. In her iron state, Rebecca believes she is an invincible warrior who can combat man: ". . . IN ACCORDANCE WITH THE JUST AND AVENGING CODE OF IRON WE SHALL WIPE CLEAN THE SLATE WE SHALL RIDE UPON THEM WITH FULL IRON" (BB, p. 158). The metallic transformation is rendered in exotic terms:

Her fingers crawled hesitantly along her thighs. They touched the magic button between her legs and she felt pure joy. Her blood surged, thickening. The button enlarged. Blood quickly hardened in her veins. A scaly crust began forming over her lips. She blinked and her eyelids clanged. A thin corrosion surfaced on her skin. It turned into a shining crust. Her teeth scraped together, clashing noisily, sending reverberations through her body. Her toes took the form of purple spears. Her muscles swelled, hardened. She looked with amazement at her beautiful armoured flesh. Bluish-white in colour, approaching silver, all with a brilliant shine. She had passed through the zone of preparation, through the zone of reduction, the zone of fusion — she had entered the zone of being. *The Iron Woman! She existed! She was here!* (BB, p. 158)

The parody of chemistry and religion ("Take up thy bed and walk, he [the doctor] commanded Rebecca" [*BB*, p. 159]) is suffused with an eroticism that turns the story into a psychotic hallucination. Rebecca's eroticism and violence are all a fantasy, a sickness of the mind originating, in all probability, from her sexual and psychological frustration as an unfulfilled, spurned woman. As soon as she indulges in sexual fantasy and masturbation (with the "magic button" between her legs), she metamorphoses from Rebecca to Iron. Her revenge against men takes the form of castration: "The iron hand moved powerfully between his legs. It closed slowly over his wizened stick, and he screamed" (*BB*, p. 164). The father who had scorned her, the husband who had tried to annihilate her, and the doctor who had defiled her become her victims. At the last, she acquires a protegée who is also, perhaps, a lesbian lover for her.

The psychic anarchy of "Iron Woman" is complemented by the distress of "The Broad Back of the Angel" (*BB*, pp. 184–201), where there is yet another psychological transmogrification. Rooke evidently revels in the dark interiors of the soul, where grotesque suffering can sometimes change into grotesque bliss or solitude. The fundamental situation in this story breaks down in intriguing ambiguity, and though we are probably apt to feel that Rooke squanders his talent at the end, the technique is clever enough to elicit our admiration.

On the surface, it is the story of two crippled friends — the narrator, Sam, and his friend, Gore — and the wounding realities of life that compound their distress, but it becomes a strange, psychological horror story. At first the focus appears to be on the rather bizarre Gore, who "elects to have a silver ring inserted in his lower lip" (*BB*, p. 184), much to the consternation of his wife, Matila, and his close friends, the narrator and his wife. Gore is evidently a weird tease who can, on impulse, stab a fork into his nose. Matila suffers for his violent eccentricities but obtains the sympathy of the narrator's wife. Sam, however, takes no side openly, although he confesses to a love for Gore. But agitating though Gore's actions are, the story drifts into the narrator's own disturbed soul.

Sam is marked by a chauvinist distrust of women, but the truly disturbing thing for him is not the darkness of women or of his own physical paralysis. The greatest *frisson* is from his boyhood, when he had a very close relationship with Arturo, a tragically fated being. Sam frequently falls into reveries about Arturo's pain-filled days, and these recollections are a poignant way of underlining man's essential helplessness.

The keynote is distress. Matila sobs and shakes her fists at "the vast wrongs done to her"; Sam's "stick legs" thrash about "in their hideous dance"; Gore moves from room to room, distracted and apparently out of mental control (*BB*, p. 194). But there are hints of a climactic change as winter packs in its snow, and dust settles, "all-knowing, all-powerful," like "the weight of a thousand copper pennies" on Sam's eyes (*BB*, p. 196).

Sam apparently regards himself as a brother of the dead Arturo, and in the surprising convolutions of the story, where he seems to leave his wheelchair in one scene and where we learn that Matila was once married to Arturo, Sam internalizes Arturo's memory within his own psyche and becomes the dead one's twin spirit, as it were, a lunatic embodiment of an obsessive phantom. A veteran, he claims, of several wars, Sam discovers the longest war is one of nerves, in which it is impossible to find man at fault for his "mad rapture" of remorse (*BB*, p. 200).

What rescues this story from blinding ambiguity is its heart-rending sentiment and a poetic abstractness that is appealing for all its vagueness. The story reveals that Rooke is never afraid to take risks, to extend technique to the limits of his powerful imagination, and even though the results lack clarity and precision, the emotional effect is potent.

Rooke's use of allegory is much more effective in "Brush Fire"

(*LOH*, pp. 95–178), where a magnificent technique reaches its apogee in a dramatic epiphany. Set in the Kenai Peninsula in Alaska, the eighty-four-page novella concerns a small collection of American soldiers ("the dough-boys of big Delta, First Battle Group, the 21st Infantry" [*LOH*, p. 96]) sent up to fight a devastating brush fire. Before the fire is over, a man is dead, and the bulk of the story turns into an exploration of the causes of his bizarre death. The victim is a Hungarian, Imré Kuimets, nicknamed the Major, although he is really only a private. Apparently he committed suicide against the backdrop of the fire by fasting for five days, then walking straight into the woods and slashing one of his wrists with a file. His company is baffled by his death, and the narrator, a company clerk called Hite, seeks insights into the tragedy. But though the surface is an investigation of a "suicide," the real thrust is psychological and moral. Kuimets' death and the subsequent story of his closest witness, Private Van Gode, become the occasion for a critical probing of two flawed systems — the army and the American society it reflects.

Gode, whose name suggests a pun on "goad," is a wicked wasp who stings his colleagues by his pranks, wisecracks, and sideshow festivity. Yet his abnormal behaviour might well be the perfect foil for the army's cold dehumanization and American society's indifference to human self-destruction. Gode appears to accept Kuimets' death as a martyrdom, a willed self-extinction, and suggests that language might have been a cause for it:

> . . . he wanted to die because there was no one he could talk to. He didn't know the language . . . . He wanted to know what those sounds he heard, meant. For what he saw, an explanation . . . . [B]ut he was cut off by the language. The only answers available to him were those he supplied himself. (*LOH*, p. 97)

Gode becomes a keen critic of the army by maintaining that Kuimets meant to feed on his comrades before they fed on him. Gode is himself a nonconformist who irritates everybody — especially his superiors. A Southerner born and bred, he shocks everybody by laughing wildly the night of Kuimets' death. But laughter — cynical, mocking laughter — is Gode's special characteristic. He is "a man who laughed at all he saw. At himself no less than everyone else"

(*LOH*, p. 128). Gode has decided that the best way of getting through the army or any other place is to laugh at it:

> . . . that night after they brought the Major's body in and things had quieted down Gode followed the path Kuimets had taken into the burn and from that black sucking, smoldering field his laughter was flung back at me, was flung back at all of us, like knives flicking from a circus performer's sleeve, high, wild, and crazy he seemed so happy in it . . . . (*LOH*, pp. 136–37)

Gode, in fact, reveals that he made no attempt to stop Kuimets from self-destruction: "If a man wanted to kill himself and had good reason or thought he had good reason or whether he had no reason at all it wasn't his obligation to stop him" (*LOH*, p. 134).

Most of the story focuses on Gode and army life rather than on Kuimets, and Rooke modulates his pitch and rhythm so that "Brush Fire" falls into largo movements after intensely brisk sections. The narrative method is basically incremental and impressionistic, as Hite gives us a series of scenes that finally turn into a powerful indictment of American values. The final question is not whether Kuimets committed suicide, or whether Gode was an instigator, but, more radically, whether the army and American society are culpable. The captain is baffled by Kuimets' death but shows that he had never known where to put him. In exasperation, he believed the Major had "quit" the army, and he authorized a campaign of harassment in retaliation (*LOH*, p. 140). The captain is typically American in his values and attitudes to a foreigner. As he complains in shocked disbelief, ". . . you could give a man a country, a home, you could bring a man out of communist-infected land and give him all the freedoms, . . . all the benefits of democracy in the country with the highest living standard in the world, and then that man goes out — could think of going out — and kills himself. KILLS HIMSELF!" (*LOH*, p. 142). The captain is totally insensitive to Kuimets' distress and does not see Gode's point that ". . . Kuimets was a freedom fighter; not a goddam freedom mouther" (*LOH*, p. 143).

Only Gode, an ironic goad to the top brass, sees clearly the roots of Kuimets' unhappiness. He offers the explanation that the Hungarian discovered that all he had fought for in Hungary and

that everything he had come to America to find was a lie. Leaving
one Hungary, he had landed smack in the middle of another.
Gode's analysis is not as extravagant as it first sounds. The United
States Army prides itself in believing it is an organization of freedom fighters, yet the very things it fights for are simply those values
most esteemed by a nation stained by dishonesty, camouflage, and
repressed frustration.

Rooke develops a marvellous emblem for the significance of his
story when he has Hite come upon the "twin corpse" of two caribou burned in the brush fire (*LOH*, p. 150). The creatures had obviously been fighting, their antlers locked, and had been unable to
free themselves as the flames brought them to their knees in the
burning brush. All that is left of them is bone shining in the moon-
light on a bed of ash. It is Gode who delivers a meaning for this
spectacle in his own disjointed, sometimes babbling fashion. Despite his continual clowning, Gode is a sad-hearted joker, a man
who resorts to mockery to offset his bitter cynicism. He rejects
those qualities that make a good American — the Oath of Allegiance, for instance — and regards the world as a vast, burned-out
place where we betray one another. "Screwed, blued, and tat-
tooed" (*LOH*, p. 174) — that's his motto for the world, and though
he sometimes sounds quite mad (casting himself as a Hedda Gabler,
a pied piper, another Hitler, or even a Poe victim), it is he who
produces the harshest critical judgements in the story in a series of
apparently disjointed monologues, coloured by his peculiar, coarse
irony. "We're burned out, man, just like old Kenai. It's time for a
new era, a new age . . . ," he claims (*LOH*, p. 174), and he sums up
through his sardonic laughter the emblematic significance of the
two fire-frozen caribou. We are all, he suggests, like the two
animals,

> . . . stomping about, snorting, and bluffing one another with
> their bleats and flash of horn as much to say: I'm mightier
> than you; I'm the Big Cheese! But who's to say their antlers
> are not to lock a final time and hold them together in their
> death struggle till the fire plunges down around them a final
> time and they sink to their knees and don't get up again.
> (*LOH*, p. 178)

A poetic ending for an elliptical story of disillusionment.

The moral impulse never deserts Rooke, but it does not develop into an antagonizing didacticism that overwhelms a story. In *The Love Parlour*, for instance, probably his most moral collection, Rooke reveals how loneliness and frustrated yearning are radical human conditions. The irony of the love parlour's being nothing more than a laundromat in the title story suggests that we do not necessarily need flamboyant settings in order to locate extraordinary distresses. The imperative mood of four titles ("If Lost Return to the Swiss Arms"; "Leave Running"; "If You Love Me Meet Me There"; "Call Me Belladonna") suggests a moral seriousness that survives some of Rooke's most indulgent exercises with grotesque elements. There are three ordinary stories built with mundane details, but even these crystallize around our needs to act on small wisdoms that will not mitigate against the opportunities for friendship, love, and self-recognition. There are two uncommonly sardonic stories where man is perceived as illness or abnormality personified, and, finally, there is a brilliant triptych about submission. Each of these stories has a convincing emotional centre, although the technique, in some cases, is disturbingly extravagant. But, then, Rooke's interest appears to be in disturbing metaphors, and *The Love Parlour*, an ironic title for a dark collection, shakes up our expectations and jars our sense of realism.

Even at his most banal, as in "Call Me Belladonna"[36] or "If Lost Return to the Swiss Arms" (*LP*, pp. 5–23), Rooke is strikingly sensitive to the private yearnings and public exhibitions of the self. "Call Me Belladonna" uses a female narrative voice to tell its story of an egotistical young man, Tom, who preens himself on his own arrogant self-image. Eager to know what his past and present lovers think of him, he makes himself obnoxious until his ego is deflated by the two women. The other story is a study in climacteric, for it tells of an old man in his final days who tries in vain to be a matchmaker for two young people who do not have a good regard for each other. It is a gentle, low-key story that exercises its old-fashioned conventions with supple dexterity; and although it is storytelling in a minor key, its poignancy is a real virtue and something that would be the envy of many writers. Our sympathies are clearly meant to lie with the lonely old man whose ebbing life has fallen into an unexceptional pattern as he visits a park daily to observe vigorous children and then heads for the Swiss Arms Hotel. There he is attended to by the desk clerk and a waitress. The old man, deeply disturbed by the sudden death of a dear female friend with whom he passed up the opportunity for lifelong companionship, is pained by the animosity of the pair who show "every kindness in the world to him" (*LP*, p. 11) but no concern for each other. He feels a greater pain about their enmity than he does about his own loneliness, and the pain "with a life of its own" (*LP*, p. 21) reaches out and touches him in his very soul. "Do something, . . . don't let it slip away like this," he pleads with the girl (*LP*, p. 22), but his exhortation comes to nothing as the girl leaves the employ of the hotel and the old man dies alone in his room, with "the overhead light burning and the water running in the faucet at the corner" (*LP*, p. 23).

Rooke forsakes his quiet irony in other stories and becomes wrenchingly grotesque. "If You Love Me Meet Me There" (*LP*, pp. 42–50) maintains an emotional distance as the narrator cannot bring himself to get involved with his charitable country neighbours. The grotesqueness grows out of a country couple's pink house with a Coca-Cola clock by the door, the wife's death by cancer, and the abnormally terrified daughter. But the very human pressure of a guilty soul redeems the story.

Less graceful and far more sardonic in their metaphorical exploration of distress are "Memoirs of a Cross-Country Man" (*LP*, pp. 51–64) and "Leave Running" (*LP*, pp. 24–41). In the first, the pidgin English of a Mexican narrator, who is employed to work at Estalavita Monastery, has a rough comedy to it but hardly prepares us for the sardonicism of Brother John who is convinced that ". . . man is illness personified . . ." (*LP*, p. 55). Brother John's language is coarse, colloquial, and profane, and he is an aggressive foil to the narrator, González Manuel, who presents himself as a bit of a fool for fear that he has nothing serious to offer the world. González has obviously not yet recovered from his unrequited love for Marguerite, his beloved who abandoned him, and Brother John grants him no pity, only a barrage of mordant cynicism. "Some men are born," Brother John says, "to wave the wand, others to record the magic fact, most to slave till the magic comes, to push the dirt and hoard up strength against that time when the dirt pushes them" (*LP*, p. 54). González is paranoid, having invented a story about someone trying to poison him at a well, but his real illness is fear — a fear, as Brother John identifies it, of dying as a perennial traveller carried on "the wings of a darkness formed by all the lives" he's left behind (*LP*, p. 55).

The morbid atmosphere of the story is created by death emblems: Father-Padre looks "nothing short of dead"; outside the window there is "a flutter of wings, in the sky a black bird flying for the trees"; in the vaults along the corridor walls lie "the dead brothers of the sect" (*LP*, p. 62). The morbidity is turned into lurid fare by Brother John's autobiographical revelations of his criminal father, crazily impulsive mother, and tragically fated fiancée. A note of perverse eccentricity is added by a crazy monk who searches for the Holy Grail and by Father-Padre's closed-circuit TV address with its stunning credo that "God is wicked, man is no less" (*LP*, p. 61).

Caught in this madness, González Manuel despairs of ever finding his own holy grail, Marguerite, or of finding a consolation for his life. His final act is a touchingly comic newspaper plea — an advertisement for the missing Marguerite — and it is a futile act because he is brought low by the truths of her desertion and the monastery's peculiarly, soul-destroying realism.

The philosophic realism (some would say pessimism) of "Memoirs of a Cross-Country Man" is distorted by the extravagant characterizations of Brother John and Father-Padre, but the distortion is far less unwarranted than the exaggerated metaphor in "Leave Running" (*LP*, pp. 24–41). Here a tale of marital disaster becomes the tale of an extreme mental obsession as Rose, whose middle-class marriage is on the rocks, becomes so madly enamoured of Igor, a cold, calculating house-burglar, that she joins him on one of his nocturnal adventures and ends up breaking into her own home. The domestic side of the story is represented by telling moments, as Rooke gives us an intimate view of the failed marriage by observing the toiletries of Rose and Talbert, and by brief scenes with the children who pester Talbert when Rose is out with her strange lover. But Rooke, unfortunately, does not trust realism enough in this story and burdens the narrative with clumsy metaphors. Talbert, for instance, draws an analogy between salmon-spawning and man's desperate flight from threats to his survival; Rose is turned into a grotesque "Bitch-Mother-Goddess" at her dressing table (*LP*, p. 29); and the housebreaking at night is a strained symbol that creaks with the weight of its pretensions. "Leave Running" is, unhappily, an example of miscalculated metaphor, where the eerie horror of its abstract conception turns to melodrama by clumsy symbol-clanging.

The triptych that carries *The Love Parlour* to its conclusion, however, more than compensates for the failure of "Leave Running."

Not, perhaps, since Malcolm Lowry's *Under the Volcano* and, more recently, Audrey Thomas' short fiction, has Mexico been so vividly represented by temperament and theme than in Rooke's three, back-to-back tales. The first, entitled "For Love of Madeline" (*LP*, pp. 81–98), has a conversational freedom and deliberately inelegant syntax. The opening is reminiscent of an oral legend with its signalling of setting, repetitive devices, choric effect, and parenthetical additions. It is narrated from the point of view of Madeline, "a nervous opinionated girl" (*LP*, p. 82), who is in the remote village of El Flores with her companion, Raymond, a tired, petulant young man who is eager to get a one-way ticket out of the place. The contaminated lakewater is deemed out-of-bounds, and scenes of poverty, prostitution, and squalor compound the Americans' discomfort. Rooke makes succinct links between his characters' disaffections and the oppressiveness of El Flores, so that the landscape becomes symbolic. As patrons sit at open-air cafés, beggars move into view in midday sun. Burglars and prostitutes try their luck, while the lake rises during the rains. Low on funds, Madeline and Raymond are hungry and tired of El Flores — tired, too, of each other. Madeline's polite smiles annoy Raymond and elicit his sour contempt. He is continually querulous, while she, suffering with a mild turista, wishes to relieve herself of the burden he has obviously become. She, as yet, does not foresee the part Sr. Gómez, the town's most noted citizen, will play in her life, for although Gómez has placed hand-painted signs outside the Café Bodega advertising for a submissive mistress, Madeline is not prepared to turn herself into a psychologically dominated woman. So her story continues to be an accumulation of petty and large frustrations, and the narrative is marked by parenthetical passages that suggest an interrupted, febrile tempo for Madeline. Only after Sr. Gómez materializes physically in the story does Rooke drive the narrative on without digression until it builds to a single emotional peak.

Raymond's financial problems and Madeline's "gibberish" (*LP*, p. 94) increase the emotional distance between the two Americans, but Rooke simultaneously enlarges the figure of Gómez so that as Raymond fades out of the story, Madeline moves towards Gómez. Rooke establishes a part of Gómez' character on the first page with the hand-painted advertisement. Gómez thinks of himself as a "dramatical forceful personality" (*LP*, p. 81) who needs a perpetually subjugated woman. He makes his first actual appearance in a

white suit and sombrero, so that he looks "enchanted" (*LP*, p. 92).
His "polite, chivalric voice" (*LP*, p. 94) makes him a knight, but
because Gómez keeps hiding his eyes, Madeline feels unable to look
into his soul. He appears to be solicitous of women, but Madeline
notices his "contemptuous smile" (*LP*, p. 94), so that from the first,
Gómez is ambiguous — a figure who offers women redemption and
mystery while he secretly prepares his total domination of their
psyches.

When Madeline approaches him for the "position," she is
rebuffed. She correctly suspects that he is lying when he says the
position is filled, and she is determined to force herself into his life.
In a brief, suddenly intense scene, set to the percussion of an abrupt
rainstorm, she goes to his door and beats against it with her "frail
fists" (*LP*, p. 98) in the driving rain. This final image crystallizes the
psychological truth of the story, for Rooke does not have to add an
explicit comment. We know from the details of Raymond's financial problems and Madeline's emotional estrangement from him
that she needs Sr. Gómez. The rising lakewater signals the
mounting tension and danger to Madeline, and the final scene of
her desolate banging at Gómez' door dramatizes most succinctly
her submission and dependence. She will never be the same again,
despite her grit and irony, for she has become a desperate beggar
who needs Gómez' charity and support.

The second panel in Rooke's triptych is "For Love of Eleanor"
(*LP*, pp. 99–126), which shows the grim, funereal side of marriage
and life. Once again, the Café Bodega and the lake become important locales with emotional resonances in the plot, but now, instead
of tracing a woman's lonely desolation, Rooke reveals the death of
a marriage and simultaneously the death in a woman's soul. The
main character is neither the woman Eleanor nor Sr. Gómez; the
dominant character is Death itself, lingering persistently with
enchanting mementoes of its morbid and fatal power.

Once again, Rooke begins with a couple disenchanted with each
other and with El Flores. As in the first story, the woman is neurotic,
although this time her neurosis is more serious than a mere eruption
of mood and passion, for it has caused a mental breakdown from
which she has not completely recovered. Eleanor feels a little sorry
for herself and thinks her breakdown diminishes her responsibility
for her actions. Her husband, Frank, is more than a little bored by
the subject of her breakdown and wears an expression of "offended

gloom" (*LP*, p. 102) over what Eleanor has allowed to happen to herself.

The morbidity of the two characters is complemented by the "drab and sexless cafe" (*LP*, p. 100), where the couple daily eat their "most extended breakfast in all of Mexico" (*LP*, p. 99). The Café Bodega appears deserted, and the entire plaza has "a mood of disenchanted isolation" (*LP*, p. 103). The contaminated lake, guarded by soldiers, deepens the feeling of unpleasantness.

Topping all this, however, is Eleanor's "undiminished fascination with death" (*LP*, p. 100). Having once had a close encounter with extinction, when her hair caught fire from a match, Eleanor, psychically and physically marked by the nearly fatal experience, lives with omnipresent reminders of death. Although she has never met him, she knows Maya, an artist from Guadalajara, who paints the dead. Maya, she feels, can find the death in her and Frank. Meanwhile, before Rooke's story carries us to that moment of truth, it accumulates its death emblems in a gathering nexus of doom. Health officers argue with the local undertaker, whose establishment, it is said, is not burying the dead quite deep enough or with sufficient speed. A young boy holds a black, wet, dead pig in his arms. The year is 1973, the time of Watergate and the death of political integrity in the person of the American president. It is also the year death comes to El Flores in the form of contaminated lake water. The local citizens are convinced that their patron saint is insane and diabolic *("El Santo es loco")* [*LP*, p. 109]). The sombre landscape is marred by disgusting mounds of refuse, debris aswim in sewage, insects, and maggots.

Suddenly, against this background of "ruin and decay," Gómez, "the man in white," advances "more outlandishly impeccable than ever, a vision in his bold linen suit and white boots and wide sombrero" (*LP*, p. 111). Although he has Madeline tagging listlessly behind him, and although it is well known that Gómez breaks American girls and then sends them away, Eleanor is immediately attracted to him. Her husband considers Gómez "unsound and dangerous and certainly evil" (*LP*, p. 111), but Eleanor finds him adorably beautiful. Eleanor is clearly wooed by the fatal fascination of the man, whom she fails to recognize as a form of death to herself. She adores him for his glamorous malignity — "his sinister vigour, his perverted chivalry" (*LP*, p. 113) — but fails altogether to make any connection between Gómez and the death he will bring her, for when Gómez enthusiastically inquires, ". . . how is your good friend Death this morning?" Eleanor merely giggles, shifting her shoulders free of his "oiling hands" (*LP*, p. 113). Gómez' oiling hands may well be an emblem of unction, the sacrament of the dying, but Eleanor is oblivious to this portent. With stylish aplomb, Rooke creates a sensual scene of sinister carnal relish as Gómez begins his fatal seduction of Eleanor:

> '*Ola señor! Con su permiso?*' He sat down, immediately launching forward to place his hands over Eleanor's knees and wedge his own between them. 'But only one death during the night, Mademoiselle, *uno y no mas!*' He grinned roguishly, though his voice was more urgent than mocking. 'Perhaps our amigo Death is ready to — how do I say it? — *echar pelillos a la mar!* — to bury the hatchet, no!' His hands slid back and forward along Eleanor's thighs. Her eyes gloated, misty from a feeling near to gratitude. (*LP*, p. 113)

The nearly orgasmic excitement of Eleanor is almost immediately counterpointed by the gloom of a funeral procession, and the rhythm of Rooke's intercutting of sex and death rises and falls like a powerful tide. As the "quiet shuffling footbeat" of the mourners is momentarily obscured (*LP*, p. 114), Eleanor and Frank trade conversation about Frank's lover, "the cool Indian" (*LP*, p. 115). Then, once again, the mourners begin their uneven song and head for church where "the bleak wedding of all our murdered souls" is to occur (*LP*, p. 118).

Eleanor eventually realizes that "El Flores is where you come when you die" (*LP*, p. 118). The figure of Father García as he stands alone on the cathedral steps, waiting for the dead to come to him, gives her view credence.

Frank, uneasy and sullen as he joins with Eleanor in reviewing the passing of the dead, is the bridegroom of death. Nothing good or productive comes out of their marriage, and while they sit at their ritualistic breakfast at the Café Bodega, Eleanor sums up the significance of their marriage and its routines as these are connected to the grim setting:

> The Saint is loco, the Saint is terrible. Death here is all leisure, Frank. You can walk up San Antonio at your leisure or make love to Nora Meyer Jones if that's your pleasure. But no

matter how extended it is it finally has to empty into something else, if only into more leisure. This breakfast has been at our leisure on its way to becoming our own version of the El Flores death. (*LP*, pp. 124–25)

While the death procession begins and ends and recommences, and the inspector from Morelia goes on with his talk of plague and pestilence, Eleanor and Frank's marriage reaches its own point of breakdown and expiration. Eleanor's nervous morbidity reaches an apogee of clinical self-pity, sharpened, no doubt, by her husband's love affair with Nora Meyer Jones. As Frank's lover advances on her, Eleanor sees the painter Maya at work on the roof of the Banco Nacional. Her final moment in the story is as a serenely composed victim, "her expression beatific, hands laced across her bosom" as if she holds there "the scarlet rose which only herself and Maya and Death's Angel could see and enjoy" (*LP*, p. 126). It is a dual beatific vision, for not only is Eleanor calm and transfigured, but the very motive for her mood is the beatific figure of Maya, a hovering "angel" of death whose binoculars pick her out for his special death icon.

The final panel in Rooke's triptych completes the Gómez story. "For Love of Gómez" (*LP*, pp. 127–57) focuses on the Mexican and his American mistress Madeline, who is as hysterical as ever between bouts of abject submission. The immediate catalyst in the plot is Gómez' decision to clean out his swimming pool, which requires Madeline to wait for ten days before she can swim in it again. Rooke exposes Madeline's vulnerability with naked poignancy, without obscuring her vanity, belligerence, and ludicrousness.

Madeline conveys her disgust for "miserable Mexico with its ignorant cacophony of misery and guile and neglect" (*LP*, p. 132), and, as one of the themes is the country's destruction of foreign women, her pointed antagonism is sharpened further for its own ironic blunting at the end. Madeline, disgusted by the primitive and depressing conditions of El Flores, is consumed by her contempt for Gómez, his *doña*, and his employees. She hates them all and denigrates them as "foreigners" (*LP*, p. 133) before she realizes the acerbic irony: it is she, after all, who is the real foreigner here. Trapped by her dependency on Gómez, she finds the country to be "an unholy terror" (*LP*, p. 134) and resents Gómez for enjoying her suffering.

But Madeline's point of view is not given absolute sway. It is sometimes supplanted by that of Gómez, and this alternation creates a dynamic uncertainty in the story. Gómez sees his American mistress as selfish, venal, and deluded, but her truculence and taunts only whet his appetite for dominating her even more ruthlessly. Madeline insults his *doña* and threatens that her father will settle the score with Gómez before rescuing her from the "pigsty called Mexico" (*LP*, p. 137). But threaten as she might with vows to diminish his superiority and power, Gómez is coolly unperturbed. In fact, he finds her declarations trite and pathetic, and he continues to be egocentric: he is enamoured of his house and property and capable of believing the sun exists solely for him. He seems to know the depth of her despair yet shows her no mercy, violating her privacy by spying on the contents of her secret letter-box.

There is a special twist to Gómez' relish of the psychosexual struggle. He knows that "the spirit" of this woman will yield but cannot be broken, yet he finds it "a curiously ignoble, . . . marvellously vain and worthless" spirit: "It withstood everything and in fact the more one attempted its mutilation the more it thrived" (*LP*, p. 150). Looking on Madeline, Gómez cannot accept Father García's timid boast that God is in every person. Madeline appears to be the distinctive product of North America — an interminably wretched and conceited creature with racism lurking in her blood. The only value she has is what he assigns to her. For instance, he orders her to paint her long fingernails red, and the colour, in his opinion, is altogether appropriate for it signals her value:

> The nails of all her predecessors had in fact been coloured the same. The blood of such women was infamous, symbolic of a thing so callous that he could see it always in his mind's eye, especially those late nights after Madeline had drunk herself past rancour and fatigue, past all attempts to fasten blame — those hours she lay in his arms and all her whining delusions of supremacy were surrendered. (*LP*, pp. 153–54)

The ending seals Gómez' victory: Madeline, desperate to use the swimming pool, is forced to swim in unchlorinated water marked by a surface of scum. Gómez does not allow chlorine in his pool because it would interfere with his garden, and Madeline is forced to suffer the resulting unpleasantness. The final image of her in the story shows her disappearing momentarily under the scum while Gómez looks on, "pleased with her, for the first time in his memory" (*LP*, p. 157). On the symbolic level, her degradation is signalled by her underwater disappearance beneath the scum. And Gómez' approval finalizes his triumphant domination. Where she had once sought shelter under his roof, she is now psychologically submerged beneath his contempt and under his control.

Yet it is also possible to have another interpretation of the ending, for Rooke himself asserts that Madeline finds the swim good for her:

> It's where she ought to be. She has dived into this pool with algae floating on the surface. That she has willed herself to do so is an act of hope. She's telling us that she recognizes her failures as a person. And I think, and Gómez thinks, that she will come out of it a better person. It's a *happy* ending, I'd argue. (Hancock, p. 132)

Rooke's moral complexity does justice to his material, for, unlike Morley Callaghan's or W. D. Valgardson's conscience, it refuses to mediate in the tensions between good and evil. "Biographical Notes" (*CE*, pp. 97–131) attests splendidly to Rooke's sincerity, for it allows evil a full measure, and when it shows the counteraction of good, it uses satire and parody as checks or qualifications but in a free form that resists a grid. It is a pastiche of notes, dialogues, film criticism, legal testimony, and narrative scenes assembled by the narrator, Martin Wolfe, a director of pornographic films. Wolfe's own personality and attitudes are revealed by the collage of notes on various characters in his life: his estranged wife, Elaine; actors Robin Harvey and Wanda Lee Casslake; Michael Oble, a freelance art and film critic who writes laudatory, pretentious analyses of Wolfe's films; and Marceline Able, a juvenile drug addict who charges Wolfe with statutory rape.

The discrete method of presentation — which is a literary equivalent of film montage — is post-modernist insofar as it requires, like all "narcissistic narrative" (in Linda Hutcheon's phrase), the reader to collaborate with the narrator in finding a pattern in the subjective biographical notes of Martin Wolfe. Every character is seen from Wolfe's point of view, yet the material is not so constricted that the reader is automatically forced to sympathize with the protagonist. As Oble discovers in Wolfe's films, "Nothing is secure . . . . Nothing is to be counted on. Place is totally unreliable. Who we are is the most specious of inventions" (*CE*, p. 109). Consequently, Wolfe must himself be taken as an unreliable witness. However, any suspicions the reader might have about Wolfe's veracity are tempered by the strain of humour in some of the sections of the incremental story.

There are many comic elements. Robin Harvey, for one, is described as a character with a "slow, uncomplicated mind" (*CE*, p. 98). Marceline is a totally unscrupulous, mindless teenager whose crazy, demotic speech is satirical in the extreme, although the amusement it provides hardly displaces the reader's moral revulsion for Marceline's deranged and vicious behaviour. Michael Oble's analysis of the profound moral significance of Wolfe's pornographic films reads like a parody of pretentious European film journals. And Wolfe's autobiographical confessions sound like a parody of disadvantaged lives.

Yet the comedy never interferes with the grave elements. Perhaps the major theme in "Biographical Notes" is guilt — the guilt swirling around Wolfe, Wanda Lee Casslake, Rita Islington, and Marceline, in particular. As Wolfe's films suggest, "guilt weighs heavily on us all . . . ," and his biographical notes, as a parallel to the content of his films, move from a distantly objective portrayal of specific victims into "the dark and tangled heart of material in which perpetrator, victim and spectator blindly collaborate" (*CE*, p. 110). The extent and nature of this collaboration are intimated in the story, especially when Wolfe focuses on Wanda's suicide and Marceline's imputations of his sexual criminality.

The argumentative Wanda, star and sex object in Wolfe's films, likes to make people believe that she hasn't a brain in her head; in fact, she is said to be an extraordinary woman who repudiates her gifts out of a deep-seated psychosis that nobody has probed, but which the camera often exploits to advantage. Wanda rages about herself as trash in pictures that are trash, and this vehement self-denigration is evidence of what Wolfe calls her "murdered" soul (*CE*, p. 114). Wolfe, in fact, devises a theory about Wanda that is a perceptive commentary on the psychology of her guilt:

> It would destroy her, I sensed, if she ever came to realize that she'd somehow come out of whatever foul, stench-infested, brutalizing place she'd started from and developed into the extraordinary person she now was. If it ever dawned on her

that she *was* out of it now. No-one is ever *safely* out of it.
There is no green benign place, no happily anointed field, no
sanctuary where one may cast off the memory of what one
was. No amount of sophisticated cinema talk, none of the
high-fashion clothes or expensive restaurants or the nice car
and lavish apartment she could now afford could convince
her that she had not been murdered once upon a time. These
outer trappings were fine, they gave pleasure, but the heart
and soul that is murdered once is one that stays murdered for-
ever. (*CE*, pp. 113–14)

Wanda's sister, Rita Islington, is less sympathetic and buys her
sister's photographs in order to sell them to the media for a tidy
sum. Her precise language and regal bearing — which make her
seem more of a star than Wanda — intimidate Wolfe, and her
immoral motive contributes to the destruction of misguided
Wanda, who is as apt to show charity to her exploiters (such as the
acid-dropping groupie Moonie Marceline) as she is to spurn the
praise of her genuine admirers.

Wanda's intrinsic innocence and goodness have obvious foils in
the cynicism and evil of Rita and Marceline. Rita's evil is deliberate,
however, whereas Marceline's, as Wolfe says, is rarely felt to be
intentional (*CE*, p. 127). Marceline, the "derelict from the lost
lagoon, guide for the lunatic's museum" (*CE*, p. 123), is "deranged,
demented, vicious. An idiotic little jerk. Empty-headed for the most
part. Even ordinary at times" (*CE*, p. 126). She does the foulest deeds
— such as trying to stuff Wanda's daughter down the commode or
backstab those who have helped her — but it is her ignorance that
sometimes saves her from having to bear full responsibility.

If we are tempted to wonder whether Rooke is dodging the issue
by special pleading for Marceline, we should bear in mind Wolfe's
bitter indictment of God that is as intense as it is paradoxical:

God is the proven traitor. I sometimes think his body is the rot
in this air. That the battle for our souls was lost, our fate
sealed incalculable ages ago. At the very minute we looked
and began to fabricate something better than ourselves.
That's when we killed God, at the very instant we in our
image created Him. Not, as is usually supposed, to explain
our origins or sweeten our destiny — but simply to shift the

blame elsewhere. We strung the bastard up. That's when we did it and that's why. (*CE*, p. 127)

Wolfe appears to be railing against God as the source of metaphysical corruption, and he fashions a charge of predeterminism that would appeal to all those who find it impossible to accept the Christian belief in free will. Nevertheless, the paradox at the heart of his indictment — God is dead, but we have created a god in our own image — complicates the issue, for it asserts the existence of an anthropomorphic deity, and this compensates for our guilt. We are guilty, Wolfe seems to be saying, so we need an object onto which we can transfer our guilt, and we invent a god to that purpose. Such a metaphysic, then, hardly dodges the issue of guilt; what it manifests, instead, is a critical realism of human weakness in a post-lapsarian world. Wolfe is skewering man at least as much as he is condemning the accepted notion of a benevolent God.

Wolfe is not a malcontent or cynic. He eagerly follows Oble's reviews of his work and finds in this formal criticism a sophisticated articulation of his moral and metaphysical preoccupations or pretensions. There is always some doubt as to the validity of Oble's elevated commentary, and we wonder if Wanda is not justified to a degree in her denunciation of it as false rubbish. We wonder if, in fact, Wolfe has the intellectual subtlety to create such profound messages in a pornographic film. Nevertheless, paradox can be a stimulating and baffling truth at the core of any art — as the "pornography" of Federico Fellini's *Casanova* or Liliana Cavani's *The Night Porter* indicate — and, so, we should give the benefit of the doubt to Wolfe, who is perceived by Oble as an angelic redeemer in an infernal world.

Those critics who do not recognize Rooke's concern with hope are probably misled by his hugely successful stories about man's death struggles and burnt-out fate. Rooke is most powerful about characters at extremes of personality and action. Even in comedy, he often waxes strong on psychological abnormality. Most of the intensity of "Mama Tuddi Done Over" (*DS*, pp. 9–42), for example, derives from the vulgar figure of Mama Tuddi, a black star of TV and radio, who attends the funeral of a seven-year-old fan and gets wrung out by the public attention and Preacher Teebone's seductive rhetoric. The texture is a little raw and the colours sometimes gaudy, as Rooke traps the TV faith-healer and Double Ola saleswoman within her own vanity and erotomania. The story thrives on the mixture of violence and tenderness, lugubrious grief and lubricious lust. Little Reno Brown, the boy who has died, is really the last thing on Mama Tuddi's mind as, dressed in fox collar and jewels and with her dyed orange hair, she flaunts her sex appeal before a multitude of fans. Her real regret is not Reno's untimely death, but the fact that she has not had time to blacken her two front teeth, a trademark known far and wide. She is present only because it is a public affair, and she has prepared a speech in praise of the dead boy, which is so ludicrously phoney that it does comic violence to the pathos we might be prepared to feel for the boy. The comedy certainly ripens as black humour. Reno Brown's mother, wearing a gold anklet with a big moon disc, and her young lover, flashy LeRoy, revive memories of their sordid lust and LeRoy's murder of Mr. Brown. Mrs. Brown gets jealous of LeRoy's interest in Mama Tuddi. And, finally, Preacher Teebone, carried away on the gusts of his own fundamentalist eloquence, quickens Mama Tuddi's sensual appetite so that, after all the fattening food of the wake, she is seduced by the erotic power of the preacher's presence and sermon. An orgy of self-display and false sympathy becomes an orgy of food and sublimated sexual desire.

Mama Tuddi's orgasm is the climax of Rooke's belief that most people have personalities in excess of who they think they are (see Hancock, p. 128). As Preacher Teebone flares on with his impassioned rhetoric, Mama Tuddi feels a snake sliding into her: "... the crawly thing have twisted down over her stomach and is hissing out its tongue and she can feel its rough nose pushing cold and wet under her hands, aiming to slide up through her woman's trough to lodge inside of her" (*DS*, p. 41). This snake is obviously a phantom phallus, but it is also a heightened emblem of psychic invasion. It might be another person of Mama Tuddi's own strange invention — not simply Preacher Teebone trying to invade her body.

Elsewhere Rooke is very sharp on the experience of multiple identities. The diarist in "The End of the Revolution and Other Stories" (*CE*, pp. 47–70) is schizophrenic and lives in a neighbourhood where *everyone* has multiple identities. She wants to become one body that contains all bodies; she wants to "look out at the world from the settled, comfortable, perfect silence of a single eye, to have no need even to think *satisfied, satisfied, we are all here!*" (*CE*, p. 70). The "revolution" in this psychological story does not refer to rebellion, but to a pattern of motion, for the plot follows the woman's fixation on another woman who is observed through her curtains and window. At first the story appears to be a study in obsession or voyeurism, as the protagonist-narrator manifests a neurotic tension, expectation, and loneliness. Little things cause frustration: grubbiness, a male neighbour, a bulbous stranger. As she admits, "... it's the legion of trivialities we can't forgive" (*CE*, p. 61). The protagonist is preoccupied with appearances and is regarded as peculiar by others. A tenacious voyeur, she does not want to be studied closely herself. She is under the delusion that she has learned to cope with "life's small realities" (*CE*, p. 67), but it becomes increasingly evident that she lacks psychological integrity and balance, and that she yearns to be the other woman whom she observes so scrupulously.

Similarly tense in its observation of psychological peculiarities is "The Deacon's Tale" (*CE*, pp. 5–23), a satire-within-a-satire, where Rooke's delight in studying the creative writer's attitude to fiction rubs against the character's mundane pressures in a strained marriage. Employing, as he often does, a first-person-participant point of view, Rooke presents us with Deacon, who complains about a sore foot and whose revelations and confessions go into the composition of a story about this affliction — a story that is continually interrupted by the criticisms of his nonliterary wife, whose quasi-Pollyannaish attitude to life is in raw conflict with Deacon's darker vision and method of writing. The wife is an addict of fact — but only of fact that she can reconcile with her falsely cheerful vision of reality. Regarding her husband as an oaf, she attacks his fiction:

> According to her, the people in my stories are never polite and nice the way people really are. In my stories it's always hocus-pocus, slam-bang, and someone has a knife at your throat. Turns people off, she claims. I'm influenced too much by TV and radio and by what I read in the papers; in real life people are not nearly so anxious and unhappy as I make out. Put in a little comedy, she says. After all, you live in a pleasant house, you've got liquor in the cabinet, a beautiful wife, and most of our *urgent* bills are paid. Why be morbid? It gives people the wrong impression. (*CE*, pp. 5–6)

The wife's bourgeois personality obviously sets the moral tone for her aesthetic. Her benignity is evidently rooted in middle-class materialistic comfort. It has a narrow focus and ignores the dark underside of life and literary imagination. For her, fiction has to be literal and delimited by the surfaces of observable facts. She cannot abide either Deacon's physical agony over his sore foot or his version of how he inherited the suffering. Her story would be different from his, of course, and Rooke gives us delight near the end when he presents the wife's prettified version of one of her husband's stories, in which she eliminates all the elements she considers gross or absurd in favour of tidy pathos and a perfectly sentimental conclusion.

The divergent philosophies of Deacon and his wife produce divergent stories within the larger fiction, and the controlling dialectic of fiction versus fact undergoes a process of mitosis to obtain a second dialectic, whereby, in satirizing a tritely conventional approach to storytelling, Deacon affords us insights into his failed marriage. Our final image of Deacon is of him at The Motherlode, his favourite bar, where he tells and picks up stories. But he is somewhat beaten down by his wife's aggressiveness, and the heart has gone out of him. Sadly, he appears to have been converted to his wife's point of view and has substituted bourgeois mediocrity in place of his earlier, fertile "abnormality."

Rooke is himself abnormal in his fiction, venturing into spooky corners of the mind and soul, laying bare the troubled, fogbound spirit of characters caught in a world where evil proliferates and where remedies are known but not applied to substantial effect. He is as apt to explore the ghostly hold of evil on people as he is to show how guilt weighs heavily on us all. His is unmistakably a postlapsarian vision.

The Gothic aspect of this vision is in evidence in many stories, particularly "Deer Trails in Tzityonyana" (*DS*, pp. 99–111), which leads us past a cemetery and along twisting roads to a massive Tudor house where the atmosphere is dismal and macabre. Shadowy figures crouch or move solemnly and ominously, and a young girl comes under a palpable power of blackness. Although the mood is sinisterly clear, particular actions remain vague. It is all bewitching melodrama.

Another eerie tale is "Aldopho's Disappeared and We Haven't a Clue Where to Find Him" (*CE*, pp. 132–57), in which the title character is "the plucky, dim-witted sort" — "just the sort of innocent, airy person to whom evil was ever liable to occur" (*CE*,

p. 132). Aldopho's peculiar romanticism fascinates Philby, the narrator, because of the character's "cockamamie fancies, his airy boasts, his buoyant jibes, his concoctions, his endless tales about the enchanted and enchanting Orpha," and "his facility for finding beauty in the most fetid, puerile pond, pasture or field one ever came across when walking with him" (CE, p. 140). Yet his way of life — as his former companions knew it — remains an enigma, as does the fact of his disappearance.

In spite of its clubhouse setting, the story acquires a malevolent cast because of the rancid and bitter vision that Gerhardt, a club member, provides of "evil set loose upon the world" (CE, p. 134). Aldopho, also a member of the secret society, appears to have been abducted, but the unpredictable Gerhardt enjoys setting up depraved jokes about the situation, and Philby is entrapped in a perplexing maze of metaphysical, psychological, and criminal investigation. Philby finally goes to meet his illusion, Orpha. There are lurid melodramatic touches that amplify a Gothic aspect, and the ending, with its descent into decay and ghostliness as in a typical Poe grotesque, is eerie and horrifying.

Despite its game structure of an exchange of stories, "Aldopho's Disappeared" has a deep pessimism. One of the interior tales is from a ballad about deceit and destruction, and, as Philby reflects, innocence seems to have no place in "God's little hoax" (CE, p. 138). Philby's comments expand into cosmic ones:

> It seemed to me that Aldopho's fate was of no consequence, that whatever mercy or violence had come his way evil would continue to stalk us and always with the same abandon and whimsy and steadfast loyalty to absurdity that it had stalked him. Evil wanted only to make us look and feel ludicrous, then it could rest . . . . We were stuck with the life that had been ordained for us. We perceived our agony and were allowed our motions, however futile. It was given to us to divine God's scheme and add our laughter to His. This itself was evil, but evil of a sort that alleviated much pain. God no doubt liked our laughing at Him. It let Him know what *we* knew: that while He played with our lives, other stronger forces were toying with and ridiculing His. Stars, rigid after their long waltz, mocked His small power. (CE, p. 139)

There is a classical strain in such a metaphysic, for the ancient Greeks themselves believed in Moira — a power higher than the highest god — and Philby apparently subscribes to a similar conception of an almighty, abstract force. Yet, "Aldopho's Disappeared" is, perhaps, an exception to Rooke's characteristic vision of grotesque *modern* malevolence. "Fromm Investigations" (*CE*, pp. 24–46) and "Friendship and Property" (*CE*, pp. 71–96) demonstrate the extent to which immorality and *Angst* are rooted in *us* rather than in Fate as some disembodied agency.

"Fromm Investigations" combines the detective story and the game model of metafiction. The narrator is a psychiatrist who operates as a private detective in order to explore and solve, if possible, other people's fears. Beneath the surface satire on Freudian psychology — a client comes to him with a problem of wet dreams — there is an inveterate concern with terror and anguish. The story opens with a declaration about the subconscious, and the story's form validates Fromm's theory about the "rampaging mole" in us that "eats through every inch of human wall" (*CE*, p. 24).

The psychiatrist is refreshingly honest. While people come to him with their neuroses, he has his own troubles: a sister-in-law's delusions about her left ear being larger than her right; a brother who stores up fraternal hatred; and memories of Nazis and his violent father. The psychiatrist, in a deep sense, is no different from his patients. Mixed up like them, he wants understanding and forgiveness. Every detail in his story forms part of a larger pattern of distress. Fromm sees that people's lives often have voids, and his job is to discover how to fill these voids. Despite his forced optimism and yearning for contentment, he knows that great expectations have vanished from his life: "Now I want only love, truth, beauty, justice, I want them all with a minimum sacrifice. I want to share in and promote the normalcy of my fellow man. I want the dignity of a shipwrecked Crusoe, I want to be done with the black vultures that each night roost around my bedside" (*CE*, p. 39).

Reality never loses its terrifying aspects; it often carries memories of past horrors. Our dreams, he knows, "are meant to be useful," but they are often stranded on the "wicked island of the soul" (*CE*, p. 39). For instance, Peter Wardlow, the patient who comes to Fromm at the beginning of the story, has an erotic fixation on Evanne Laurent, but the psychiatrist discovers that this woman was once a Nazi, and so it is ironic that Wardlow's subconscious is attracted to the personification of evil. Fromm's own reveries about the past are fraught with their burden of fear, for the psychiatrist and his family were once embroiled in the monstrousness of World War II. He, like anyone who comes to him for help, is a refugee from his fears. Fromm wants shelter from the past and from the devastating force of his subconscious, but as he himself asserts: "We are in a modern world; all cures are known; it's their application that is impossible" (*CE*, p. 46).

One reason why evil persists in this world is possibly because the virtuous ones do not resist or fight it, or cannot on account of their fatigue, meekness, or dejection. Such is the case in "Friendship and Property" (*CE*, pp. 71–96), where Rodin, fragmented by the death of his beloved wife, Aimée, is emotionally and spiritually battered by Leopold, an arch-materialist and professional rogue. Leopold, knowing that Rodin does not battle back, is always the aggressor, making certain to "strike first and ask questions later" (*CE*, p. 77). He maligns the weak and cadges drinks and food. A racist at heart, as shown by his attitude to the sexy black woman in the Wild Boar Tavern, he wears contempt like a badge. Totally without moral scruples — he carries double indemnity on his wife and uses funeral parlours and taverns to conclude shady deals — Leopold is the epitome of an opportunist. He tries to blackmail his friends and acquaintances, and when he succeeds in any of his nefarious schemes, he gloats contemptuously over his victims.

Rodin exists as a meek moral foil to Leopold's crookedness. His sentimental relationship with his late wife renders him vulnerable to Leopold's cynical and cruel attack. Leopold knows that he can get at Rodin through memories of the dead wife, and he uses his skill at deceit to repulsive advantage.

Although our sympathies lie with Rodin, Rooke never attempts to force a moral redress. He allows Leopold a victory of immoral exploitation, and, indeed, gives him the last contemptuous word about his mild victim.

The rejection of ethical absolutes is part of the post-modernist's attitude towards reality. So is the rejection of the traditional satirist's faith in the efficacy of satire as a reforming instrument. As Robert Scholes explains in *The Fabulators*, black humourists — such as William Golding, Iris Murdoch, Lawrence Durrell, Jorge Luis Borges, Vladimir Nabokov, Kurt Vonnegut, John Barth, John Hawkes, and Joseph Heller — have "a more subtle faith in the humanizing value of laughter. Whatever changes they hope to work in their readers are the admittedly evanescent changes inspired by art, which need to be continually renewed, rather than the dramatic renunciations of vice and folly postulated by traditional satire."[37]

Rooke joins other black humourists in teaching us neither scorn nor resignation, but how to take a joke. In "The History of England, Part Four,"[38] he burlesques Tudor history in presenting a King Henry who, thinking that he is courting Emy Dealiath of Detroit, is surprised to find Anne Boleyn at his castle. The fun is the ultramodernity of Anne. Sexually precocious, she is a fan of pop and rock music (the Nylons, Donovan, Bing Crosby, the Gospel Rollers, the Jackhammer Blues Band), who demands Pay TV in the king's bedroom, and does not hesitate to use physical violence in order to get her way. Although the Young Prince and the Queen Mother speak in period diction and phraseology, Anne resorts to twentieth-century American vernacular: "You can put your head back in my nice teen-age lap. How about the Nylons for good easy listenin'?" (SM, p. 277).

The only certainty about Rooke's literary world is an uncertainty about its characters and comedy. His prolific imagination produces the most improbable people, and he often places them in highly improbable situations with such tantalizing charm that disbelief is usually suspended. For example, in "A Bolt of White Cloth,"[39] a mysterious stranger appears before a farm couple and offers the woman a free section of the cloth he is carrying — a section vast enough to look "like a long white road" (BWC, p. 13) — with the proviso that if she or her husband ever stops loving, they will lose the cloth and all else. The lure of this tale is in the gentle moral incentive offered by the stranger, and by the "holy" and "radiant" quality (BWC, p. 19) of the mysterious material. There is no action as such in the story, and at the end the couple wonder about the identity of the stranger and the source of his magical cloth. Perhaps this unusual blend of realism and fantasy is what Joan McGrath had in mind when she said of Rooke: "Reading [his] short stories is about as close as most readers need come to an out-of-body experience. His settings are *almost* realistic, but realism as viewed through a curved window frosted by magic."[40]

The fundamental point, perhaps, about Rooke's comedy is that it is really a mirror for the art and power of the storyteller, rather than a text for philosophic or social edification. Sometimes the jest is overtly rhetorical, as in the title of "Saloam Frigid with Time's Legacy while Mrs. Willoughby Bight-Davies Sits Naked through the Night on a Tree Stump Awaiting the Lizard That Will Make Her Loins Go Boom-Boom" (*BWC*, pp. 101–19). But the deeper jest lies in the situation of a man's being bothered on a bus by a talkative green-eyed woman (Mrs. Bight-Davies) who promises to tell him her life story for five dollars. Unable to escape, he has to listen to her incredible tale of how a witch had instructed her to cure infertility by a bizarre method. The woman, although insistently loquacious in "a peculiarly infuriating voice, brazen and not the least melodious" (*BWC*, p. 107), turns out to be a powerful storyteller. Even as her tale grows in strangeness, it acquires an irresistible appeal. The man's curiosity is sharpened, and he becomes enraptured by her oral power.

Rooke returns us to the wellsprings of story, and although cruelty and violence are often integral elements of his fiction, they are modified by a passage from realism to surrealism, as in the novella *The Magician in Love*. Here the fantastic penetrates the realistic to the very quiddity of being and, by astonishing us with shocks to our perceptions of literary convention, extends the power of fantasy to contradict perspectives. The work creates its own ground rules without in the least abandoning or diminishing Rooke's familiar penchant for whimsy, puns, irony, psychological extremes, surrealist touches, or spontaneity of voice.

The anonymous narrator is evidently — but it becomes evident only very late in the work — a friend of the anonymous title character, yet his identity always remains vague. The air of mystery surrounding the narrative voice is thickened by the essential mystery of the Magician's own character and life. Although set nominally in a British Columbia village, the story cuts loose from the specifics of locale, for its thrust is not towards delimiting regionalism but towards the freedom of fantasy. Setting is one of the least important elements in this work, whose prime impulse is for the supernature of illusion. Inspired by the hero's thaumaturgical power and passion, the narrator himself creates a compressed prose-poetry that magically holds a sadness under the surface wit and melodrama. It is clear that this is a tale that makes its own rules: flowers spring up out of a garbage can; a blue orchid emerges at the Magician's buttonhole; a sugarbowl does cartwheels; and the pace and nature of real life are transformed by the Magician's magic into artifacts or illusions.

Rooke, who shows in "Hanging Out with the Magi" (*DS*, pp. 137–55) and "Iron Woman" (*BB*, pp. 144–68) that he is interested in the spirit world and in mediaeval myth, here extends his fascination with fantasy. Illusion is the very essence of this tale, and it is given both a surface and a voice. In addition to describing a series of magic tricks and charades by the Magician, Rooke carries us into the illusory world of the title character via the voice of the anonymous narrator. He both universalizes and specifies the themes of love, illusion, destructiveness, and suffering by establishing a contract between the frustrated narrator and the thwarted Magician, and a pact of sympathy between the narrator and the reader who is finally reminded that ". . . these experiences are now common to us all."[41]

The Magician in Love is not about magic acts based on arcane philosophies, or about spine-tingling thrills of the senses. There is none of the eerie morbidity that so charged Ingmar Bergman's film *The Magician*, nor any of the sinister, deep black evil found in Robertson Davies' Magnus Eisengrim novels. Nature here is not intransigently malignant, nor relentlessly arcane. It is given free play and encompasses exultation and exaltation as much as it does depression and deterioration. Ostensibly a story about the Magician's frustrated love for his mistress, Beabontha, it is really a parable of illusion as a mode of perception, and of love as an eccentric tyranny. The tone is frequently tragicomic, and the host of eccentrics and grotesques intensifies the context of expressionistic gesture and symbolism in a world where fantasy reveals the truth of the human heart by satirizing man's world and, paradoxically, clarifying through anarchy. The expressionism, overlapping with a dynamic post-modernist vision of art making its own values, dissolves conventional form, stresses powerful emotion, and exemplifies the mystical, quasi-religious yearnings of the human soul.

The special appeal of this tale is not in the story itself, but in the tone, devices, and structure. Rooke charms us by the Magician's spontaneous power, and the author's wit turns reality whimsically around in a half-circle of puns and light irony — as can be seen in the Magician's meeting with a stranger who had seen his show in Blüne:

"How are tricks?" the stranger asks.
"I am devising a circle," the Magician calmly replies.

"Oh? And how does that work?"

"You start here," says the Magician, illustrating his words with a long descending, now ascending finger — "and go to here."

"Looks easy," remarks the stranger.

"Yes, but the trick is that mine can hold water."

And none can deny that his hands are suddenly wet, that his invisible bag suddenly is full. That fish swim beneath his outstretched palm, thick as herring.

The stranger is impressed; he has never seen this trick done before. "Ah," he laughs, "if only we could do as well with our women!" (*ML*, p. 9)

Rooke frequently throws the reader off a steady track by introducing wry characters or situations. The collection of eccentrics and grotesques (Muggs, Runa, Igor the rope-dancer, Lady Mothmuir with her pet monkey, Thelda and Esmaralda, Fitch, and Saul) is, perhaps, more than a resort to diversion. These figures, many of whom have their own domestic anxieties, counterpoint the Magician in his stress and relief and show that nothing is alien to Rooke's imagination. Indeed, the stranger reality can be, the better it is for Rooke's story. Heavy drama is but a beat away from sheer comedy, and the peculiar mixture of grief and happiness, the sunny and the dark, creates a tragicomic context.

The ending, as the Magician's misfortune infects others (including the unhappy, melodramatic narrator), is a satire both on the disillusioning effect of love and on the idea of a comic ending for fiction. Rooke's narrator tries to sort out the facts from the gossip, realizing at the last that none of this matters, for the only significance is that life must go on in hope and love:

> Beabontha has gone on a cruise, she's slit her wrist,
> gone off cliffs, she's a streetwalker in Three Rivers,
> she's entered a nunnery in Pictou.
> She and the Magician were seen together arm-in-arm
> crossing the border, they mean to build a new life
> on the other side of the world.
> One sorts these rumours, looks for the truth, hopes
> for the best.
> None of this matters.

We have each other.
Let's go on. (*ML*, p. 93)

It is an open-ended story, after all, that is resolved only by the narrator's ambition to continue with his life and his loved one. It confirms Rooke's interest in fiction that cuts to the bone without shedding blood — a fiction that cleans our living wounds and heals by its cruel truth.

The Magician in Love shows again that those critics who say Rooke's work is all form and no content, contrived for effect and not for meaning, are not playing his game with form. Rooke's best stories — as most of his critics realize — are all shaped by a character's voice, and if criticism is to address itself sharply to Rooke's craft, it cannot neglect or depreciate the value of rhythm, tone, and dialogue. Certainly, Rooke's essays at playwriting (despite their portentous allegorization and strenuous absurdism, as in *Krokodile* and *Sword/Play*) helped his sense of characterization because they forced him to listen to different voices and listen carefully to their diverse qualities. Unlike much of the short fiction of Margaret Atwood or the recent novels of Robertson Davies, such as *The Rebel Angels* and *What's Bred in the Bone*, where, from one story or novel to the next, there is no radical or convincing change in voice and where one character can often be interchanged with another without a drop in inflection, Rooke's stories never sound alike. The argot of "Hitting the Charts,"[42] with its parodic clichés, catches the obsessiveness and melancholy of its narrator very differently from the way "Sixteen-Year-Old Susan March Confesses to the Innocent Murder of All the Devious Strangers Who Would Drag Her Down" (*DS*, pp. 59–72) expresses a breathless rush of anguished yearning and feverish lust in a timidly intense monologue. In the first story, the narrator self-consciously projects a cool, "hip" quality that communicates his desire to be considered in step with the disco age. The diction is racy and so obviously touched up for slang, that in itself it is enough to convince us that the speaker has a history of fickle trendiness:

No more four a.m. movies for me, with the final blip dropping like man's last breath across the snow-balled screen. No more weeping in the solitude of all my betrayals and longing for dawn's tender mercy to tuck me up in my drunken bed.

*Oh frail is thy hand in mine, oh frail is your touch, my dar-
ling Caithleene.*
I was clearly cut out for this fine nightlife. It was *Groovy
Greybeard Groovy* and proper time I took off my age-old
bib.[43]

The combination of "jive talk," sexual language, and "hot" radio or
disc-jockey speech is reminiscent of Hugh Hood's oral style in "God
Has Manifested Himself unto Us as Canadian Tire," although
Rooke uses pop song lyrics, whereas Hood exploits the language of
the merchandizing catalogue.

The Susan March story teems with disturbed imaginings and illicit
erotic desire. Its enigmatic elements — What did her father really do
so cruelly to her? Did he commit suicide? Is Susan lusting simply after
Reeves or is he a substitute for her dead father? — give it mysteri-
ously lurid colours, and Susan's forceful analogies ("the fierce clutch
we have on love like the clutch these houses have the hooked claws
these houses have upon the lake" [*DS*, p. 71]) express a murderous
but somewhat ambiguous psyche. The story is a dramatic monologue that plays like a passionate fugue, with motifs repeating themselves and linking up within Susan's sick soul. Although the diction is
often on a level far beyond a girl of Susan's age, this character is
obviously no ordinary person: her textured monologue is the spontaneous poetry of a mind inflamed by a psychopathology of lust and
revenge. It mirrors the lake of "lurking snares and slimy silken skin
over submerged logs booby traps" (*DS*, pp. 65–66) and shows how
Susan's soul is chained to the rotting logs at the lake floor "thick with
the rocking corpses of those who had entered" her life (*DS*, p. 72).

Rooke's predilection for voice shows remarkably well in other
stories, too. "The Shut-In Number" (*SM*, pp. 28–36) is virtually a
monologue by a loony child-abductor, who justifies his crimes as a
service to God. He has the veneer of a slick television evangelist, for
he knows how to gloss every action, how to seem holy or divinely
selfless about his evil. There is absolutely no strain in Mr. Charles'
voice as he speaks of his compassion for "shut-ins" or about his
equanimity in the face of "life's little imponderables" (*SM*, p. 33).
The drama of this chilling tale is virtually all in the speaker's voice.

"The Birth Control King of the Upper Volta"[44] is narrated by
another crackpot — a middle-aged schizophrenic bigot with Oedipal
tendencies and audiovisual hallucinations. Adlai is entrapped by the

myth of his racist father — an intrepid salesman who attempted to control the vast population of a small African country by selling the natives contraceptives, so that whites could fill the places that would have gone to blacks — but, worse, he is overwhelmed by the voices of various characters (real and imagined) who push him to delirium. Adlai's hysteria is exemplified by his clichés (particularly those borrowed from his mother), and it is only the silence of the ending that curbs this delirium by an inner desire for peace.

Not all voices in Rooke's stories are at this pitch or register. In "The Woman's Guide to Home Companionship" (*BWC*, pp. 72–85), where two women, old friends and neighbours, sit around drinking while one writes a story about the gruesome double murder of their husbands that the two have committed, there is a voice that is itself satirized by the very arch-bourgeois expressions and diction. Although only one can be the scribe, both women are actually in discourse, passing comments, posing questions, prompting revisions, attempting to balance prudery against their petty vices and their dual homicide. The prose attempts to be poised and decorous, but the tangential small talk and the enormity of the crimes behind the surface undercut this texture.

One of Rooke's most impressive vocal performances is the novel *Fat Woman*, where we hear Ella Mae's voice in monologues, soliloquies, and arguments that are often wryly comic, robustly plaintive, or affectingly disconsolate in their clichéd language. This voice, which gives the novel most of its élan, is Rooke's device for obtaining a shimmer of consciousness within an overall field of vision. Events and circumstances are broken down into sensory impressions, often refined. There is little plot, but strong characterization of the central figure. Curiously, this characterization is achieved by a humorous strategy whereby Ella Mae's personality is shown, as it were, inside out, from behind the screen of consciousness. Her interior monologues — about her painful affliction, puzzling husband, rough and insensitive young sons, nosy neighbours, religion, God, et cetera — are intimate self-revelations. She is not a mere bundle of vagrant sensory impressions but an articulated whole, of the same order, though not to the same degree of complexity, as Molly Bloom or the strong female characters in Dickens, Eliot, or Austen. Ella Mae's monologues and soliloquies are really half a dialogue — a continuous argument with society and God, whose answers or responses can be inferred, if not directly overheard.[45]

Fat Woman is really an extended novella which mixes symbolic and realistic modes in telling its story of the Puritan Ella Mae, an obese married woman who is afflicted by her physical condition and her assorted problems with man and God. She quivers in her solid flesh and morbid depression through a "soulless marriage"[46] and under the imagined indictments of a severe God of retribution. The psychology of the central figure is inextricably bound to an uncompromisingly austere theology of punishment, and Ella Mae's clichéd view of life is repeatedly expressed in a language of clichés.

Rooke draws economical sketches of small-town life. Although place is not specified, the novel has a decidedly provincial flavour with its references to bake sales at the First Baptist Church of New Love, a Sunday turkey shoot sponsored by the Rod and Gun Club, and the noted women's barbershop group The Fast Notes. Then there are the quick, snappy sketches of Winnameer Riser, a big-wheel civic woman; Estelle, the lusty proprietress of the local Dairy Queen; shiftless Fred Joyner; and Fred's snoopy wife, Eula, who has "hair like a glue pot" and a face "like a washed-out road" (pp. 151, 152). Ella Mae's boys, Ike and Theodore, are stereotyped as television addicts, who use the house as a restaurant and motel more than as a home. They are "wild beasts" (p. 43) and a whirlwind of rough-and-tumble boyish energy, slamming into the livingroom or kitchen, caterwauling, colliding with each other, and hurling themselves outside with scarcely a word of apology or kindness to their mother.

As a fictional experiment, *Fat Woman* moves in two directions — those of sensibility and sensation, which ordinarily are the poles of each other, but which in this case neither abolish the social dimension, nor annihilate the sense of character. The recording of sensibility — originating in English fiction with Samuel Richardson, Jane Austen, and Virginia Woolf — is chiefly an abstract, sophisticated pursuit, but, like the charting of sensation — as in the novels of Ernest Hemingway, James Farrell, or Raymond Chandler — it can be a very modern experiment when it provides the perspective of a dissociated outsider, as in Camus's *L'Etranger*. *Fat Woman* is not on the plane of any of the major fictions, but its experimentalism, modern though not new, obtains the world of twentieth-century sensibility, a world often slow or in midtempo, a world of wounding guilt and pain, in which little things are magnified or registered on the film of consciousness.

In the paradox of Ella Mae's vision — where she is both a subject and object to herself — lies the scope of a fiction of sensibility and sensation. She represents herself to us by her private griefs and joys, reacting all the while to the ways in which others see her or as she imagines they do. She is defensive against Eula, hurt by the taunts of her husband and sons, envious of a friend's successful weight reduction, and anxious about her husband's affections for her. Yet she remains a prisoner of her ancestry and religious convictions and, paradoxically, becomes more of God's fool in trying not to be made a fool to others.

Rooke feeds us with Ella Mae's sensations. He has her nibbling on cookies and then repenting with diet and nerve pills. He has her gorging on ice cream and enjoying Jack Coombs's radio show and then suffering blackouts. He has her torturing herself with her painful ring-finger and then fantasizing about sex with Edward, her husband. The naturalism of the story — the inveterate yoking together of nature, action, and consequence — is worked into the symbolism of Ella Mae's boarded-up bedroom window, her fat, her Stomach Serpent, Preacher Eelbone, and other details. Yet this is sometimes an uneasy mixture. There is no ambiguity about Ella Mae's huge Stomach Serpent, a grotesquely comic emblem of her own gross self-indulgence. The imagery is unequivocally comic in its parody of gluttony incarnate. But there are ambiguities in other symbols. For example, Ella Mae's pulsating ring-finger ("about the ugliest thing she'd ever seen on a human being" [p. 88]) could stand for her innocent victimization, the failure of her marriage, a fardel of flesh, or a sensitive spirit imprisoned in a gross body. Similarly, the boarded-up window could represent Ella's inability to see the world for what it is, or a barrier in her marriage.

However, her sensibility is more successfully represented via her sensory impressions and mental reflections. Ella Mae is realistically drawn because she is concrete and sentimental. She cries and complains openly about her deceased mother and her own life, but even as she memorializes her beloved mother, she shows the roots of her own spiritual malady. It was her mother who — although desirous of beauty for her daughter — had influenced Ella Mae with orthodox views of a stern God, and Ella Mae can never dissociate herself from a feeling of "impending horror" (p. 18).

Ella Mae with her finger that ought to have been cut off and her feet flat from what they had to carry. Ella Mae with her children that wouldn't come home and her husband who had seen everything he wanted ever to see from their bedroom window — who wouldn't come home either. Life was futile. It had no more point to it than snakes in a basket. (*FW*, p. 71)

In a radical sense, this is a novel of religious sensibility. The second half leaps far above realism as it gives wings to Ella Mae's religious fantasies and beliefs. Everything is coloured by Ella Mae's peculiar religious outlook. The irony is that while Ella Mae feels at one moment that religion is inadequate to help her, she transforms all reality into scriptural allegory, turning life into a secular analogy for religion. Having learned from her mother that even an automobile is "an instrument of the devil" (p. 107), she looks at life and sees the devil loose upon the world. She suffers Edward's dictatorial authority because it is like God's, and she mistakes his snarling rage for religious frenzy in the one scene that sensationalizes dramatic action and threatens to split the story out of its safely narrow path (p. 128). Her religious sensibility distorts her perception of reality. While it gives her fortitude to bear her own pain (because this is less than some others' suffering), it also forces her to yield to Edward and God (sometimes blurred into a single being). Despite Edward's wounding words and violent rage, he looks to her "like a little boy would look, one who knew he soon was to do something he shouldn't," and her sentimentality makes her see "repentance and suffering, sorrow and doubt" in his Jekyll-and-Hyde figure (p. 131).

As the novel races into religious symbolism and analogy, it becomes increasingly clear that the form is not developed by plot, but by Ella Mae's sensibility, and that the climax is not to be attained by incident or external action per se, but through the workings of her warped mind. So obsessed is she by religion that even her moment of greatest public humiliation — when Edward forces her to go to the hospital for treatment of her swollen finger — is given an allegorical cast: "Edward had delivered them both over into the Devil's hand. The Devil's work was underway. That was what Edward wanted. His hatred and contempt of her was so great that he was willing to walk Hell's Road himself just to see that she got to her destination" (p. 140). She projects a guardian angel for herself, and her imagination, already inflamed by scriptural persuasion, waxes with zeal over God's master plan for her and the world.

This section generates an apocalyptic frenzy of religious archetypes and analogies. The house is seen to be as gloomy as Satan or some infernal disease; every human being is nothing but "dung upon the ground" (p. 146); Preacher Eelbone's portentous voice lives in her conscience; and Edward becomes a parody with his "whiny Adam's apple voice and his mean snake eyes" (p. 146). As sacred parable and motto suggest themselves to her, she suddenly sees a shooting star, but it burns out before she can make a wish; this she interprets as God's sign that she is "not a fit vessel for wishes to be satisfied" (p. 156). Construing this as a miraculous apocalypse of the vanity of her life, she continues to transform everything into a religious emblem, casting Edward and her sons as three angels, and determining to face Edward, to "get on her knees and face God" (p. 160).

Religious fundamentalism deters her from suicide, even though she complains of the merciless, ubiquitous darkness of a force in her life that is "uncaring and black as a grave" (p. 172). Yet she is cowed into acquiescing to religion, marriage, and servitude. When tempted to joke about God, she checks herself in the fear that she may be courting suicide, and hence, damnation. She hears God's voice, and in a pitiably comic attempt to find some spiritual justification for her carnal grossness, turns to biblical quotations to support herself. Her stomach is the one organ that God momentarily sanctions, and her wish-fulfillment fantasy reaches a comic peak when she resignedly accepts God as being "Pie in the Sky" (p. 170).

The comedy turns perverse when she sees her salvation in Edward, accepting at the last her boarded-up window and his anger as means to whittle her down to salvageable size. The triumph of religious orthodoxy is assured in the final scene where, having cast herself as a massive Mother Earth figure, she engages in sexual intercourse with her husband in one voluptuous surge of passion:

> She grinds her eyes shut, but lets him put the part in her legs. She opens her legs for him. She would make a space where even this darkness might thrive. She would make her wide flesh be everything, a lake of cream to drown in, a field of earth in which Ella Mae Hopkins and everybody like her, all the world's poor and miserable, all the maimed and the bereft, one in which all lost souls might forever cuddle — cuddle and hide.

Oh hide me, she thinks.
Let my cup run over.
"Feel good?" he says. (p. 174)

Here the comedy is apocalyptic in its signalling of a marriage of
flesh and spirit, but the question remains: Has Ella Mae really won
or lost by being nothing more than a fat womb — a creature
trapped by the immanence of flesh and its own darkness? The
reason why there is no single resolution to the question is because
Rooke did not want to resolve the situation: "I don't like resolving
situations because most situations are not resolved. I like the open
ending. I like the reader to say, 'This is the ending,' and the other
reader to say, 'No, this is the ending'" (Hancock, p. 133). A story,
as Rooke reminds us, is "anything I can make it be and get away
with" (Hancock, p. 133).

NOTES

[1] Quoted in Anne Collins, "A Canine's Search for Poetic Justice,"
Maclean's, 16 May 1983, p. 44.

[2] Clint Burnham, "Reading Foreign Writers: An Interview with Leon
Rooke," *Waves,* 14, No. 3 (Winter 1986), 6.

[3] Geoff Hancock, "An Interview with Leon Rooke," *Canadian Fiction
Magazine,* No. 38 (1981), p. 120. All further references to this work
(Hancock) appear in the text.

[4] "Leon Rooke," in *Canada Writes!: The Members' Book of the Writers
Union of Canada,* ed. K. A. Hamilton (Toronto: Writers Union of Canada,
1977), p. 295.

[5] In *Last One Home Sleeps in the Yellow Bed* (Baton Rouge: Louisiana
State Univ. Press, 1968), pp. 95–178. All further references to this work
(*LOH*) appear in the text.

[6] Leon Rooke, "Leon Rooke: The Authorized Biography," *Canadian
Fiction Magazine,* No. 38 (1981), p. 146.

[7] "The Regional Writer," in *Mystery and Manners,* ed. Sally Fitzgerald
and Robert Fitzgerald (New York: Farrar, Straus & Giroux, 1969), p. 59.

[8] In *Death Suite* (Downsview, Ont.: ECW, 1981), pp. 137–55. All further
references to this work (*DS*) appear in the text.

[9] In *Cry Evil* (Ottawa: Oberon, 1980), pp. 24–46. All further references
to this work (*CE*) appear in the text.

[10] Linda Hutcheon, *Narcissistic Narrative: The Metafictional Paradox* (Waterloo, Ont.: Wilfrid Laurier Univ. Press, 1980), p. 31.

[11] Hutcheon, p. 32.

[12] In *Vault: A Story in Three Parts* (Northwood Narrows, N.H.: Lillabulero, 1973).

[13] "The Hi-Tech World of Leon Rooke," *Canadian Fiction Magazine*, No. 38 (1981), p. 135. All further references to this work appear in the text.

[14] J. R. (Tim) Struthers, Lesley Hogan, and John Orange, "A Preliminary Bibliography of Works by Leon Rooke," *Canadian Fiction Magazine*, No. 38 (1981), pp. 148–64.

[15] Keith Garebian, "Short Stories: The New Anthologies of Rooke and Hodgins," rev. of *Last One Home Sleeps in the Yellow Bed*, by Leon Rooke, and *The Barclay Family Theatre*, by Jack Hodgins, *Montreal Calendar Magazine*, Nov. 1981, p. 35.

[16] J. R. (Tim) Struthers, "Cadence, Texture and Shapeliness," rev. of *The Love Parlour*, by Leon Rooke, and *It's Easy to Fall on the Ice*, by Elizabeth Brewster, *Journal of Canadian Fiction*, No. 31/32 (1981), p. 245.

[17] "Fantasy Lives," rev. of *Cry Evil*, by Leon Rooke, and *Shoeless Joe Jackson Comes to Iowa*, by W. P. Kinsella, *Canadian Literature*, No. 91 (Winter 1981), p. 106.

[18] Cary Fagan, "God's Ugly People," rev. of *Fat Woman*, *The Canadian Forum*, March 1981, p. 34.

[19] Quoted in "Gentle Winner," *Books in Canada*, April 1981, p. 4.

[20] Sheila Fischman and John Richardson respectively, quoted in "Gentle Winner," pp. 3, 4.

[21] Quoted in "Gentle Winner," p. 3.

[22] Rev. of *Death Suite*, *Quill & Quire*, Nov. 1981, p. 24.

[23] B. Derek Johnson, "Magic and Death," rev. of *The Magician in Love* and *Death Suite*, *The Globe and Mail*, 24 Oct. 1981, Sec. E, p. 16.

[24] Stephen Scobie, "The Inner Voice," rev. of *Death Suite* and *The Magician in Love*, *Books in Canada*, Nov. 1981, p. 8. All further references to this work (Scobie) appear in the text.

[25] Peter Stevens, "Short, Sweet and the Same," rev. of *The Birth Control King of the Upper Volta*, *The Windsor Star*, 5 March 1983, Sec. C, p. 9.

[26] S. Schoenbaum, "To Woof or Not to Woof," rev. of *Shakespeare's Dog*, *Book World* [*The Washington Post*], 22 May 1983, p. 6.

[27] Joan McGrath, rev. of *A Bolt of White Cloth*, in *Canadian Book Review Annual 1984*, ed. Dean Tudor and Ann Tudor (Toronto: Simon and Pierre, 1985), p. 274.

[28] "Rooke's Prose a Bit Too Mannered and Maillard's Work Turns

Sloppy," rev. of *The Birth Control King of the Upper Volta*, by Leon Rooke, and *Cutting Through*, by Keith Maillard, *The London Free Press*, 25 June 1983, p. E10.

[29] "Fairy Tales for Adults Who Don't Believe in Magic," rev. of *The Birth Control King of the Upper Volta*, *The Globe and Mail*, 8 Jan. 1983, Sec. Entertainment, p. 12.

[30] Paul Ricoeur, "What Is a Text? Explanation and Understanding," in *Twentieth-Century Literary Theory: An Introductory Anthology*, ed. Vassilis Lambropoulos and David Neal Miller (Albany: State Univ. of New York Press, 1987), p. 344.

[31] *Shakespeare's Dog* (Don Mills, Ont.: Stoddart, 1983), p. 37. All further references to this work appear in the text.

[32] See Roger Fowler, *Literature as Social Discourse: The Practice of Linguistic Criticism* (Bloomington: Indiana Univ. Press, 1981), pp. 58–79.

[33] John Cheever, "The Swimmer," in *The Stories of John Cheever* (New York: Ballantine, 1980), p. 714.

[34] Cheever, p. 715.

[35] In *The Broad Back of the Angel* (New York: Fiction Collective, 1977), pp. 144–68. All further references to this work (*BB*) appear in the text.

[36] In *The Love Parlour* (Ottawa: Oberon, 1977), pp. 65–80. All further references to this work (*LP*) appear in the text.

[37] *The Fabulators* (New York: Oxford Univ. Press, 1967), p. 41.

[38] In *Sing Me No Love Songs I'll Say You No Prayers* (New York: Ecco, 1984), pp. 272–90. All further references to this work (*SM*) appear in the text.

[39] In *A Bolt of White Cloth* (Don Mills, Ont.: Stoddart, 1984), pp. 7–20. All further references to this work (*BWC*) appear in the text.

[40] McGrath, p. 274.

[41] *The Magician in Love* (Toronto: Aya, 1981), p. 90. All further references to this work (*ML*) appear in the text.

[42] "Hitting the Charts," *Canadian Fiction Magazine*, No. 38 (1981), pp. 5–12.

[43] "Hitting the Charts," p. 7.

[44] In *The Birth Control King of the Upper Volta* (Downsview, Ont.: ECW, 1982), pp. 7–38.

[45] Many of the ideas expressed in my discussion of sensibility and sensation in *Fat Woman* are drawn from Mary McCarthy's article "Characters in Fiction," *Partisan Review*, 28 (March–April 1961), 171–91.

[46] *Fat Woman* (Ottawa: Oberon, 1980), p. 77. All further references to this work appear in the text.

LEON ROOKE

SELECTED BIBLIOGRAPHY

Primary Sources

Rooke, Leon. *Last One Home Sleeps in the Yellow Bed*. Baton Rouge: Louisiana State Univ. Press, 1968.

——. *Evening Meeting of the Club of Suicide*. Vancouver: New Play Centre [1972?].

——. *Krokodile*. Toronto: Playwrights Co-op, 1973.

——. *Vault: A Story in Three Parts*. Northwood Narrows, N.H.: Lillabulero, 1973.

——. *Sword/Play*. Toronto: Playwrights Co-op, 1974.

——. *The Broad Back of the Angel*. New York: Fiction Collective, 1977.

——. *The Love Parlour*. Ottawa: Oberon, 1977.

——. "Cakewalk." *Event*, 9, No. 2 (1980), 101–32.

——. *Cry Evil*. Ottawa: Oberon, 1980.

——. *Fat Woman*. Ottawa: Oberon, 1980.

——. *Death Suite*. Downsview, Ont.: ECW, 1981.

——. "Hitting the Charts." *Canadian Fiction Magazine*, No. 38 (1981), pp. 5–12.

——. "Leon Rooke: The Authorized Biography." *Canadian Fiction Magazine*, No. 38 (1981), pp. 145–46.

——. *The Magician in Love*. Toronto: Aya, 1981.

——. *The Birth Control King of the Upper Volta*. Downsview, Ont.: ECW, 1982.

——. *Shakespeare's Dog*. Don Mills, Ont.: Stoddart, 1983.

——. *A Bolt of White Cloth*. Don Mills, Ont.: Stoddart, 1984.

——. *Sing Me No Love Songs I'll Say You No Prayers*. New York: Ecco, 1984.

Secondary Sources

Burnham, Clint. "Reading Foreign Writers: An Interview with Leon Rooke." *Waves*, 14, No. 3 (Winter 1986), 5–7.

Collins, Anne. "A Canine's Search for Poetic Justice." *Maclean's*, 16 May 1983, pp. 44, 46.

189

Fagan, Cary. "God's Ugly People." Rev. of *Fat Woman*. *The Canadian Forum*, March 1981, p. 34.

Fowler, Roger. *Literature as Social Discourse: The Practice of Linguistic Criticism*. Bloomington, Ind.: Indiana Univ. Press, 1981.

Garebian, Keith. "Short Stories: The New Anthologies of Rooke and Hodgins." Rev. of *Last One Home Sleeps in the Yellow Bed*, by Leon Rooke, and *The Barclay Family Theatre*, by Jack Hodgins. *Montreal Calendar Magazine*, Nov. 1981, p. 35.

"Gentle Winner." *Books in Canada*, April 1981, pp. 3–4.

Hancock, Geoff. "The Hi-Tech World of Leon Rooke." *Canadian Fiction Magazine*, No. 38 (1981), pp. 135–45.

——. "An Interview with Leon Rooke." *Canadian Fiction Magazine*, No. 38 (1981), pp. 107–33.

Hutcheon, Linda. *Narcissistic Narrative: The Metafictional Paradox*. Waterloo, Ont.: Wilfrid Laurier Univ. Press, 1980.

Johnson, B. Derek. "Magic and Death." Rev. of *The Magician in Love* and *Death Suite*. *The Globe and Mail*, 24 Oct. 1981, Sec. E, p. 16.

——. "Fairy Tales for Adults Who Don't Believe in Magic." Rev. of *The Birth Control King of the Upper Volta*. *The Globe and Mail*, 8 Jan. 1983, Sec. Entertainment, p. 12.

"Leon Rooke." In *Canada Writes!: The Members' Book of the Writers Union of Canada*. Ed. K. A. Hamilton. Toronto: Writers Union of Canada, 1977, pp. 294–95.

Martens, Debra. Rev. of *Death Suite*. *Quill & Quire*, Nov. 1981, p. 24.

McCarthy, Mary. "Characters in Fiction." *Partisan Review*, 28 (March-April 1961), 171–91.

McGrath, Joan. Rev. of *A Bolt of White Cloth*. In *Canadian Book Review Annual 1984*. Ed. Dean Tudor and Ann Tudor. Toronto: Simon and Pierre, 1985, p. 274.

Reaney, James Stewart. "Rooke's Prose a Bit Too Mannered and Maillard's Work Turns Sloppy." Rev. of *The Birth Control King of the Upper Volta*, by Leon Rooke, and *Cutting Through*, by Keith Maillard. *The London Free Press*, 25 June 1983, p. E10.

Schoenbaum, S. "To Woof or Not to Woof." Rev. of *Shakespeare's Dog*. *Book World* [*The Washington Post*], 22 May 1983, pp. 5–6.

Scholes, Robert. *The Fabulators*. New York: Oxford Univ. Press, 1967.

Scobie, Stephen. "The Inner Voice." Rev. of *Death Suite* and *The Magician in Love*. *Books in Canada*, Nov. 1981, pp. 8–10.

Stevens, Peter. "Short, Sweet and the Same." Rev. of *The Birth Control King of the Upper Volta*. *The Windsor Star*, 5 March 1983, Sec. C, p. 9.

Struthers, J. R. (Tim). "Cadence, Texture and Shapeliness." Rev. of *The Love Parlour*, by Leon Rooke, and *It's Easy to Fall on the Ice*, by Elizabeth Brewster. *Journal of Canadian Fiction*, No. 31/32 (1981), pp. 244–47.

——, Lesley Hogan, and John Orange. "A Preliminary Bibliography of Works by Leon Rooke." *Canadian Fiction Magazine*, No. 38 (1981), pp. 148–64.

Wasserman, Jerry. "Fantasy Lives." Rev. of *Cry Evil*, by Leon Rooke, and *Shoeless Joe Jackson Comes to Iowa*, by W. P. Kinsella. *Canadian Literature*, No. 91 (Winter 1981), pp. 106–09.

*Audrey Thomas
and Her Works*

Audrey Thomas (1935–)

BARBARA GODARD

Biography

AUDREY GRACE (CALLAHAN) THOMAS was born in Binghamton, New York, on 17 November 1935 to Frances (Corbett) and Donald Earle Callahan. Her father, a teacher, returned to graduate school, putting the family in straitened circumstances. Like many middle-class families in that "Presbyterian"[1] city, this one espoused the work ethic and stressed intellectual attainments as a measure of social position. Indeed, several of its members were notable advertisements for these values; one of Thomas' aunts was a professor of mathematics, while her maternal grandfather was an engineer and inventor with IBM in nearby Endicott. He provided the thread of gold in an otherwise drab, brown life. His big summer place in the Adirondack Mountains of northern New York, with private, sandy beach on a well-wooded lake, afforded idyllic memories, while his punning and philology stimulated Thomas' interest in words. His practical jokes, Thomas remembers, provided lessons in "reality and illusion,"[2] another encouragement for a budding writer.

Elsewhere, this was lacking. Her ill-matched parents quarrelled, and the family was isolated. Despite this, in later years they expected Thomas to write "stories that ended happily" (Appelbe, p. 34a). But this sat ill with Thomas' sense of herself as a misfit, which developed from early loneliness, augmented by a feeling of being completely left out when she started school at four, small and with bad eyesight. Growing up during the war years, with radio bulletins announcing heavy casualties, Thomas was preoccupied with death. Nor did this diminish, as polio scares and car crashes killing fellow students kept green its possibility.[3] All these experiences nourish Thomas' fiction, despite her revolt against the rigid, narrow philistinism of her milieu which prompted her adult wanderings.

Thomas escaped in an acceptable way, helped by a scholarship to a girls' private school in New Hampshire when she was fifteen. This was followed by a scholarship to Mary A. Burnham School, a finishing school in Northampton, Massachusetts. Some of the money for her education was earned by summer work at the insane asylum in Binghamton when she was seventeen. In 1953 she entered prestigious Smith College, also in Northampton, on a tuition scholarship. Here, in the company of other bright girls, she was challenged intellectually for the first time. Majoring in English, she made the dean's list when she graduated with a B.A. in 1957.

Thomas embarked on a *Wanderjahr* to complete her sentimental education when she followed her best friend to St. Andrew's University in Scotland for her junior year (1955–56). There she enjoyed a taste of independence in boardinghouse living and in an academic system of large lectures at a cosmopolitan university frequented by many commonwealth students. During her holidays she took the usual grand tour to Spain, Italy, Belgium, Switzerland, and Scandinavia. Upon graduation from Smith College, she returned to Britain, finding employment as a teacher in the Birmingham slums at Bishop Rider's Church of England Infant and Junior School.

In 1958 she met and married Ian Thomas, a sculptor and art teacher at the Birmingham College of Art. With their first child, they moved in 1959 to Vancouver, B.C., where her husband taught. After supply teaching for a year, Thomas enrolled in an M.A. program in English and became a teaching assistant at the University of British Columbia. Her thesis, "Henry James in the Palace of Art: A Survey and Evaluation of James' Aesthetic Criteria as Shown in His Criticism of Nineteenth Century Painting," was completed in 1963, at which point she began doctoral work with the support of a Canada Council award. "An Archetypal Reading of Beowulf," the thesis she wrote, was more like a novel than a dissertation. The thesis was not accepted, and Thomas opted out of academia.

Her first published story appeared in *The Atlantic Monthly* while she was in Africa, where her husband taught at the University of Science and Technology in Kumasi, Ghana, from 1964 to 1966. In 1969 she took up writing full-time and bought a house on Galiano Island, in the Gulf of Georgia, B.C., where she has lived since. In 1971 she returned to Africa — to French West Africa, Senegal, and Mali, as well as Ghana again — for three months of research. She separated from her husband the following year; they were divorced in 1979. To support herself, she returned to teaching, alternating years of writing with posts in university creative writing departments

— at University of British Columbia (1975–76 and 1981), Concordia University (1978), University of Victoria (1978–79), and Simon Fraser University (1982). Further travels abroad took her to Greece for a year during 1976–77 and to France in the summer of 1979 to try out the French she had been learning the preceding year.

During the 1970s Thomas was involved with a number of Canadian literary institutions, serving on the Arts Advisory Board of The Canada Council and on its Reading Tours Committee. She is also a member of the Writers Union of Canada, on whose national executive she has served, and of P. E. N. These commitments reflect a putting down of roots manifested in her taking out Canadian citizenship in 1979.

As a child Thomas had a romantic dream of being "A Writer," wanting "to be *known* and all those things"[4] to compensate for being small and shy. She was an avid reader, alerted by her grandfather to the magic of words, and a listener of her "Shanty Irish" father's storytelling.[5] She wrote some poetry when she was about twelve, adding fiction at about nineteen.[6] None of her apprentice works has been published, and Thomas considers them "really terrible stories."[7] Juggling babies, graduate school, and teaching, she had little time for writing, though the stimulation of U.B.C. "turned [her] on to words again" (Coupey et al., p. 95). She submitted about a dozen stories to *Prism* and other periodicals and collected rejection slips. The shock of Africa, amplified by the experience of a miscarriage, placed her under a compulsion to order the chaos of her life. "Words were all I had . . ." in that state of despair, says Thomas (Coupey et al., p. 94), to "organize the pain and turn it into art" (Wachtel, p. 5). "I realized that it wasn't going to kill me. So I really began to write, to go down deeper" (Wachtel, p. 5). "If One Green Bottle . . . ," a story from that experience, was published in *The Atlantic Monthly* in 1965 and won an invitation from editor Bob Amussen to submit a manuscript to Bobbs-Merrill.

Thomas' collection of stories *Ten Green Bottles* was published in 1967. Then followed what Thomas has called "the glass slipper technique of getting published."[8] The contract stipulated a novel as well. While writing the doctoral thesis and awaiting the birth of a third daughter, Thomas struggled with a novel that failed to click. She put it aside to write *Mrs. Blood* (1970) and *Munchmeyer and Prospero on the Island* (1971) before revising it as *Songs My Mother Taught Me* (1973). These were followed by another novel, *Blown Figures*

(1974), and a second collection of stories, *Ladies and Escorts* (1977). *Latakia* (1979), a novel, was in turn succeeded by more stories, *Real Mothers* (1982) and *Two in the Bush and Other Stories* (1982), a selection from her two earlier collections. In 1984 she published the novel *Intertidal Life*, and in 1986, a collection of short stories, *Goodbye Harold, Good Luck*. Presently she is working on a book of memoirs, "Graven Images."

Over the past decade, Thomas has published or had broadcast on CBC *Anthology* another half-dozen uncollected pieces, including a children's story, has published more than a dozen book reviews in periodicals such as *Canadian Literature* and *Books in Canada*, has contributed essays to academic journals on subjects such as art criticism or women writers, and has written plays for CBC *Stage*.

Thomas is the recipient of several Canada Council Arts Grants (1969, 1971, 1972, 1979). Her story "If One Green Bottle . . ." won an *Atlantic Monthly* "Firsts" Award in 1965. Other stories have won more recent competitions: "Harry and Violet," second prize in the National Magazine Awards fiction category, 1979; "Natural History," second price in the CBC Literary Contest fiction division, 1979–80; "Real Mothers," second prize in *Chatelaine*'s Fourth Annual Fiction Competition, 1981; and "Untouchables: A Memoir," second prize in the CBC Literary Contest memoir division, 1981. *Intertidal Life* was short-listed for the 1984 Governor General's Award in fiction, and it was the first winner of the Ethel Wilson Fiction Prize in 1985 offered by the Association of Book Publishers of British Columbia and the Federation of British Columbia Writers. Together, these honours and awards support Priscilla Galloway's contention that Audrey Thomas has moved definitely into the "top rank of Canadian novelists."[9]

Tradition and Milieu

Audrey Thomas has been open to a wide variety of experiences as a result of having lived in four places three thousand miles apart. To place her in a milieu will be to mirror the fragmentation which is the subject of her fiction. As a perennial transplant, she is the inheritor, not of any Canadian tradition, but of a broad Anglo-American one to which she has had access through formal study. The many allusions in her works range from the Metaphysical poets, through the Romantics, to the great modernists. Like many other expatriates, she has used writing to bring order to her varied existence, giving herself a context through words. Her greatest affinities are with other expatriate writers, though the fact that she began her serious writing after making contact with other young writers in British Columbia has brought her within the sphere of West Coast experimental writing. That she has been articulating her experience as a woman in a decade when women writers have been receiving much attention as a group places her work in an additional Canadian and international context.

The major influences on Thomas' writing are those of expatriate modernists James Joyce, Joseph Conrad, and, above all, Henry James, about whom she wrote her M.A. thesis. While she absorbed from James a preoccupation with perception, she also adopted several closely related themes which are central to her work: the traveller, the interface of civilizations complicated by the blind innocence of characters, and the personality in flux. Thomas is intrigued by the moment when one thing turns into another. Travelling becomes a metaphor for that process of metamorphosis, for one of self-discovery, just as Africa is often a metaphor in her work for the paradoxical intermingling of dream and reality (Bowering, p. 10). Here her work invites comparison with Conrad's *Heart of Darkness*, though she confesses the real darkness is in Canada (Coupey et al., p. 88). Like Conrad, she is primarily interested in questions of perception. This marks her difference from her contemporaries among Canadian novelists who have also developed the expatriate theme.

In the late 1960s, travelling to Africa became a new twist in the Canadian myth of the noble savage. Critics such as Donald Cameron and William H. New drew parallels between Thomas' work and that of Dave Godfrey, Margaret Laurence, and David Knight.[10] Thomas wrote reviews of their fiction, implicating herself in this context of primitivism. While they share a theme, however, these novels are very different technically. Thomas, refusing to impose James's rage for order on chaotic experience, produces surrealist novels which only Godfrey's fiction approaches in inventiveness. Moreover, as Thomas points out (Bowering, p. 15), Laurence and Godfrey are more political than she is: they were involved with the colonialist/nationalist question, while, in the same period, she was concerned with the body, its foreignness, and, self-reflexively, with the process of writing. Unlike them, she is not "a novelist of ideas at all" (Bowering, p. 31).

This distinction is equally apt in another context in which the African setting has been interpreted: Africa as the "Shadow Continent," as the Jungian unconscious.[11] This brings Thomas' work within the orbit of the archetypalism which has been a marked feature of Canadian fiction in the 1960s and 1970s. Like Laurence, Thomas uses biblical allusions and plots; like Margaret Atwood, she writes from a knowledge of female rituals and rites of passage — that perennial concern with transition and change — which invites comparisons between *Surfacing* and *Mrs. Blood*, both of which present explorations of the irrational, nightmare side breaking out of the order of male civilization. Thomas' formal experimentation sets her aside here, as it also does from the work of Robertson Davies. Thomas' innate archetypalism contrasts also with Davies' doctrinal Jungianism. Again, she is not a writer of ideas though she read Jung's works for her archetypal study of Beowulf. Like Davies' *The Manticore, Blown Figures* explores analysis. Thomas is interested in the process of ordering experience, but in her fictional form she rejects the Jungian doctrine's strictures on the mind, whereas Davies orders his novel within the psychoanalytic dialogue which is his narrative mode.

One source of Thomas' technical innovation is her awareness of remote literary traditions. Studies of Old Norse and Old English gave her an interest in philology and also a sense of the instability of the word as sign, while her break with the linear form of the organic novel was stimulated by interest in the cumulative forms of folk narrative and the circular forms of Renaissance fiction (Bowering, p. 13). This broadening of perspectives through formal education is also evident in the work of other well-educated contemporary writers in Canada, such as Hugh Hood, who, like Thomas, is writing a *roman-fleuve* with recurring characters and motifs.

The other impetus to experiment comes from Thomas' association with her post-modernist peers in British Columbia, many of whom she met at graduate school. Her work has been published by *The Capilano Review* and by Talonbooks, both in Vancouver. In fact, she was the first prose writer to be published by the latter, which, along with Coach House Press in Toronto, has specialized in producing the books of the Tish poets — including George Bowering, Frank Davey, Fred Wah, and Daphne Marlatt — and others associated with the new, language-centred writing, developed from Dada-Surrealism. Thomas sees herself as a failed poet, and in the beginning, her relationship with the Tish group was distant. As she describes it, she would stand — perennial outsider — at the door of their office, next to hers at the university. It was difficult to "enter what you people were doing," she told Bowering in retrospect, "because it was all poetry" (Bowering, p. 8). And she kept her writing a secret. Now she thinks her prose is close to poetry, "meant to be read aloud" (Bowering, p. 8) in the manner of oral performance favoured by bpNichol and bill bissett. Her fiction finds its closest connections with the work of writers such as Rudy Wiebe, who is interested in voice, or poet-novelists Leonard Cohen, Michael Ondaatje, and Margaret Atwood, whose narratives also avoid traditional expository links, development occurring instead through a flux of images.

Thomas also shares with the Tish group an inheritance from phenomenology, "a *real* articulation of your experience of the real," as Pierre Coupey phrases it (Coupey et al., p. 107), manifested too in Bowering's *Autobiology* and Marlatt's *What Matters*. Thomas' writing is self-reflexive and "autobiographical" like that of Clark Blaise (Bowering, p. 14), another expatriate intrigued with the clash of cultures. Their work, along with that of Alice Munro and Rudy Wiebe, has been included in Ondaatje's collection *Personal Fictions* (1977), and currently, as writers question the representation of reality through words, this mode of fiction is an important one in Canada. A distinction made by Munro between "autobiographical" work, defined as being "life in its incidents," and "personal" work, which "draw[s] on experience,"[12] points out the impossibility of erecting definitive boundaries between truth and fiction. However, while Laurence, Munro, Blaise, and Ondaatje (for whom Thomas has expressed admiration [Wachtel, p. 6]) play with this paradox yet build credible characters, Thomas' sense of writing as lying leads her at times to dissolve even this comfortable mimetic illusion.

Thomas is not only a novelist, she is also a highly skilled writer of short stories, a genre which has been very vital in Canada in the last two decades. Thomas is drawn into this context by critics who compare her early writing to that of Hugh Hood,[13] while her control of the genre in *Real Mothers* has evoked comparison to the work of the "best" short-story writers in the country, Mavis Gallant and Alice Munro. Like them, Thomas builds her stories layer upon layer, generating paradoxes and ironies and creating a density of texture which "demands much more of her readers than [does the work of] most writers."[14] While Thomas' stories are less often experimental than her longer fiction, they nonetheless contain many convoluted stories-within-stories, testifying to a high degree of self-referentiality in her work, in line with post-modernist trends.

The last context into which Thomas' work fits is that of women's writing, which, paralleling the growth in women's self-awareness during the 1970s, has enjoyed a fine flowering in Canada, as it has in the United States. In her home on Galiano Island, Thomas is part of an artistic community which has been said to rival that of ancient Lesbos.[15] Here she is close to writers Dorothy Livesay, Jane Rule, and Phyllis Webb and to painter Elizabeth Hopkins. In her article "Is There a Feminine Voice in Literature?" Thomas admits that her work has also been "shaped by some of the great women of the past": "Harriet Beecher Stowe, whom I read in an illustrated edition when I was very very very young (and who had an enormous influence on the women of her own and the succeeding, generation), Louisa May Alcott, Willa Cather, Sigrid [Undset], Emily Dickinson, Edna St. Vincent Millay, Virginia Woolf, Doris Lessing and so on."[16] Most of the writers mentioned are American women — she notes her ignorance of many famous British and French women writers — though she significantly fails to mention any contemporaries such as Sylvia Plath, who was at Smith College with her and whose obsession with death, though expressed in poetic form, might invite comparison. Also absent are Elizabeth Spencer and Joyce Carol Oates, two other American-born teachers and writers of fiction. Thomas has admitted feeling no kinship with Oates's Gothic sensibility (Bowering, p. 31), though her own concern with the stability of identity, a feature of Gothic fiction,[17] might suggest such a pairing. That Thomas has been incorporated into the Canadian tradition while these other writers have not conveys the importance in this respect of her decision to switch from an American to a Canadian publisher.

Not a feminist in the strict sense of the word, Thomas nonetheless works to advance women's knowledge of themselves — she wants "to demonstrate the terrible gap between men and women" and "to give women a sense of their bodies" (Coupey et al., pp. 98, 107) — and this dedication to the real is political in a broad sense. Her position is thus much like that of Munro, Laurence, Atwood,

Marian Engel, Constance Beresford-Howe, and Carol Shields as opposed to the more radical stances taken by younger writers such as Judith van Herk or by lesbian writers like Jane Rule. She documents the strictures on women's lives and attempts to articulate this experience in women's own words without positing alternate worlds. Nonetheless, Thomas's experimentalism separates her from the others, as does her interest in sexuality. Thomas feels a kinship with Munro, but, as she points out, sexuality in Munro's work is mostly adolescent (Bowering, p. 31). Doris Lessing has written frankly about sexual relations between men and women (Bowering, p. 14), but Thomas with her first story, "If One Green Bottle . . . ," inaugurated what Atwood has termed "gynecological" fiction (Bowering, p. 20).

This concern for the body has drawn Thomas into the orbit of women's writing in French, especially the work of Hélène Cixous and Madeleine Gagnon, who advocate the translation of the body to create a new woman's discourse. Ultimately, though, her additional concern with the materiality of the acts of writing and reading finds a correspondence in the work of Nicole Brossard. Although she has not mentioned these specific figures, Thomas has made clear her admiration for the work of Quebec women writers, and specifically Marie-Claire Blais's *Mad Shadows*, whose surrealism her own *Blown Figures* shares (Bowering, pp. 30–31). "Mademoiselle Blood," the title of her review of Anne Hébert's *Héloise*, underlines her affinities with "the theme of 'mastery'"[18] and with the dark world where sex and death intertwine. Both writers also share a fascination with *Alice's Adventures in Wonderland*. Thomas carries linguistic subversion to a greater degree, however, and is closer to the younger generation of Quebec writers. *Mrs. Blood* was translated into French and published in Paris. It is, however, unknown in Quebec.

Thomas is something of an anomaly in the field of English-Canadian letters, for she shares thematic concerns with some groups and formal preoccupations with different ones. This also suggests that, as yet, her work has had little influence on younger writers, though with someone like Thomas whose career is in full spate, any prediction is highly contingent on the present moment.

Critical Overview and Context

Thomas' reputation has been a seesaw one, for she "has been 'discovered' repeatedly" (Wachtel, p. 3). There is general agreement that despite some unevenness Thomas is a serious writer who continually extends herself in new directions. She is also a demanding writer "in her scrupulous avoidance of easy answers" (Hofsess, p. 18) and in the density of her prose. Critics in some of the little magazines have risen to the challenge and written perceptively about her handling of language and form. Appraisals of her fiction are nonetheless funnelled into the thematic mould — in this case into the categories of "Africanadian" and "feminine" writing — which has hampered the development of Canadian criticism. Serious evaluation of her work has also run afoul of the "autobiographical" issue, which is raised at the outset of innumerable profiles and reviews. Encouraged by the family portrait on the cover of *Songs My Mother Taught Me*, critics believe her stories are all straight from the heart, and her craft is devalued by this biographical obsession. More rarely expressed, though undoubtedly a factor in newspaper reviews, is the question of Thomas' "difficulty." Don Stanley put the issue plainly: "Unfortunately, her strength in the realm of matter-of-fact is marred by a kind of strained literary sophistication."[19] Disliking her use of allusion, he consequently found her novels lacking humour. Such demands for the mimetic novel have created imbalance in Thomas' career.

The reviews of *Ten Green Bottles* (1967), most of which were published in the United States, all concur on the excellence of the collection, which, despite a certain unevenness,[20] is not just promising, but is the work of an author who, according to Anita Raskia, "has clearly arrived."[21] Jane Kay comments on the effective creation of a "mood of anxiety among the ordinary" (Kay, p. 30). Thomas' characterization is praised — she is "skillful at peeling off the emotions"[22] — as is her "keen observation," "limitless sensibility,"[23] and compassion mixed with "Faustian irony" (Raskia, n. pag.). "Omo," the story of a black Peace Corps member in Africa — a timely subject — is the one most often singled out as the best story in the collection. On the question of her subject, opinion is divided. Laurence Lafore in *The New York Times Book Review* says that Thomas' "speciality is not a region but a gender" and that she is particularly brilliant at portraying "neurotic women."[24] Anita

Raskia and Donald Stephens, on the other hand, specifically comment on the range of voices (including male voices) and locales convincingly rendered (Raskia, n. pag.; Stephens, p. 95). The most contentious issue is Thomas' style: opinion is equally divided between condemnation of the "shapelessness"[25] and praise for the "mosaic that lacks sequential structure" and which thereby allows her to capture the flow of the moment of epiphany (p. 96). The reviewer for *Choice* feels Thomas' stream-of-consciousness technique works well in "If One Green Bottle . . ." but fails her elsewhere,[26] while Kay suggests this first story is "more pretentiously oblique than poetic" and that the other stories, written in a "less obtrusive style," work better (Kay, p. 30). To Joel Clemons the effect is "immature,"[27] to Stephens, "beautiful and controlled" (Stephens, p. 96).

Reviewers returned to *Ten Green Bottles*, along with a later collection of stories, when it was republished in 1977 in Canada, and a similar extended evaluation of *Mrs. Blood* occurred when it too was republished in Canada, in 1975, several years after appearing in the United States. The reviewers' initial ambivalence about Thomas' style disappears in the reviews of her first novel, which is unanimously praised as a "spectacular tour de force"[28] whose "writing [is] exactly right in tone."[29] Several reviewers follow the pattern established by William H. New in his 1971 article "Africanadiana: The African Setting in Canadian Literature" and his review of *Ten Green Bottles*[30] and explore the African theme in Thomas' writing. Joan Coldwell explores the implications of Thomas' novel within a tradition of feminine sensibility where her portrayal of biological conditions marks a new departure.[31] All concur that it is the character who leaves the dominant impression rather than the landscape. Coldwell especially praises the protagonist for being "as complete a character as . . . [Margaret Laurence's] Hagar Shipley" (p. 98) and singles out the means used to create her: "authentic dialogue," Proustian converging of symbols, and the "near-Joycean passages" of her quotations and language rituals (p. 99). In general, female critics respond more positively than males, who, like New fail to perceive "a universal experience" in one woman's private suffering (New, p. 229). The single French review of the novel was also unflattering, calling it "parfois confus, flou et inégal."[32]

In his review of *Mrs. Blood* and Thomas' two novellas, *Munchmeyer and Prospero on the Island* (1971), Anthony Boxill notes that one of Thomas' principal themes is art and the artist.[33]

The novellas, which explore the "interpenetration of illusion and reality,"[34] are the subject of longer and generally favourable reviews. Two reviewers, however, present their observations in somewhat ambiguous terms: O. H. T. Rudzick states that "Prospero's magic does not get much above the mundane . . . ,"[35] and Mary McAlpine says that Thomas is the "possessor of a strange talent," "an oddly erratic style" which is "irritatingly brilliant."[36] Other reviewers pick up on Thomas' perceived strengths. Judith H. McDowell, for example, praises her "admirably realized people,"[37] and Kildare Dobbs similarly comments on the "completely convincing rendering of the mind of her male protagonist [in *Munchmeyer*], even in his attitude to sex."[38] Thomas' "versatile style" and "her rich and various" language are praised by Boxill as the vehicles for her penetrating insight[39] and lead McDowell to conclude that ". . . hers is a superior, perhaps major talent."[40]

With the 1973 publication of *Songs My Mother Taught Me*, Thomas' reputation attained a new plateau. Not only was the book widely reviewed, but many of the reviews are in-depth analyses. The book's virtues are generally perceived to be "the sheer intensity of feeling" evoked[41] and the "loving attention to detail"[42] which Thomas' "fine eye and ear" use to create "an impressionistic period piece."[43] Many echo Alix Kates Shulman's observations that the book is "almost lacking in plot," that it is "a collection of vignettes."[44] There is much disagreement about the impact of this circularity, however, and Karen Mulhallen concludes that it violates the basic structure of the *Bildungsroman*.[45] Other problems identified are difficulties in narrative perspective — the insufficient separation between the two voices, the one of direct experience and the one recollecting it[46] — which result in "saturation"[47] with Isobel or a sense of the inappropriateness of the allusive style.[48] While William Gairdner decrys the "cloying" atmosphere,[49] Susan Walker praises Thomas' "sharp-edged sense of irony" and "tinge of self-parody."[50]

While Thomas' work had already received brief mention or explication in more extended academic articles concerned with a group of writers, the praise she received for her stylistic innovation in Frank Davey's *From There to Here: A Guide to English-Canadian Literature since 1960* did much to dispel any remaining doubts about her work. Davey sees her style as fundamental to the "extreme kind of psychological realism" she writes.[51] Similarly, the perceptive, detailed analysis of Thomas' themes of death, madness, and art in the thesis of Linda MacKinley Hay gives an added stamp of academic respectability to her work,[52] and the probing interview by Pierre Coupey and the other editors of *The Capilano Review* in the same year increased understanding of Thomas' work among the literary cognoscenti.[53]

With *Blown Figures* (1974), Thomas inverted her usual order by publishing first in Canada. Although the book was widely reviewed and Thomas' characteristic features identified, critics reacted less to this fiction itself than to the surrealist movement of which it is part. Despite Bowering's warning to readers who find avant-garde fiction "self-indulgent" to reexamine "the parameters of the self,"[54] most reviewers had an axe to grind. Kildare Dobbs notes that the cover blurb contains "a quotation from Anaïs Nin (usually a bad sign),"[55] while Linda Sandler suggests that discontinuous form is "the literary hoax of the century."[56] These are countered by Barbara Bannon's claim that Thomas "gets close to something important here, and on the way points to new directions for surrealism,"[57] and by Margaret Atwood's high praise: in *Blown Figures*, Thomas "approaches the height of her powers," and "with each of her books, the reader feels that the next will not only be better but different in some unimaginable way."[58] Most critics take a middle road, agreeing with Michele Turin that the book is "very demanding but downright confusing"[59] and concluding, like O. H. T. Rudzick, that the value of reading it is "problematic."[60]

If Thomas' star was setting with the general public, it was nonetheless rising in certain academic circles, mostly in the peripheral little magazines where several extended analyses of her work appeared. These do not significantly change the interpretation of Thomas' work, though their detail amplifies its resonances through the by now familiar perspectives of thematic,[61] textual,[62] Jungian,[63] and feminist[64] approaches. Again, while canonical status is confirmed through mention in the revised *Literary History of Canada: Canadian Literature in English*[65] this involves no new readings of the texts themselves. Such is also the case with reviews of *Ladies and Escorts*, which was published in 1977 along with a reissue of *Ten Green Bottles*, for many of the reviewers discussing both books comment that they are "companion volumes,"[66] though, as Marian McCormick remarks, "years have given [Thomas] greater confidence and skill."[67] Aware of the reception of *Blown Figures*, most critics feel obliged to take a stand. After observing that "no one story is the true story, but the sum of the stories is," Atwood, for example, warns us that "a reader will either love this approach for its richness and its surreal echo effects or be very frustrated by it."[68] And within the generally positive views, each critic finds his or her own Thomas. There is Thomas whose strength is in her "realism,"[69] Thomas the outstanding "raconteur,"[70] and an entirely different Thomas who is not a "story-teller" but a fabulator (Atwood, p. 25). A number of critics point out the centrality of Thomas' themes of language and fictionalizing, underlining the validity of Atwood's appellation "a writers' writer" (Atwood, p. 25), though few are unqualified in their praise, noting the usual flubs as well, such as overworked surfaces and strained style.

Characterization, hitherto Thomas' forte, becomes an issue for debate in reviews of *Latakia* (1979). Are the main characters "irritating and embarrassing"[71] or are they "believable"[72] or are they "caricature[s]" knowingly created for "their roles in an extra-literary farce"?[73] *Latakia* also elicits a number of comments about authorial control of narrative, and of language whose excess has been "ruthlessly excised."[74] Overall assessment of the novel remains in suspension between extremes: R. P. Bilan, for instance, calls *Latakia* "a major disappointment,"[75] whereas Jane Rule, who nominated it for the Governor-General's Award, contends that Thomas "perfects her method of maintaining multiple time streams for a marvellous economy of narrative."[76]

The evident intent in *Latakia* to explore the "gap between women and men" (Coupey et al., p. 98) incited complex feminist approaches to this fiction, ranging from my own explorations of the female archetypes and the problem of language for women whose experience has been described only in the words of men,[77] to Constance Rooke's tentative proposal of a female reader-response theory.[78] Similar concerns inform two of the five academic articles which appeared on Thomas at this time. Lorraine McMullen's "The Divided Self," consisting mostly of plot summary, places Thomas' penchant for double narrative voices within a tradition of female characterization which reflects the position of woman as Other, trapped in false roles, behind false masks.[79] Ellen Quigley's review article, more detailed in its analysis, demonstrates through reference to linguistic, literary, and mythological constructs how *Latakia* is a new female romance: the movement from unity through dissolution to new unity is seen as the inverse of the traditional romance pattern which ends with male joining female, for here the male is the disturbing element and the higher unity is found when Rachel is confirmed in her female-defined identity, in love with herself.[80] This article fleshes out Robert Kroetsch's contention that Thomas is one of the "gangsters of love" whose writing is always an "uncovering," a violence done to form.[81] Quigley's article also offers the demonstration sadly missing from Robert Diotte's study of a promising subject, "The Romance of Penelope,"[82] wherein the author claims that the Isobel trilogy — *Songs My Mother Taught Me, Mrs. Blood,* and *Blown Figures* — offers a new form of epic combining the domestic romance of Penelope with the epic wanderings of Ulysses. However, the body of Diotte's paper moves at a tangent from his thesis, documenting the conventional handling of the *Bildungsroman* and of tragedy in the first two books and the failed epic of the third. Another study from this period, Joan Coldwell's "Memory Organized: The Novels of Audrey Thomas,"[83] also approaches Thomas' writing from generic and formal angles and offers a rich inventory of the techniques she has used in her consistent narrative strategy of looking backward. Focusing on Thomas' art, this paper provides a convincing demonstration of the ways in which recurring facts have been shifted by the ordering kaleidescope into ever-new patterns.

All these articles, as well as Bowering's interview with Thomas, which exhaustively examines details,[84] have concentrated on Thomas as craftsperson and have effectively banished the spectre of autobiography from discussion of her work, as is indicated by the reception of *Real Mothers*, a collection of stories published in 1981. Uniformly positive, these reviews are also mellower in tone than early reviews of her work: the reviewer from the *University of Toronto Quarterly*, for example is appreciative of her "metafiction[al]" aims.[85] The simultaneous publication of her earlier stories in a new collection, *Two in the Bush and Other Stories* (1981), prompted Eleanor Wachtel to comment on the growth which has occurred in the interval: Thomas now appears "relaxed," though her informality is "carefully crafted." This is a result of the more performative mode of the stories, anecdote having replaced "elliptical, personal imagery" for narrative transitions.[86]

With the publication of *Intertidal Life*, a major shift occurred in the critical evaluation of Thomas' work. The increase in the number of reviews — more than thirty — was the first indication of change. More significant, however, was the consensus in opinion of the reviewers who proclaimed this novel to be "an ambitious, complex work"[87] in almost unanimously favourable reviews. Another major difference in the criticism of *Intertidal Life* is its focus on the question of Thomas' critical reputation. Nancy Wigston categorizes the novel as a "breakthrough,"[88] while a number of other reviewers explore the significance of the break. Urjo Kareda's extended review, which focuses on the lengthy history of writing the novel, its various revisions and flirtations with publishing houses, begins by addressing the question of Thomas' marginal position within the literary institution. Although one might expect her to have easy entrée to the "female-dominated literary establishment," Thomas' writing is "racier, ruder, more raw" than that of contemporaries like Atwood and Munro, characterized as "more elegant than blunt," or than the "mythic cadences" of Margaret Laurence. Thomas has also been excluded on geographical grounds, like Mavis Gallant. Most significantly, however, Thomas has heretofore heightened her individuality by choosing to publish with a small, regional press whose distribution of her work has been patchy. All this should change, Kareda predicts, with the shift to a large publishing house which will provide her with wider distribution, broader promotion, and a higher profile. Thomas, he asserts, is "making her move into the mainstream" (Kareda, p. 50).

Also discussed in many reviews is Thomas' successful handling of the complicated focalization of the novel, which shifts "coherently and cleverly"[89] between first-person journal of the explorer of the female psyche — the compendium of clichés, proverbs, songs, definitions, and quotations of her commonplace book — and third-person commentary of the observant writer. The extended nature of these reviews is clearly in large part responsible for the complexity and comprehensiveness of the discussion of the technical aspects of Thomas' writing. Since the comments are laudatory, however, this new attention also reflects what is understood to be improvement in her craft. Nonetheless, the habitual comments on characterization are also present in these reviews of *Intertidal Life*, which, like Thomas' other fiction, is described as more a novel of character than of plot — "a rather shapeless series of events," according to Katherine Govier.[90] On the question of characterization, the consensus is succinctly summed up by Burt Heward:

. . . the plump, passionate mother of three, in Thomas' loving hands, becomes a heroine to cherish, a heroine transcending her condition as victim . . . . This only goes to make her one of the most rounded, most fully explored women in Canadian fiction. Other characters, including the children, remain disembodied, but this is the artistic price paid with such an oceanic stream of consciousness. Rarely, if ever, has woman as bloody victim of biological, cultural fate been so power-fully portrayed.[91]

Not everyone agrees with this judgement on the secondary char-acters. "The characters who populate *Intertidal Life* meticulously portray the dualistic nature of individuals," writes Judith Fitz-gerald, who then goes on to describe the in-depth portrayal of Alice's friends Anne-Marie, Raven, Selene, and Trudl, each a foil for Alice's self-discovery but each also "represented as a complex individual endowed with personal and social problems."[92] This view, unique among the critics, corresponds to Thomas' own evalu-ation of the novel as one which focuses on women's relationships with other women as well as on their relationships with men (Wachtel, p. 50).

The incorporation of feminist analysis into the novel is some-thing which critics almost universally believe to be poorly handled. Kareda gives Thomas the benefit of the doubt by explaining away the abrupt disjuncture between analysis and narrative exposition as a consequence of radical cuts Thomas made in the original manu-script (Kareda, p. 51). Fitzgerald's approach is equally tentative:

Form and content in this novel represent a near-perfect mar-riage, a balance flawed only by Thomas' enthusiasm for digression. Here, she erodes the narrative's power and allows her characters the unsubtle luxury of expressing views, valid in themselves, that may have been more appropriately located in pamphlets on such subjects as feminism.

That is not to suggest Thomas damages either her credi-bility or the importance of her message; rather, the ongoing reiteration of women's rights and wrongs occasionally becomes overbearing. Yet, in a novel of this quality and mag-nitude, such peccadilloes remain precisely that.[93]

Critical ambivalence to *Intertidal Life* becomes clearer with hind-sight in reviews of Thomas' subsequent book, *Goodbye Harold, Good Luck*. This collection of short stories is introduced by an essay in which Thomas explains her method of composition through "correspondences."[94] As well as outlining the creative pro-cess as she understands it, Thomas writes about her readers' prefer-ence for her short stories over her longer fiction though she thinks of herself as a novelist. The reviewers all address this point and in the process reveal their own preferences for Thomas stories over her novels. As Joel Yanofsky succinctly phrases it:

> Comparing this accomplished book with her last novel, *Inter-tidal Life*, an uneven, difficult work, it's easy to see why. Like Alice Munro and Mavis Gallant, Thomas is at her best work-ing within the boundaries of the short story; she is at her most effective creating a fiction that is subtle and fragile, that is made up of hard choices and vivid moments.[95]

In aggregate, what the initial reviews demonstrate is that despite the acclaim for *Intertidal Life*, critical norms have not changed in the Canadian literary establishment. Value is still determined by the standard of a transparent, unmediated language which purports to connect word and thing, being and self-consciousness, in the analy-tico-referential discourse of modernism, the one which is disrupted in Thomas' novels with their overt thematizing of the construction of a subject-position and the text as productivity. These values determine the interpretation of *Goodbye Harold, Good Luck*, which all the reviewers agree marks a turning point in Thomas' short-story writing as she introduces some of her novelistic con-cerns and devices. This observation leads to opposing critical opinions about the collection, as the lines confronting social realists against magic realists or surrealists are firmly drawn.

A new and positive feature identified by reviewers is humour. Thomas considers herself to be a funny person but admits that humour has not frequently appeared in her writing (Wachtel, p. 28). Reviewers appreciate the combination of "humor with heart-breaking pathos and realism with the odd dose of whimsy."[96] This humour is most evident in "The Princess and the Zucchini," a witty fairy tale for adults about a princess who encounters a talking zucchini, with "a feminist twist to the theme of the captive prince."[97]

Thomas has engaged in play for a long time, as we shall see, but only with these stories is her wit and playfulness finding public acknowledgement. This is the clearest sign of the change in direction associated with the appearance of *Goodbye Harold, Good Luck*.

The winds of change are also blowing in academia, where a flurry of articles on Thomas has appeared in the last few years. Newspaper reviewers may still be ambivalent about Thomas' work: scholarly critics on the contrary are universally enthusiastic about her experimentalism. This new interest is the result of a shift in critical paradigms currently under way in the field of Canadian literature towards post-structuralist analyses from semiotic, deconstructionist, and feminist perspectives, theoretical approaches which begin with the premise that language mediates our encounter with "reality." These tendencies converge in Thomas' work with its subversions of the paradigms of dominant (read patriarchal) discourses. Most of the recent critical studies are by women who foreground Thomas' feminism. They focus on Thomas' technique more often than her themes, exploring the dense allusive texture and the subtle ironies in her work.

Anne Archer, in her essay "Real Mummies," follows many reviewers in fully endorsing the biographical fallacy — constructing Thomas' biography from reading her fiction. Thomas is accused of narcissism (in the Freudian, not textual, sense of the term). "It is the purely personal aspect of much of Audrey Thomas' writing, coupled with her propensity to tell and retell a single story — to present us with a theme minus variation — that is both fascinating and problematic."[98] The fascination lies in the technique. However, Archer devotes less space to exploring the subtleties of Thomas' style than she does to sighting her artillery on the "limited perspective"[99] that marks the Thomas canon. That repetition has always functioned as *différence* in Thomas' work is something Archer has overlooked. She has, however, introduced an interesting, though brief, analysis of the guest/host conceit wherein Thomas works out the connections of incident and coincidence and major thematic concerns regarding the close link between religion and sex.

Wendy Keitner, in "'Real Mothers Don't Write Books: A Study of the Penelope-Calypso Motif in the Fiction of Audrey Thomas and Marian Engel," shares these basic critical assumptions about the unmediated nature of language and reality, though she moves closer to the preoccupations of other recent critics through her focus on feminism. She briefly discusses the search for the "elusive synthesis of love and work, family and career, intimacy and power" (which has been the predominant concern of North American women for more than twenty years since Betty Friedan wrote *The Feminine Mystique* [1963]) as it informs the dramatic conflicts of Isobel in the trilogy.[100] Reading the fierce polarities between familial and sexual ties as the contrast between the ideal mother, Penelope, and the highly sexual Calypso from the *Odyssey*, Keitner traces the evolution in Thomas' work of women split between domesticity and independence, showing how the conclusion to *Blown Figures*, where Isobel undergoes a ritual transformation, marks a new dimension of liberation for the writer/mother figure.

What Keitner's article shares with recent work on Thomas is the connection it makes between her texts and classics within the Western tradition whose plots her books seek to deconstruct. Thomas creates what Frank Davey terms "alternate stories"[101] — scripts written by one character for another, stories from mythology and literature repeated by characters, stories contained within symbolic objects, and stories written by characters to justify their lives — which are contained within "the apparent story" (p. 5) and ironically work to "demolish it" (p. 9), producing "disjunctive narratives" (p. 5). As in Atwood's fiction, the multiplicity works not to affirm through irony the truth of the traditional story but to suggest the possibilities of yet unknown and unarticulated stories which reject the unitary and patriarchal romance and all the other unitary genres that are displacements of romance (p. 14).

A number of other essays, notably those by Brigitte G. Bossanne and Joan Coldwell, [102] flesh out this description of Thomas' intertextuality by focusing on specific examples of borrowed texts. The term *parody*, which would be helpful in elucidating Thomas' postmodernist textual politics, both sexual and colonial, is not introduced into this debate. While grounded in description, these essays move beyond it to interpretation and, in the case of various feminist readings, to hermeneutics. Nor do all agree with the conclusion that Thomas' texts are mocking where the classic or "familiar" story, as it is termed, is devalued. Many, in fact, point out the way in which she respectfully reworks forgotten texts, especially the ancient lore of the Mediterranean goddesses, figurations of the Great Mother.

Detailed studies of the powerful archetypes of female creativity are to be found in two essays by Lorna Irvine, which form a major portion of her book on Canadian women writers, *Sub/version*. In "The Hieroglyphics of *Mrs. Blood*," Thomas' first novel is presented as the model of a female text. Turning the silent months of pregnancy into narrative, the narrator makes birth into a metaphor for the act of writing. This "condensation of birth and book,"[103] which functions only symbolically for male authors, is a projection of her own body for the female author. Childbearing is a central element of the *Künstlerromane* of women and represents a response to the "hegemonic texts and contexts of our culture" (p. 35) which either appropriate the birth metaphor to give legitimacy to male texts that are mere fictions derived from paternity or use it to circumscribe and limit female creativity, and which can therefore only be the "*repetition of reproduction*" (p. 35). With its stillbirth, *Mrs. Blood* centres more on narrative failure. Depicting ambiguous bodily and textual boundaries, in which there is a conflation of inner and outer, of narrative and marginal textual commentary, *Mrs. Blood* insists on allegorical meaning, meaning which is defined as "female narrative" (p. 31). This argument is extended in "Delusion and Dream in Thomas' *Blown Figures*," where the later novel is seen as another example of female textuality.[104]

Although it deals in chaos and inversions, this reading of Thomas' novel as examples of *écriture féminine* paradoxically creates order and hermeneutic closure, where to other critics there appear to be only chaos and the *reader's* ordering activity. Irvine's skill at detecting allusions and at reading these paradigms through the filter of feminist analysis suggests she has found Ariadne's thread through what to Louis K. MacKendrick seems to be a metafictional labyrinth, autonomous in the auto-representation. MacKendrick explores the recurring images in *Blown Figures* which constitute Isobel's awareness — images of blood, of decapitation, of glass — and the narrator's metatext with its allusions, parallels, and associations. Supporting my earlier thesis,[105] MacKendrick argues in favour of the role of the reader in the creation of meaning in *Blown Figures*. However, his assertion that out of all the "apparently random associations" there is "*one* passage . . . , uninterrupted by an intense imagistic or rhetorical concentration," in which the narrative makes "complete objective sense"[106] is a much more violent imposition of the hermeneutic compulsion than the feminist readings where ambiguity and process are perceived throughout *Blown Figures* and are themselves elements of signification. It is also a contradiction of his support for the creative participation of the reader in the process of making sense. The need to find a single key to unlock meaning has generally been abandoned by Thomas' other critics with the recognition of her deconstructionist bent for indeterminacy.

Among those who have stopped looking for a single key is Coral Ann Howells, who has written more than one article about Thomas. A British critic approaching Thomas' fiction as part of a broader analysis of Canadian women's fiction, she is also concerned with Thomas' "treatment of narrative as a feminist issue."[107] In two essays, she is concerned with women's need to tell stories which are closer to their social realities and, consequently, with the need to revise or unwrite "the old romantic fantasy narratives" we have inherited[108] "based on woman's adoration of the powerful male and on an exaggerated evaluation of him."[109] In "Margaret Laurence: *The Diviners* and Audrey Thomas: *Latakia*," Howells compares Morag and Rachel, the narrators of these two books. Both characters confront "traditional cultural dependencies,"[110] try to break free from the stereotypical images, and, in the process, discover the doubleness within the images and themselves. This question of the absence of narrative closure in a series of stories grounded in disruption is Howells' subject in the second of the two articles, "No Sense of an Ending: Real Mothers," which examines Thomas' collection as stories of resistance to and refusal of inherited codes and fictions.

Howells' argument is similar to that of Irvine, though Howells' essays are less detailed and complex in their argumentation, which echoes the terminology of deconstructionism. These same characteristics mark two essays on the same books by Pauline Butling, a Canadian and a long-time friend of Thomas. In "Thomas and Her Rag-Bag," Butling places *Real Mothers* within a recent movement by women writers to redefine "the images of women in fiction."[111] Thomas successfully "de-constructs" (p. 197) old images to make way for new. Idealistic images are replaced by more realistic ones, where "confusion, embarrassment and mixed feeling" (p. 198) become identified with mother love and, in a second step, with the construction of new ideals. While this essay explicitly foregrounds the key terms of deconstruction, its conclusion, in the advancement of a new hermeneutic, is at radical odds with deconstruction's displacement through miming and perpetual indeterminacy. Butling does not probe this inherent contradiction of a feminist deconstruction which seeks to destroy only in order to make new again. Her position is closer to that of the American mode of deconstruction as destruction, developed from Heidegger by William Spanos and made central to the Canadian sense by Robert Kroetsch.[112] In this, Butling might be seen to replace the nationalist with a feminist text in a continuation of the line of argumentation developed by Kroetsch in his earlier analysis of Thomas in "The Exploding Porcupine: Violence of Form in English-Canadian Fiction."

In "The Cretan Paradox or Where the Truth Lies in *Latakia*," Butling shifts ground slightly, emphasizing her understanding of Thomas' fiction as writing which foregrounds its linguistic nature and "the act of writing."[113] The usual motifs, symbols, myths, and plots are present in this work, including the most evident one of the lover's triangle, but they fail to become "unifying paradigms" (p. 107). The liar's paradox with its confusion of truth and lie assures that all meaning is plural and open. This is "the essence of both the novel's form and its narrative method" (p. 107). Consequently, it is "a *successful* telling of a *failure* in communication" (p. 110).

While adopting the post-structuralist approach of Irvine, MacKendrick, and Butling, Susan Rudy Dorscht takes issue with them all on a significant point, that "key" to understanding of MacKendrick, which has become the "essence" of the narrative in Butling's words, and is present as female hermeneutic in Irvine's analysis. As Dorscht argues, subjectivity and meaning are products of discourse. Through an exploration of post-structuralist theories of subjectivity and an illumination of the ways in which Thomas' fiction foregrounds the construction of subjectivity, Dorscht argues that Thomas' fiction, like post-structuralist feminism, insists that language is all there is: "Everything is word, everything is only word . . . ."[114] In this reading, Dorscht foregrounds the centrality of language in a more radical manner than Butling and provides a critique of the vestigial remnants of liberal humanism in Butling's textual "essence" and Irvine's "female text."

This essay also stands as a critique of intertextual readings which have focused on Thomas' rewriting of Shakespeare's *The Tempest* in her continued preoccupation with power politics and textuality, this time of the colonial as well as patriarchal variety, both linked in the figure of authority, the master of magic and government, creator and father, Prospero. These approaches read Thomas' work allegorically as a sociological symbol of post-colonialism. Readings of Thomas' *Munchmeyer and Prospero on the Island* by such critics as Chantal Zabus and Arnold E. Davidson have focused on its subversion of Shakespeare's classic. Debate has centred on the relative importance of Caliban and Miranda, Thomas' textual practice in this matter being remarkably similar to that of other Canadian writers who engage in a "battle of the books" in order to affirm raw Canadian experience over polished masterpiece. According to Zabus in her broad overview of revisions of *The Tempest* in New World literature, such adaptation and reinterpretation of the earlier European literature of colonization may be "sheer parasitism," at its worst. At its best, as an articulate retort, ". . . it constitutes one of the most cogent strategies of decolonization in literature."[115]

Arnold Davidson offers a detailed reading of *Munchmeyer* to show how Thomas' two novellas are held together by repetition and expansion so as to be "both lineal and parallel extensions of each other."[116] As Davidson suggests, the text lies between its two parts, requiring provisional readings. In that it dramatizes the process of making sense, this book is an example of contemporary metafiction foregrounding the way in which the book is "constructed and/or deconstructed."[117] What Davidson's essay implies, though without precisely stating as Irving has done, is that Thomas' deconstruction effects textual subversion which is also political subversion. In this, in its challenge to language, the book's politics are more radical than Zabus credits them for being. This deconstructionist reading stops short of suggesting that Thomas' work is an interpretive puzzle foregrounding the *reader's* ordering processes, a thesis which the present essay advances.

Thomas' Works

Given the polarization of Thomas' critics, it would be best to identify myself at once as one of the readers who delight in her convoluted narratives and the rich texture of her prose. These features are no mere decoration but fundamental to her creative impulse, which commences in a series of questions about the precarious relationship between language and reality. Is life, like Africa, "something which you 'do' and then write up for the folks back home?"[118] Are the connections between being and nothingness, between life and death, just "a question of semantics?" ("Still Life with Flowers," in *TGB*, p. 22). Is it "easier to conjure up a fairy tale . . . than to put one's finger on the pulse of truth?" ("A Winter's Tale," in *TGB*, p. 142). How can we define anything when language is so slippery, shifting its meaning with every new context? Jokingly she alludes to those waiting for signs as "doubting Thomases" ("If One Green Bottle . . . ," in *TGB*, p. 15), underlining the self-reflexive character of this narrative. The relationship between the word as sign and what it signifies is always an arbitrary one, but in the extreme situations in which Thomas' characters find themselves — in foreign countries, in insane asylums, in sexual ghettoes — the gap between their experience and the language used around them is a vast one. This problem in communication is simultaneously cause and consequence of their alienation. In her writing, Thomas explores and explodes limits and boundaries in a perpetual search for meaning.

This quest is evident from her first published story, "If One Green Bottle . . ." (*TGB*, pp. 5–16), where emerge her major themes of madness, death, and art, which I would rephrase as a preoccupation with nonsense, absence, and making sense. They surface again in a variety of forms in the other stories in *Ten Green Bottles* (1967) as the characters grope for meaning which would give them reassurance of their existence in a seemingly absurd world. Here the word is paradoxically both presence and absence. All the characters are obsessed with signs and portents conferring identity and the promise of a future, transcendence in fact, beyond the void they confront: "Not this nothing" (p. 16), the lost baby, the lost word, that haunts the protagonist of "If One Green Bottle . . . ." Most of the stories record some form of loss, some fall from grace perceived through the veil of memory. This woman is in labour, in a foreign hospital, waiting for "the flaming cross," "the olive branch" (p. 9), but she remembers only the "six dead mice" (p. 10) and the formaldehyde bottles of dead foetuses, death intermingled with birth. "Waiting anxiously" (p. 15), she is "Noah" (p. 9) hoping for the sign of a new covenant and forgiveness, some transcendent meaning. In her drugged state, she also identifies with Estragon in

Beckett's *Waiting for Godot*: "the clown . . . advancing slowly across the platform . . . dragging the heavy rope . . ." (p. 14), waiting in vain for any transcendental sign, "all a masquerade . . . a charade" (p. 14), words adrift in the abyss. This seems destined from conception, as the early signs make clear. For the gods do not give, they take by the *"droit de seigneur"* (p. 8). Zeus rapes Leda; God visits this Mary who can summon up only "the ghost of a smile" (p. 8). Creation implies forceful violation and destruction, with only "ghosts" resulting. Thomas' allusion to the biblical myth, where the divine presence is identified with spoken language, extends the implications of the narrative situation of a woman's experience to the broader question of creation in the ordering and meaning of existence. That the "ghostly" word or spirit has its own authority and cannot be made to mirror the protagonist's reality may be a consequence of perception distorted by drugs. Thomas' extreme form of psychological realism depends for its convincing effect on a dislocation of rational narrative order and grammatical syntax, and her woman in childbirth is drugged. However, the biblical myth of the incarnate word invoked here invites us to see the word set adrift because, backed by the fiat of a male God, it is antithetical to women's realities and has become "empty" for them. Metalinguistic considerations then may be the source of the supposed "madness" of the characters, who more appropriately might be viewed as nonsensical, in a world where all is in flux.

Repetition encourages us to think in this way. Thomas has described *Mrs. Blood* and *Blown Figures*, which can be read separately or together, as Chinese sliding panels which can be moved around[119] — a modular construct — and this aptly conveys the way the stories in *Ten Green Bottles* hang together. The whole is greater than the parts because the narrative principle of the individual stories — juxtaposition, montage — is written large so that incidents and motifs are amplified in significance through repetition in another story. The closure of the text is just one of the many boundaries Thomas blurs in this book as she shifts the frames of our perception, stretching and manipulating our sense of reality. "Still Life with Flowers," the second story in *Ten Green Bottles* (pp. 17–30), offers a parallel situation to that in the title story but shifts the perspectives. Here a young mother is also mourning her loss. She is going to the funeral of her lover, and her mind likewise wanders to the past which is stilled in a tableau, for she too is Lot's wife in her "aesthetic satisfaction" (p. 17). For her too the epiphanic symbol is most effective precisely when it reaffirms the impossibility of transcendence or truth. Alternating between first- and third-person narration — as the first story does between first- and second-person — it moves through several periods of the past: when the woman had gone to a funeral as a child, even then locked into herself and unable to feel; when she was playing the game of Dead Man's Body; when she met her lover and they made love in a world where only they seemed to be alive — a *danse macabre*, with ghosts. As in the first story, Thomas plays with the pun on die, a reference paradoxically to both sex and death. Now the narrator fixes her mind on "nothing" (p. 24), words around her meaningless as "strange formal diction . . . clichés" (p. 25), and examines the void for signs or scars that might indicate her lover had existed, might signal the truth of the passion she had felt. What she finds is a bright flower from his grave, a symbol resonant in the first story, too where the dead child is the rose. It fittingly terminates the episode with the lover in an inversion of its beginning when she had cried out to her husband that she was "not a garden" (p. 26). Ironically, now she is not growing but posing, her flower part of the stilled life and the life still, part of the paradoxical tableau she has created. As in the first story, her vision is distorted by tears. "Still Life with Flowers" also raises the issue of aesthetics as anaesthetic, art used to cover/smother life; as we learn in "Omo" (*TGB*, pp. 47–75), anaesthetics can be used to kill.

Our experience of reading the book is a cumulative one as these details find further resonances. The ghost and the flower recur in "A Winter's Tale" (*TGB*, pp. 142–60) in the form of a ghostly nun who purportedly died for love and the "Rose-red" (p. 146) of fairy tales whose constricting image must be exploded. "Xanadu" (*TGB*, pp. 31–46), the third story, begins with another biblical allusion announcing the fall and yet another loss of innocence, when a housewife in Africa, blessed with too perfect a servant, finds her power over her family diminishing and sets out to restore it by "framing" the servant. This story also explores a blurring of boundaries — a dislocating of perception — this time between dream and reality. The allusion to Coleridge in the title finds echoes in the next two stories — "Omo" and "The Albatross" (*TGB*, pp. 76–97) — where, as in "The Rime of the Ancient Mariner," unwanted storytellers force their tales on other characters and introduce a model of reader as victim of a teller's compulsive expiation. Guilt motivates them to tell all, just as it stimulated the labouring woman's confession.

"Omo" justly deserves its reputation as one of Thomas' best stories, for as well as introducing a topical subject, the Peace Corps in Africa, and probing into American neocolonialist motivations and the thorny issue of racism through plays on the nickname "Omo" relating both to the American detergent advertised for its whitening powers and the Twi word for "not good" (New, p. 226), it is a perceptive examination of the unreliability of language, given the failure of the revelatory sign, the stillbirth of the Word, in the framing story of this volume. It is another ghost story. Omo, an albino African who is called a "ghost" (p. 59), comes into the lives of two Americans in incidents which involve death, so that Thomas' story revolves around a blank which is nonetheless a presence. It is also a self-reflexive story about white and black: the racial metaphor, juxtaposed with allusions to the black marks on the white paper, becomes an allegory of writing and reading.

The narrative enfolds a complex series of tales within tales. The white American E. K. Jonsson is reading the diary of his missing housemate, black American Walter Jordan. These diary entries are contrasted with E. K.'s own notebook jottings of their experience. Rather than communicating with each other, the two young men have recorded their observations. Writing implies a flight from communication. As well, we have Omo's life story as the eavesdropping E. K. has (mis)heard it. At the centre of the story is the paradox of the white man who is really black and the black man who is really white, suggested in the palindrome *Omo*. But how can we know who they really are, indeed who anyone or anything *really* is? The complexity of knowing another person through their words is revealed by E. K., who comments on what he reads in the diary of the absent man: "He made fun of me to himself. That's what really shakes me. I know now a lot of it was just a cover (I sometimes wonder if he didn't write his journal to convince himself he was ironic and detached about everything)" (p. 67). The varying perspectives — personal as well as temporal — enfolded in this sentence, and in the larger narrative, cancel each other out, leaving the reader with an interpretive puzzle. Then there is the confusion of E. K. who confesses to his unreliability: "What I mean is, I'm not sure what I meant by 'this is Africa'" (p. 52). Here, extreme lucidity, an attempt to think in "black-white terms" (p. 61), to make absolute distinctions, leads to distortions as great as those effected by the emotion-fogged eye. We are left with discrete phenomena, a compulsion to order, and ambiguous or paradoxical signs.

Thomas' use of oral narrative and diary forms expands the terrain for her investigation of the interrelationship of the fictions of life and those of art. She includes hallucinations, memoirs, and anecdotes (as told by Miranda in "Xanadu") and will later enfold the construction of full-fledged fantasy worlds, like the fairy tales in "Elephants to Ride Upon" (*TGB*, pp. 115–41) and "A Winter's Tale" or like the totally private fantasies in the mad world of the asylum in "Salon des refusés" (*TGB*, pp. 161–77), which closes the book. In this last story, the Van Gogh paintings on the asylum walls, as well as the story's title, which is evocative of the impressionist painters, allude again to our innate drive to fabulate and to the very blurred boundaries between revolutionary art and insanity, both of which challenge our understanding of rules and order while presenting reality in cryptic symbols.

Thomas' major concerns and techniques are to be found in embryo in this first collection. The stories are specular or narcissistic and through a variety of perspectives and narrative frames comment on the distortions which arise when one looks back on the past to find truth. They focus on characters of different sexes and conditions who have some form of altered, heightened, or deranged consciousness. Thomas explores them in crisis, placing them in foreign countries — Africa, England — where they will be pushed to their limits.

Much of the power of Thomas' writing is created by the dense style. Connections between the dislocated parts of the story (and between stories) are effected through recurring symbols and incidents which function as leitmotifs: masks, games, blood, flowers, ghosts, and the journey by, or movement through, water as process of discovery. Allusions function in a similar manner to effect associative links even as they expand the boundaries of the stories to encompass the range of literary history. Contrary to many reports, these allusions are not particularly obscure; rather, they are concentrated in certain fields of general, even popular, culture. These include the impressionist painters (evoking a concern with perception); Coleridge (the investigation into the operations of fancy and the creative imagination); Shakespeare (romance and antiromance);

the Bible (archetypes, truth to be questioned or inverted); children's lore, including games, stories, and rhymes (highlighting the ludic function of art); and folklore, as in the circular counting songs referred to by the title of the book itself and of the story "One Is One and All Alone" (*TGB*, pp. 98–114) (highlighting the self-cancelling narrative structures).

These allusions, which illuminate the word as both presence and absence by shoring up its failing authority even as they announce its relativity, are also central to Thomas' obsession with paradox, with non-sense. In these stories, we find intentional verbal paradoxes — "One is prepared through being unprepared" ("If One Green Bottle ...," p. 11) — as well as puns and ambiguities. These are reflected on the structural level by the ambiguous time framework within a single sentence which subverts our logical rules of cause and effect: "You are wrong, you philosophers, we are not the sum of all our yesterdays, but the product of all the tomorrows which never came. Wrapped in our dreams we only wake to yesterday and madness and damnation" ("Salon des refusés," pp. 170–71). In the macrocosmic scheme, this dislocation occurs in narrative logic which also knows no beginning, middle, or end, but circles around on itself, as in "A Winter's Tale," or is continually dispersed in the funhouse mirrors of story within story within story to the vanishing point. Then there is the blurring of boundaries between stories and literary tradition, between psychic states, and between people. Thomas' stories deconstruct our rules of logic and explode the forms resulting from them. While these practices continue in her later work, her habit of graphically representing the disjunctions through differing typefaces or through ellipses — another blurring of boundaries between word as signified content and as concrete visual sign — gradually disappears so that the stories *look* more connected. A comparison of "Still Life with Flowers" from this first collection with "Déjeuner sur l'herbe" from the more recent *Real Mothers*,[120] both of which are set in the cemetery and concerned with loss of the ability to feel, is instructive.

When Thomas signed the contract to publish *Ten Green Bottles*, she agreed to write a novel. After working away at a *Bildungsroman*, she put it aside to develop her first story, "If One Green Bottle...," into *Mrs. Blood* (1970). Although first to be published, *Mrs. Blood* is chronologically second in a triptych about Isobel Cleary; *Songs My Mother Taught Me* (1973) and *Blown Figures*

(1974) complete the series. *Mrs. Blood* describes Isobel's bleeding pregnancy and eventual miscarriage in an African hospital and thus recapitulates many of the situations and concerns of the stories. Isobel's sense of alienation from her white body in a black world evokes the colour question of "Omo"; her recollection of her love affair with Richard in England and the abortion he forced her to undergo brings to mind the liaison of "A Winter's Tale," which is also set in England, and inverts the outcome of the timely pregnancy in "Elephants to Ride Upon"; her memories of working in an insane asylum return us to the world of "Salon des refusés" and, as they do in that story, suggest a metaphoric connection between bodily and psychic health. Indeed, this is central to *Mrs. Blood*, whose narrator also waits for signs of a new covenant. She is convinced, as an African belief would have it, that her miscarriage is punishment for the earlier abortion. The sign that has come promises only her damnation, her consignment to oblivion. Unlike African society, however, her world offers no rituals to effect expiation. Her confessional narrative circles around this void, the art of narrative becoming a substitute for ritual. Private rather than communal, it remains solipsistic, alienating.

The matrix of this novel is its final sentence, " 'Get rid of it,' he said," [121] a snippet of conversation Thomas once overheard in a telephone booth. [122] She wove this and other found pieces into her own experience, writing a double story. Richard at the heart of the story is not in it. Mrs. Blood's memories create him, as a writer does a character, *ex nihilo*. Thus, difficulties of creating character are examined as Mrs. Blood remembers Richard making love to her and tries to imagine herself in his skin, experiencing her body (p. 77). The impossibility of doing so, of ever getting beyond one's own version of reality, is implied by juxtaposition. Her attempt to enter his mind arouses her desire. Richard using litotes to address her — "Madame, you are no philosopher" (p. 77) — introduces the absence with which he is paradoxically identified throughout. As Mrs. Blood says, "And now I have a horse called Nothing and when you ask me where he rides I'll answer, 'Nowhere' " (p. 77). With Richard, she has "held hands in a movie called 'The Man Who Never Was' " (p. 217). Richard, lost lover, becomes confounded with the lost child: "Love, *L'oeuf*. Nothing. Nothing will become of nothing" (p. 217). He is the shadow of her personality, drawing her down into the world of heat, fertility, sexuality, violence, unreason, and death.

Consequently, the narrator calls out to her husband, Jason, that she is not what she is (p. 218). She is the murderer of her child, a Medea to his Jason. But she is also unknown to him; she is the sensual, punning, irreverent, subversive Mrs. Blood, who parodies the Mass and Cartesian rationalism: "I stink therefore I am. This is the bloody and bawd of Christ which was riven for thee" (p. 21). She is also Mrs. Thing: strong ego, civilized European afraid of the dark continent, a woman bound into a passionless marriage.

The narrative alternates between the two voices and between past and present tenses. In the third and final section, however, Mrs. Blood and the past tense dominate, indicating that the integration of the personality will not take place, that it will dissipate into nothingness. Similarly, the authorial control which is wielded by Mrs. Thing to turn this chaotic experience into a narrative is loosened. The raw material to be converted to ordered artefact in the creative process is aborted. The final section is a found narrative, a collage of quotations (many from *Macbeth*) which finally overwhelm the narrative as they have threatened to do all along with Mrs. Blood's proffered clippings from the newspaper: racing tips, horoscopes, notices of name changes — all tentative portents.

Although the present and a forward-moving narrative line are abandoned for the fragmented past, the control exerted by creative metamorphosis is still evident. The sections of the book, which focus on fleeting moments or emotions, are ordered like a collection of poems and were written in this way, a section at a time, then pieced together. The major revisions made in the text in the process of composition were the elimination of dates, which had emphasized the linear progression through the pregnancy, and the changing of the order of some of the segments.[123] One which was moved several times before finding its present location is Mrs. Blood's memory of the hibiscus flower with its evocation of Joyce's Molly Bloom in Andalusia, its echoes of the flowers of death and life in *Ten Green Bottles*, and its reverberations within the novel of Isobel's deflowering and the ripening and peeling of her endometrium:

> There was an hibiscus flower, like a clot, outside the bedroom door.
> And then they took my crimson soul and crimson lining. (p. 217).

The repetition and expansion of symbols in the manner of poetry moves us now forward, now backward through the text. Just as the narrative strategies rely on the organization of memory, through conscious memory games or the involuntary associative flux, so too the activity of reading mirrors these same processes. To this duplication of processes, the old riddle "What is black and white and re(a)d all over?" appropriately addresses itself. Just as Mrs. Blood's life force spills over the dark continent, blending inner and outer worlds, white and black bodies, so too our reading brings together black words and white page in an experience which, because of the gaps and demands made for our participation in its creation, becomes increasingly individualistic and chaotic even as it unites us through this process with the narrator. Reader and narrator become cocreators of meaning.

Mrs. Blood openly addresses this question of inversion, of subversion. The horizontal position of the narrator forcibly reminds us that two of the major experiences in life, those of birth and procreation, occur lying down. It is not just death which is the leveller! More central to the metafictional character of the narrative, however, is the opening epigraph from Lewis Carroll's *Alice's Adventures in Wonderland*, where Alice protests to the Cheshire cat that she doesn't want to go into the mad world and the cat replies that her presence is proof that she already is mad. This alerts us to a number of allusions in the novel to Carroll's book which show us we are in an inverted-mirror world where things "aren't always what they seem to be" (p. 11), a world in which proportions and rules are perpetually shifting according to the vantage point. Like Carroll's, Thomas' is a fantasy world posited on the conditional proposition *if . . . then*. Fantasies nest within fantasies in infinite regress, each unfolding another level of reality. From each level, the others seem absurd. The awareness of reciprocity of views, however, opens the way for the effacement of boundaries between inside and outside, up and down — the sort of collisions and metamorphoses that constitute the essence of the shifting perspectives in Thomas' world. Here the narrator is both outside Carroll's story, as when she dresses her children for a costume party as Alice and the white rabbit (p. 180), and inside, as when she herself is Alice, aware of the strangeness she must hold for these March Hare Africans. Finally, she is the food and drink which cause Alice to lose all sense of proportion: "I put a sign on my breast, 'Eat me,' and on my lips a notice, 'Drink me,' but only the mosquitoes came" (p. 26). As the passage continues, however, these associations collide with allusions to the Mass, and she becomes Christ, the sacrificial victim. Fantasy and nonsense are major sources of parody in this book, and Thomas uses them to open up the classics — the archetypes of our civilization — to other perspectives, and to move against any authoritarian centre, any omniscient perspective.

These actions of eating and drinking echo some of the other puns in the book. While Mrs. Blood casts herself here as Christ, elsewhere she plays the role of Mary. As George Bowering has remarked, there are an inordinate number of characters called Mary in the book (Bowering, p. 25). This conflating of herself with both mother and son (she several times tries to become her friend Rosemary) makes of this story a revision of that earlier story of the creation of the Word, told this time from the woman's perspective. This is a story of waiting for others, of the abdication of the self to the invasion of others, a story which culminates in the loss of everything. Similar inversions — feminist subversions — are suggested in another reference to eating, the punning phrase of Richard's "Avez-vous du pain?" (p. 150). While "pain" calls forth a more proletarian bun than Proust's madeleine, it nonetheless evokes here, too, the narrative drive to remember. At the same time, it refers also to the "bun in the oven" that is causing so much pain and loss. The "pain" paradoxically contains both nourishing presence and painful annihilation.

While such games establish the contrapuntal mode of *Mrs. Blood*, the fiction through its gynecological theme provides an experience readers can identify with even as the narrative frame ironically undercuts this, distancing the reader. In Thomas' next work, *Munchmeyer and Prospero on the Island* (1971), the contingencies of life are entirely absorbed, leaving us with formal consolations. Together these two novellas develop the typical portrait-of-the-artist novel with its split between unsuccessful character and successful author. However, creator and creation are given entirely separate narratives and different tenses. In the process, Thomas provides a veritable catalogue of narrative modes, ranging from jokes and anecdotes, through dreams (both day and night), hallucinations, and fantasies, to letters, journals, and novels. Thomas explores the special insights offered by each of these genres through which the imagination takes wing and examines their impact on the lived life of the teller.

One of the major subjects Thomas is tackling here is the relationship of the aesthetic artefact to the life of its creator. Is it projection of or compensation for his/her life? Is a good life necessary for good stories? Here Thomas is exploring an axiom implied in Henry James's fiction: "... the man who does not understand or appreciate the principles of art cannot completely grasp the principles of life, ... an awareness and appreciation of the one involves ... an awareness and appreciation of the other...."[124] As well, Thomas explores the relationship between the "sister arts" of writing and painting, discerning the differences between them with respect to their powers for representing life. Here too we can find no absolute truth, no bedrock reality, but only shifting perspectives and levels of "reality." An interpretive puzzle, the work of art can only imitate other works of art. For in every moment of our life, we are telling stories, creating images, and a novelist merely stands at an extreme in a spectrum rather than being a privileged, inspired individual.

Of all her books, this one is the most satiric and the most playful. Thomas claims to have "had more fun writing this book than any book I've ever written" (Bowering, p. 26). Its convoluted fugal development unites the two stories in a series of mirror inversions reminiscent of André Gide's *The Counterfeiters*, for a writer keeping a diary writes of a would-be writer keeping a diary while writing a novel. Feigning and lying are the subjects of these self-cancelling narratives. The first, *Munchmeyer*, was written in 1968 when Thomas was struggling with a novel. It relates the confusion of Will Munchmeyer, perennial graduate student, father, and frustrated novelist, as recorded in what is purportedly his diary. It begins, however, on April 1 and may well be an April Fool's Day send-up.

Thomas takes us into that in-between world of truth and deception which is her speciality, developed metaphorically here, not by the continent of Africa or by Alice's descent into the rabbit hole, but by descent into the second level of Dante's hell, as the opening epigraph and Will's own frequent allusions to the "messy *cammino*,"[124A] the middle way, make clear. Like T. S. Eliot, Will suggests that the way down is paradoxically the way up, and in his pursuit of the transcendental sign, he has taken refuge in the basement, where he scribbles in his diary while trying alternately to write novels and a thesis. Diary masquerades as novel masquerading as diary. Conditional *if* ... *then* sentences are perpetually juxtaposed, undercutting each other and sending us oscillating back and forth among life, diary, and novel:

> And I write this *as though* it were a novel, in which I play the role of narrator, (a) because Martha [Munchmeyer's wife] thinks I'm writing a novel down here in my cellar, and thus it's easier not to make a slip; but (b) — and really what is most important — diaries scare me. From myself to myself — a kind of schizoid thing. (p. 5; emphasis added)

Will offers us a history of diary-keeping in his family, asserting that "all his experiences with diaries have been negative in one sense or another" (p. 7) because they have not helped him solve the riddle of his existence which is what diaries are for. "Diaries are for people who need to prove themselves" (p. 5). "I write. I am," he parodies Descartes (p. 58). In his quest for self-definition, in his pursuit of signs, Will arrives at the paradoxical position where everything is a sign or message from the fates (p. 22), none of which is more privileged than any other, and all of which are equally subjective. Will is left with his solipsism, imposing self-censorship because of his fear of being read and discovered to be an imposter, even though he is aware that the audience is a mirror which he needs to hold up to himself to confirm his identity — his existence as a novelist: "Fame had been my mistress, not truth" (p. 8). His wife, Martha, by knitting sweaters and giving them away, arranging feasts for others to consume, and producing children, acts as a foil to Will by showing the sacrificial nature of "art" that would communicate. This pairing of Will and Martha parodies Virginia Woolf's linking of Mrs. Ramsay and Lily Briscoe, mistresses respectively of the arrangements of life and of pigments. Will comes to see that Martha — biblical doer of good works — has put her mark on him with the sweaters. Hers is the sign which defines him, but, ironically, it is a mark of Cain, an infernal sign (p. 47). A complex pun on Cain and Abel, elided with a sexual joke, makes it clear that "can" is not "able" to "come" (p. 47). Will's writer's block, which he compares to "being constipated" (p. 5), is also impotence (p. 80). He retreats from his wife with her overwhelming material creativity into onanistic fantasies of the dream girl, who is perhaps a hippy on the beach and is certainly a parody of the dream girls of Joyce's Leopold Bloom and Stephen Hero. The end of Part 1 leaves him separated from his family, staring at a sign in a garage, "Super-Hell" (p. 25), an ironic inversion of the transcendent sign he has been seeking.

In Part II Thomas' games become even more complex. In this story or hallucination, Will awakes hung over, without his glasses, to find a man soliciting him or helping him — it is never clear which. Together they set out on a chase through Vancouver streets, which have become a maze for the blinded Will in a parody of Bloom's and Stephen's night wanderings through Dublin. The link between Thomas' two men is a homosexual one rather than a paternal one, and a series of blurrings of boundaries between these characters indicates that Pierre is another distorted mirror of Will. Will escapes from Pierre in a wonderful, surrealistic chase around an empty department store, where he seeks refuge in the Mothers' Room, then awakes on the beach to find his hippy beside him. Whether this is nightmare or story is never clear, though the past tense after the present tense of Part I suggests it might be a story.

Part III shifts us to another locale and another decomposition of the narrating subject. Will rents an upstairs "room with a view" in the house of an artist, Tom Lodestone, and begins what he suggests is a more creatively productive stage of his existence. He spends his days writing story after story, though they come back from the publishers with rejection slips, and he becomes more involved with the painter's family, eventually starting a sexual relationship with the wife, Maria. As he represents them in his narrative — Tom working away alone, married to his art, and Maria isolated with the baby — the relationship looks like his own with Martha. He has a brief fantasy relationship with Mavis Marvell, an admiring student, who joins the other two MA's in his life, all the characters telescoping into one another.

The relationship with Tom is also developed through doubling, for Will is writing a novel about Tom and goes to his studio for technical advice. He is intrigued by Tom's paintings, depictions of the White Goddess in which he finds a mixture of sensuality and cruelty, and he attempts to come to an understanding of Tom's character through words. His reading of the character will find a reflection in *Prospero on the Island*, where Miranda describes the painter Prospero and her character Will Munchmeyer in similar terms, suggesting the blurring of boundaries between creation and creator. Tom remains an enigma for Will though. The novel is never finished, nor is Thomas' novella; the ending is undercut, left open, as Will slips into semi-delirium and offers several alternate "takes" of the final scene. Thomas' debt to film is clear here, and, indeed, the whole novella is reminiscent of Fellini's 8 1/2, where private fantasy is offered as completed film. Will's invitation to the critics to complete his book, to deify him in the role of the romantic artist burned out too young (p. 80), and his denunciation of his whole life as lying — "I lie. You lie. We lie" (p. 81) — are direct addresses to the reader to fill in the blanks, to add the interpretation which will be creation. Ironically, this very private work is also very open to the reader since the instability of the narrative sign invites us to complete the puzzle as best we may.

The lack of closure in *Munchmeyer* — Will's inability to maintain the separation of life and art, his failure to circumscribe and fix life — is contrasted in *Prospero on the Island* with Miranda's distinctions between her diary and her novel, between her ordinary self and her "new-washed writer's eye" (p. 105). The layering in her diary is just as complex as it is in Will's and documents Miranda's relationship with her subject, namely with the novel *Munchmeyer* which she is writing. The parallels between the two diary-writers-cum-novelists are clear. Like Will, she regularly visits an artist for knowledge of his craft. With Alex MacKenzie, the painter (is there an allusion also to the explorer of the continent?), she discusses the art of writing and the relationship between creating and living. Central to both novellas is the question of an audience. Communication breaks down when people stop listening. Miranda reveals herself to be like Will, a compulsive chatterer burdening others with her stories. But her diary executes an inversion, focusing less on her own stories than on those of Prospero, becoming ironically very much like a novel — some of the entries consist of pure dialogue (p. 116) instead of the diarist's usual monologue — as Miranda listens.

Miranda's diary extends beyond a preoccupation with the unreliable sign. Her focus is on process. She discusses Prospero's technique of oral presentation and the fillers he uses, probes into the roots of words, and ponders whether "a metaphor or simile *really* makes you see" (p. 101), exposing the means through which the illusory nature of writing is sustained. She also documents the physical reality of the act of writing, a process involving "some kind of marvelous chemical reaction ... similar to sexual attraction" — writing as the product of

a "visceral imagination" (p. 123). By making the sign represent the
material nature of its production, she hopes to place its nature
within the bodily processes, gestures alone providing a way out of
the semiotic dilemma (p. 128). Painters make marks on the page
which are more immediate, less mediated and abstract, than
writers' words, which form visual images only at a second remove
(p. 114). Because of the materiality of their creations, Miranda
admires Prospero and her husband, Fred the sculptor, who both
work in nonverbal forms. Fred, moreover, values living well over
creating well. Through her ardent lovemaking with him, Miranda
merges with his world and becomes a successful creator. This
merging is suggested through her attentiveness to nature, her
recording of the material of the passing year despite the paradox of
second-degree representation it presents. It is also conveyed
through her preferred place of work at a table before a large window with a view. While the window frames it like a painting, the
view is not static but mobile and expands her world beyond the
solipsism of her character Will: "I like to be here writing away and
look up suddenly to see what new thing has moved into my field of
vision," she writes (pp. 100–01). Nonetheless, this is not quite a
writer's notebook where she records scraps, trying to catch
"impressions" (p. 104), though it comes closer to this than Miranda
with her new hunger for facts would admit and certainly far nearer
to this than does the diary of her character Will, despite his identical preoccupation with the parallels between writing and painting.

Miranda really is much more concerned than Will is with the
Other. This is conveyed through her choice of character. In writing
about a man, she is trying to extend the boundaries of her imagination to move into a very different mind, even though she shares
Will's anxieties about the elusive, unreliable verbal sign. She is ultimately able to admit the human necessity for creating other worlds
when she recognizes that her young daughter, Toad (read
Caliban?), is becoming human when she creates monster stories.

Nonetheless, Miranda's diary is undermined, just as Will's is,
through allusion. Framed by an epigraph from *The Tempest* and by
descriptions of life as a "bucolic dream" on a pastoral island
(p. 94), Miranda's narrative provides us with an illusory paradise
which is a copy of a literary paradise, just as Will's hell imitates a
literary hell rather than a real one. Her narrative never does touch
base with any reality; it remains within circling signs, displaced

from any context, merely situated on another level. Significantly, the difference between the two mirroring worlds is not so much one of location as it is one of perspective. Allusions to Jonathan Swift, whose self-consuming spider and honey-producing bee from *The Battle of the Books* are certainly in Thomas' mind, make this clear. Will, down in his hole and overwhelmed by the weight of the world, sees his wife as Glumdalclitch, the giant Brobdingnagian nurse. His hyperbolic perspective is as distorted then, as it is later, when from his upper room he looks down at Lilliput. Miranda shares this latter distorted view when, in her diary, she describes her urge to control and order the world, to create characters: "There is a whole Lilliputian panorama inside my head and I hurry to put it down" (p. 123). The successful creator, then, becomes a benevolent tyrant over a captive people, as Prospero is on his island. The ruthlessness Miranda senses in him and in her character Will, which Will in turn intuits in his character Tom, is thus a component of the successful artist who must subdue reality with authority. There is an ironic truth to Miranda's assertion that she is not what she seems to be either but is playing at pastoral like Marie Antoinette (p. 118). And the characters all revolt against this tyranny, thus creating the embedded narratives, for every character has his or her own story to tell, his or her own version of the facts.

This inversion is suggested also by the Freudian metaphors of writing as sublimated sexuality that Thomas uses — pen/penis, pen/womb. Through her artist figures in the two novellas, Thomas makes preliminary, self-contradictory distinctions. Will suggests that females don't need to write or paint, that they don't need mirrors since they "have created creatures in their own image" (p. 46), yet Miranda is writing even though she has three children. Writing for her is like gestation, however, for when her novel is finished she says she feels "slack-brained, the way one feels slack-bellied the day after the birth of a child" (p. 148). The revolt of Toad-Caliban from mute subject to fantasizing storyteller forecasts the ultimate independence such creations may have from the creator who contained and nourished them. We are not yet in the world of proliferating relativistic perspectives of *Six Characters in Search of an Author*, though we have not far to go.

Thomas coordinated such a world in *Blown Figures* (1974), which is the last of the Isobel Cleary trilogy. But before she followed the trajectory of her development of the theme of author and subject, she returned to the manuscript which became *Songs My Mother Taught Me* (1973). In this novel, we return to the worlds of two of the stories in *Ten Green Bottles*: that of the family portrayed in "Aunt Hettie and the Gates of the New Jerusalem" (*TGB*, pp. 129–41), and that of the insane asylum in "Salon des refusés" (*TGB*, pp. 161–77). These settings determine the tone for the two parts of the novel, "Songs of Innocence" and "Songs of Experience," in which the hidden fanaticism of the child's family gives way to the overt madness of the asylum. Miranda's experience in the asylum enables her to see the family's deforming force more clearly: "I wore fear like a hump on my back" (p. 95). This shift in perspective effects the change mentioned in "Aunt Hettie and the Gates of the New Jerusalem": "Why grow up? All it means is to grow away" (*TGB*, p. 138). This sentence is the matrix of the novel.

To enter the world of *Songs My Mother Taught Me* is to encounter a less convoluted one than we have met in Thomas' other fiction, for the fugal constructions and crab canons are written for fewer voices, and the blurrings of the two sections are fewer than we have become accustomed to, for this is a simple case of inversion. Moreover, there is little sense of change in the narrative voice, which remains rooted within the past it is busy remembering, contrary to the practice of most *Bildungsromane*, which chart the growth dramatically through alterations in voice. Nonetheless, hints of this are made at intervals throughout the narrative through Thomas' habitual technique of splitting the narrative persona between a remembering subject immersed in the experience and a reflecting narrator, objectifying: "Such were the feasts of *my* childhood, of *Isobel's* youth."[125] Significantly, these additions were made to the final draft of the manuscript and embody the devices Thomas had learned to use in the interval before she returned to complete the novel. But the strained syntax of this sentence is unusual in a narrative which, despite its lyric circling around the emotional wounds of the past, and despite the snippets of conversation and the sometimes blunt juxtapositions, seems straightforward. Thomas' aim in this book has been to create the illusion of a present that coexists seamlessly with the past — a vision of infinity through words.

The narrator, by hovering over things, naming and cataloguing them, and building up a rich complex of minutely detailed observations, transfixes sensory experience in the more enduring patterns of language. Thomas' ability to find the precise word, brand name, or quotation from a popular magazine enables her to evoke the world of a child on the east coast of the United States in the 1940s with such power that her readers share in this associative flux that emotion recollects in tranquility. Episodes in the novel are shaped around single objects or events — houses, feasts, cemeteries — in the Proustian manner. But Isobel does more than vibrate with things to show their halo, to show the way it was. She gives evidence of her aspiration to be a writer in her love of words and her sense of their talismanic power to override her fear of death. She plays conscious memory games to fix time in its flight: "If something truly unusual happened I tried to impale the whole complex of sight/sound/touch/taste/smell on my consciousness and memory as though such an experience was like some rare and multicoloured butterfly" (p. 37).

What she conjures up and fixes in her collection is the smothering life of an unhappy family in upstate New York: the father, unsuccessful as a breadwinner and in sex; the mother, frustrated in her ambitions to power and wealth, vicariously living them out through her reluctant daughters; Jane, the sister, a shadowy companion in misery; and grandfather Harry, who radiates love from his summer cottage. In the second part, Isobel takes a job in the madhouse and asserts her independence from her cloistered family. The narrative unfolds the death of the "mind's virginity" (p. 168) and subsequently the loss of the other virginity. In the "Shit Ward" (p. 178), Isobel encounters life and death in its most grotesque forms — the amputated limb, for example, which is carried around and offered as a chicken or turkey drumstick! But she finds in the ward "a beauty and self-control that was created out of pain and ugliness and decay" (p. 224), which is an augury of the direction her creative powers will take in maturity.

This second section testifies to Thomas' increasing interest in paradox and nonsense. For one thing, the limits between sanity and madness are blurred; as Isobel comments: "In many ways it was easier for me to cope with the avowed madness of Ward 88 than the glossed-over violence of my home" (p. 169). But in the hospital, the boundaries between containers and contained are continually shifting. This paradox is reinforced by the inversion of the Blakean categories which give their titles to the two sections, for the book perversely affirms the virtue of losing Eden for the real world — of

The figure through which this aesthetic is conveyed is the circle, itself an image of paradox with its still centre and moving circumference, its boundaries delimited yet its centre expanding. It is, moreover, an ancient symbol for infinity with its end circling back on itself. Thomas invokes this figure to frame her narrative inversions, the tale within the tale within the tale which is always the same yet different from itself because of the interval between repetitions. Significantly, Thomas here undermines the aspirations of her character to give eternity to her recollections. Fixing them in words to represent them is absurd when stories do not represent anything; they merely tell the same story over and over again. Neither art nor life has any privileged status, for everything can be repeated, copied. There is no essential sign or origin. The copy or repetition is just as likely to be the copy of another work of art — even of itself in pastiche or parody, as in this self-encircling narrative — as it is to be a copy of life.

It is significant that the circular tale of the epigraph is told to Isobel and her sister, Jane, by their grandfather Harry. The tale is another of his many practical jokes, of his many punning and paradoxical signs, like the "Journey's End" sign affixed to his cottage which Thomas describes at the beginning of the novel. It is old Harry, "mythical at the top of the stairs" (p. 95), who is the prankster telling this joke, this novel. His theory of art as play ultimately shapes the aesthetic of the mature Isobel. Play, freewheeling play, as Jacques Ehrmann reminds us, is "articulation, opening . . . of and through language," its ludic function holding out the goals of true culture and civilization, freeing us from a false, systematized reading and an appropriation of a singular truth.[126] It is play which allows us to form a variety of conceptual worlds, to play the game *if . . . then* which enchants the mature Thomas. It is this magic of Harry's that Thomas endorses rather than Isobel's magical words which would transport us to some timeless, transcendent realm. She suggests that Isobel is closer to being a writer when she makes her way "through the adventures of Big C and little c" (p. 52) at age five than when she egotistically plans to immortalize herself in a novel in her freshman year at college (p. 154).

Art is ruled by the throw of the dice. Chance and subjective whim are at the root of the arbitrary names we give things, as Harry's games with words imply. Names that others have given to objects are not "real name[s]" (p. 98), and Isobel is encouraged to find her own. The writer Isobel steps into the early pages of the novel in one of her rare appearances to point out this lesson in relativity: ". . . with the accumulation of remembered summers, I grew to understand the relativity of the map . . ." (p. 15). Isobel has inherited Harry's preoccupation with signs, as her bending over the map suggests. As a child, she was fascinated by the "illustrious names" bestowed on the "prosaic towns" of upper-state New York, names like Rome, Syracuse, Ithaca, and Troy, which are traces of epic adventures (p. 13). Isobel learns to spell from them:

> Utica was one of the first words I could spell, and "U" was, for a long, long while, a magic letter.

> "U"
> Dear Harry,
>   How ar U? (p. 13)

U leads outward to Harry and to Utica; it also leads onward to Ulysses. When Isobel bends over a map with the same city names written on it in the closing pages of the narrative, it is a map of Europe she is studying while dreaming of foreign odysseys. The words are the same, the context different, as the narrative circles back on itself. The change is not so much the result of causally determined progression or growth as it is an accident of a shift in perspective.

The lovingly woven surfaces of this period piece are shown to be illusory in another way, tricks of *trompe l'oeil*. The cover photograph on the Canadian edition is described by Isobel within the text as a picture "of my sister and myself, aged five and six, in green velveteen dresses, little poke bonnets and velvet muffs" (p. 112). But it is also identified as a picture of Audrey Callahan and her sister, so that the boundaries of inner and outer, text and context, are effaced. The identification of this photograph, as well as Thomas' comments in interviews about the risk of her mother suing her for libel on the publication of this book (Appelbe, p. 34), focuses attention on the novel's autobiographical nature. There are indeed notable correspondences between incidents in this book and details about her life which Thomas has disclosed in interviews. However, the time spent on writing and rewriting is evidence of the processes of selection and arrangement, and similar processes were involved in taking the photograph: we are informed in the narrative about the trip to the hairdresser, the selection of clothes, et cetera, all preparations designed to embellish the girls' appearance. Moreover, the picture constitutes the ritual Christmas present to the joker, Harry, and so another testimony to the trickster's power. By setting a supposedly autobiographical story within the frame of the grandfather's storytelling, Thomas underlines the distancing and editing at work in this (re)presentation of memoirs. The stories of life merge with the stories of art, for both employ selection and arrangement in order to make them story, and details in a new context have a different meaning. This autobiographical input again makes fuzzy the limits of fiction as it explodes the "fictional" character.

"All my novels are one novel, in a sense," Thomas says. "Each one extends, in a different style, offering more information, from a different perspective, what is basically the same story" (Hofsess, p. 17). This is especially true of *Blown Figures* (1974), which takes Isobel Cleary back to the scene of her miscarriage in Ghana — the subject of *Mrs. Blood* — to exorcise the dead and seek expiation for her guilt. Although the story is based on the same incidents, it is conveyed through entirely new narrative sequences. We learn much more, for instance, about the breakup with Richard and the abortion Isobel had at the time. The sliding panels extend new frames and open new perspectives on material Thomas has written earlier. An episode involving the "Woolworth's ring" links her relationship with Jason to the short story "Elephants to Ride Upon" (*TGB*, pp. 115–41), allowing the novel's portrayal of the tentative relationship of two lovers about to be married to amplify the earlier story. Connections also exist with stories published later. "Joseph and His Brother,"[127] for example, reintroduces the theme of madness from demonic possession, repeating a line from *Blown Figures* about madness resulting from sexual intercourse with a ghost. But as always with motifs or sentences repeated in Thomas' work, the context changes. While the line about madness is offered as an explanation for Joseph's brother's fate after he has made love with a strange woman (*LE*, p. 30), the same line in *Blown Figures* is devoid of all context, appearing alone on an otherwise blank page.[128] It may be one of the found pieces from Isobel's African travels that she presents for her readers, one part of the carefully assembled collage that includes advice columns for the lovelorn, children's lore, and comic strips. Or it may actually be an expression of her current state of mind, her belief that she is possessed by the demons, the Obayifo. Were she an African, as she tries to be at the end, the narrative would be a religious quest, a public confession of witchcraft followed by absolution. But Isobel, Bronie woman, white North American, walks out of the ceremony of confession into the forest, fixated, totally mad, unable to relate to words in the foreign language, "damirifa, pity" (p. 545). The book ends then with five white pages, the hidden iceberg of the story.

The manipulations of text and context which these repetitions establish demand the participation of an attentive reader, who must remember, sift, compare, and contrast the occurences of a given phrase. These intratextual allusions, added to the intertextual allusions which are common in Thomas' writing, sharply increase our work as readers — we must reconstruct the story of *Blown Figures* in our own heads. As a result of this activity, a shift in horizons of perception occurs in the text. If *Mrs. Blood* is about the character's quest for signs and significance, *Blown Figures* is about the reader's quest for meaning, about an inward trip into our own minds. The journey is ours as we fabricate the connections, "make" the story, seek out the linear links between points on the journey in hopes of finding formal consolation.

The book, however, being not just about chaos but randomness itself, sets up traps for us. It literally blows our minds, dislocating the figures of order which enable us to read. Allusions to *Alice's Adventures in Wonderland* and to mirrors — of the funhouse variety (p. 141), or cracked (p. 444), or pocket-size and, hence, reductive (p. 163) — as well as comments about the indirect nature of movement — "Crabwise I come" (p. 34) — offer clues to the reader about the principles of inversion at work, of the ways in which the narrative turns back on itself, undercutting any representation of reality, any statement about truth. But the reader cannot function here as in Thomas' other work where these features are common. The ontological status of the narrative is in much greater doubt, as George Bowering suggests in his comments on the title:

What are figures, and what is blown? There are fly-blown corpses, and corpses were once figures. Craftsmen blow figure in glass. If you don't have a good figure you'd better turn off the light if you want to be blown. Bad counters blow their figures. Poets who reach for effects blow their figures up fat. Some flute players blow outlandish figures. Add your own . . . .[129]

As well, there are references in the text to blown figures "dissolving" in the heat (p. 227) and figures being "burnt to death" in bushfires (p. 228), which infuses these created figures with the idea of violent disintegration and confirms their association with the grotesque, parodic, and carnivalesque aspects of the book. Most significant, however, is Bowering's invitation to add our own interpretations of the title, for this is what Thomas' text invites us to do. It breaks down the boundaries between author and reader, teaching us how to interpret, to follow up clues when confronted with a puzzle or riddle.

The new shift in the horizons of perception which enters *Blown Figures* and expands Thomas' meditations on the relationship between illusion and reality offers a way out of the semiotic paradox of the shifting nature of the sign by insisting on the materiality of the book, underlining its antirepresentational qualities. Thomas has quite literally inverted the frames of the book, bringing the external frames — typography, paper, ink, cover — into the heart of the text, providing yet another set of directions for our reading. As we pay attention to colour and position, reading concrete prose, we are led away from the linear thrust of the sentence or paragraph towards an awareness of the iconic nature of the text. Even more disturbing to the reader, however, is finding that the centre of this activity is located, not in what Thomas writes, but in what she does not write. In the silences.

The most notable feature of the physical book is its blank pages, wherein lies the heart of its meaning. Some pages are entirely blank, as at the end, while others are only partly white, with a line, or fragment of a comic, at the top. In this way, the material nature of reading is accounted for, time being allowed for the turning of the page. One such page invites our collaboration: the sentence at the top — "Think of something God's book tells you to do. Then, in this space, draw yourself doing it" (p. 120) — is followed by blank space contained by a surrounding black frame. At its limit here, the word moves into drawing.

It is in another art, music, that we find an account of the nature of these pauses, which are as significant as notes sounded. As John

Cage has shown, there is no such thing as silence. When we stop talking, the noises of the ambient world enter and we hear the sound of our own nervous system functioning and of our blood circulating. Similarly, while reading *Blown Figures*, we hear our own replies to Isobel, our thinking and reading between the lines. As well, fragments of our experience are dredged up to fill in the blanks. The reader's experience is implicated in any act of reading, since communication is based on an interpretive community with shared values, but it is not always openly acknowledged and called into play. Thomas recognizes the presence of her readers and actively draws us into the game she is playing, game foregrounded through the continual allusions to children's games and the more sinister adult ones at border crossings (p. 166). Just as we question the reality of Isobel's journey to Africa — is this dark continent a dream, a hallucination, or a metaphor? — so too we reflect on our experience of reading the book. Is the blown figure composed of our reverie, or is it a metaphor for chaos? Or is it all these at once?

Part of the problem for the reader is the status of the narrator, a continually shifting figure who addresses the reader in a variety of ways, involving different kinds of interaction. The inner frames of the book — the several dedications and the epigraph — set up contradictory directives like a magician creating an illusion through misdirection. Along with the list of her children and her women friends to whom Thomas has dedicated her book, we find the sentence "To all the Alice's, whatever your mothers called you," a dedication to a character created by Lewis Carroll but who also comes into Thomas' book. Notions of reality are confused here when the word can enfold within the text both "historical" beings and fictional beings. Moreover, the inside and outside of the text are blurred, and our author becomes as amorphous as this Alice. She is like Isobel, identifying with Alice in the fiction, continually "dissolving" a part of herself, losing contact with her arms or her body.

The creation of an illusory world which represents something is further undermined by the second dedication, "to Isobel," which suggests that she is not just a fictional construct but a real person. As the dedication to Isobel continues, inner and outer are further merged when the implied author writes: ". . . because you are fond of fairy tales, . . . I have made you a story all for yourself — a new one that nobody has read before." Indeed, throughout the inner story, Isobel is obsessed with fairy tales, identifying with their characters, attributing her predicament to the fact that she has never been assertive as a person but has for too long modelled herself on the passive princess of the fairy tale, waiting for someone else to rescue her. By implication, then, Isobel has no reality outside the story. Story is the only reality; fictions are all we can know, being essentially about themselves.[130]

The epigraph opens up a third frame of perception by implying that the metaphorical and hence literary nature of experience is the only reality language can express. It is a quotation from Sir Thomas Browne's *Religio Medici*: "We have all Africa and her prodigies / Within us." However, the nature of this "within" can range from the organization of mental operations to the welling up of the subconscious. As in her other books, Thomas plays here with the shifting nature of the boundary between sanity and insanity and conveys this through a mobile narrative perspective.

The position of the implied author in this text is a complex one, impossible to pin down. At times, she is identified with Isobel, offering us the contents of Isobel's mind directly in the collage of found pieces which increasingly take over the narrative as each of the twenty-four (epic framework) chapters ever more rapidly breaks down into fragments. Yet it is here that the reader is most actively involved as cocreator of the text, for we are given only the raw material on which Isobel's mind is working, not a description of its operations, and we can read and interpret the pieces along with her. Potentially, implied author, character, and implied reader merge here. Yet at other points, we are aware of the implied author as puppet master, God controlling the character, standing outside her. The opening paragraph alerts us to this. Isobel cannot read the sleeves of the ship's officers, and her blindness contrasts with the implied author's omniscience. In the sentence "Consider Isobel, leaning over the railing on the promenade deck of the HMS *Pylades*" (p. 11), we are invited to stand aside with the implied author and observe Isobel's actions. Elsewhere we are invited to berate her: Isobel is a "fool" we are informed, by "I who fit you [i.e., Isobel] together" (p. 218). But there is another story unfolding, that of the implied author and her varied relations with Miss Miller. At times, the two are distant, the implied author imagining herself as a child, asking for a lullaby from Miss Miller (p. 365), or expressing her fear that she will die and Miss Miller "will eat [her] up" (p. 542). At other times, even while apostrophizing, the implied author and Miss Miller are conflated into one grammatical entity, "we," who is manipulating Isobel:

> Before us, Miss Miller, we have four objects:
> A painted woman reading a real newspaper
> A real woman reading a painted newspaper
> A painted woman reading a painted newspaper
> A real woman reading — ah, you guessed it! The point is
> not which is which but does it really matter? (p. 221)

Indeed, this is the question Thomas' book raises. What is reality, what fiction? Given these differing levels of reality, does it matter if we distinguish between them? All are expressed in words, as symbols, though their ontological status varies. The relationship between illusion and reality is complex, impossible to pin down to a one to one. Everything depends on the viewer's perspective. The novel leaves us in continuous motion, settling on no fixed meaning. On one level of reality, Miss Miller is just a name and seems eventually to merge with the reader through the narration in the vocative, an intimate relationship that is established also through the blank pages, part of the leitmotif of the act of reading making us aware that we are learning to read, to interpret. The openness of form invites many possible readings, and the baroque architecture opens perspectives to infinity. As the creative act takes place in our minds, we descend into hell along with Isobel. Like her and the implied author, we may well become lost in the labyrinth, changing our direction constantly as our expectations drift. The blown figures may well be we, the readers.

However, if Miss Miller becomes more than the confidante, the listener, burdened with some guilty mariner's story, and more than the Jamesian *ficelle* which serves to draw out the narrative, then the book may also be read in another way. Miss Miller's name alludes to James's Daisy Miller, an appropriate analogue for Isobel in her destructive innocence, entering into collision with foreign cultures, addressing thus the "reality" of literary tradition. There is another Miss Miller who may also be invoked, one of Jung's patients, an American from New York who had travelled much through Europe and Africa, a person of unusual capacity for identification and empathy, whose amnesiac fantasies Jung wrote up in *Symbols of*

Transformation.[131] For Jung, Miss Miller is "shadowy," a "phantom" whom he allows just enough life to reveal some of the secrets of the inner life. In turn she is transformed into a fantastic creation by Thomas and Isobel. Isobel sees her as "something in my dream" (p. 297) and ultimately follows her into a schizophrenic state.

Miss Miller, then, is something more than a name, something more than the "you" with whom the reader identifies. Someone whose wanderings have been analysed, she becomes the symbol of that analysing and organizing force taking over Isobel's experience and turning it into narrative. Miss Miller's role in the narrative is similar to that of the title character in Jacques Ferron's novel *Papa Boss*, the story of the dispossession of a heroine by the diabolically omnipotent narrator whose use of the vocative in his fable is the web of his enchantment. But the relationships of author and character are more complex in Thomas' book, both being related to analysis and travelling, to order and insanity. Ultimately the narrative breaks off with Isobel's appeal to Miss Miller, "NO MORE TWIST" (p. 545), no more thread. This is a story about the miscarriage of creation.

In Thomas' earlier fiction, we become aware of the guilty compulsion to tell which animates her storytellers. In *Blown Figures*, she makes a detailed analysis of the role of the listener in bringing this story into being. It must be heard, be understood, be made concrete, or there is no message, no meaning. Thomas' narrative, moreover, exemplifies Roman Jakobson's description of second-person literature:

> Epic poetry, focused on the third person, strongly involves the referential function of language; the lyric, oriented toward the first person, is intimately linked with the emotive function; poetry of the second person is imbued with the conative function and is either supplicatory or exhortative, depending on whether the first person is subordinated to the second one or the second to the first.[132]

Blown Figures is supplicatory, as first Miss Miller, then the reader, is the author(ity) calling the narrative into being.

Through this narrative perspective, a form of collusion is sustained between author and reader, a wink exchanged, which cues us in to the fact that we are participating together in a fabrication, in an illusion. The word *illusion* comes from the latin word *illudere* meaning, literally, in play. And through these cues addressed to the reader, Thomas has sent the message "this is play." Play is of course beautiful, enchanting. It is order, establishing a self-contained space with its own arbitrary rules. Its action begins and ends in itself, in no way contributing to the movement of life beyond its frame. A paradox is thus established, for the statement "this is play" may be expanded to say something like: "These actions in which we now engage do not denote what those actions *for which they stand* would denote."[133] By analogy, this describes the paradoxical relationship language bears to the object it denotes.

Blown Figures thus extends the analysis of the ludic function of literature from *Songs My Mother Taught Me*. The book is labyrinth or puzzle, fully engaging us in the quest for its ordering principles. It also evokes the sacred riddle or contest or the sophist dialogue based on the catch-question. Epistemology has the appearance of a game. These forms of dialogue are to be found in the enigmatic exchanges of Isobel and Miss Miller, and beyond that in those of psychoanalyst and patient. There is more than a hint that Isobel never made it to Africa but stayed in London to "go inward" with R. D. Laing (p. 14). Likewise, we are part of a game: "we are all the White Queen's Pawns" (p. 126). Such verbal exchanges are the modern world's litanies and catechisms through which we verge on the profundities of cosmology. Once they were linked with ritual, with play in action, with drama. But for Isobel, words, stories, and literature do not have the sacred function of play anymore, even though Thomas offers this to her readers. Isobel finds nothing to uplift her when she stays at the monastery and seeks to renew herself, to align herself with the cosmic order. She then tries to do so through African rituals. While Isobel's success in this endeavour is uncertain — do those blank pages mean fullness of experience, the ineffable, or do they mean naught? — Thomas' narrative, through its accentuation of its fictionality, its feigning, reproduces the ancient formulas of ritual storytellers. Like the storyteller in the book, Thomas marks off the sacred narrative space beyond the boundaries of life, proclaiming: "A tale, a tale. Let it go and let it return. This is a story about a man and a woman. A story a story. Let it go. Let it come" (p. 169).

The stories in Thomas' second collection, *Ladies and Escorts* (1977), are coextensive with earlier periods of her writing so that readers may have trouble remembering in which volume they belong. The African and Mexican stories in this collection — "Joseph and His Brother" (*LE*, pp. 19–30), "Two in the Bush" (*LE*, pp. 44–70), "Rapunzel" (*LE*, pp. 71–80), "A Monday Dream at Alameda Park" (*LE*, pp. 116–31), and "The More Little Mummy in the World" (*LE*, pp. 132–46) — focus on the violent conflicts of cultures. Other stories, such as "Kill Day on the Government Wharf" (*LE*, pp. 31–43), "Three Women and Two Men" (*LE*, pp. 147–59), and "Aquarius" (*LE*, pp. 5–18), work with issues raised in *Munchmeyer and Prospero on the Island*, exposing the fake pastoralism of the hippy retreat to the islands and exploring the relationships between the quality of an artist's life and of his or her creations. This latter theme is most developed in "Initram" (*LE*, pp. 88–107), which focuses on the relationship between creator and subject.

This is of interest also in "Tear Here" (*LE*, pp. 108–15), a story about an old woman who collects supermarket bags then puts one over her head and smothers herself. In this story, attention is deflected from the action itself to the problems encountered in writing about such a totally isolated figure. Her motives can never be known because nobody has talked to her or observed her carefully enough. "We have no real way of knowing, for she does not appear to have had any friend, male or female, or even any acquaintance, any sort of confidante, (so useful in stories of this sort) . . ." (p. 108). The narrator refuses to abrogate the prerogatives of divine omniscience here, to read into the woman's mind; instead, she builds up the narrative through negatives which recite its inability to come into being. Rudy Wiebe has used such a technique of negation to write a poignant lament for Almighty Voice, but Thomas' prosaic narrative details — plastic bags, supermarket line-ups — do not present the same potential for archetypal symbolization and meaning despite the paradoxical denial of meaning. In her story, the narrative indirection ultimately leaves us as puzzled about and as separated from this anonymous woman's tragedy as the unperceiving clerks. We have no privileged insight: it is difficult to know another person.

The stories in this collection expand on a theme and a symbol from *Blown Figures*: "The blood which links all women was linking them now; it was not a question of a cut head now . . ." (*Blown Figures*, p. 479). The blood which flows in Thomas' African writing creates a sort of Lawrentian blood bond; it evokes the "real" African primal cultural roots, or origins, of humanity which so many of her characters seek. While Thomas works to demystify this quest for an instinctive, uninhibited life, it is nonetheless the fascination with the latent savagery of the primitive life which affects us as readers. This refuge in a preverbal origin, in a "visceral imagination," underlines language's inadequacy, its distortions of the nonverbal.

A number of stories in this collection offer an ironic perspective on this romantic worship of primitive strength and energy, presenting the clash of overly idealistic Europeans with the violence of African, Mexican, or North American Indian cultures. While these stories debunk idealism, they do nothing to diminish the emotional intensity in these primitive communities. For a white tourist to ignore this reality would be dangerous, as the narrator of "Two in the Bush" suggests:

> Perhaps I would end up a headless corpse in the lagoon. That such things didn't happen was nonsense. The veneer of civilization is never more than a few inches thick. Jimmy Owusu-Banahene had told me about the murder of the new secretary of the town council six months before (he'd been stealing funds). Found with a nail driven through his head. (*LE*, p. 65)

The fun of this particular story derives from the two women treating the warnings as "nonsense" and making their way through a world of intrigue, gun running, prostitution, graft, and corruption as though all were a game. However, a similar attempt by Caroline, the North American girl in "Rapunzel," to treat Africa from an aesthetic perspective — to draw and write it up as a means of enlarging her artistic awareness — ends in nonsense, which is tragedy because it suggests the complete breakdown of the personality, not the comic state where nothing is what it seems to be.

In its opening vignette, the story establishes a tension between images of paradise and of violence, while it depicts the self-absorption of the white girl, blind like so many Thomas protagonists. The fairy-tale allusion underlines her naïveté, her distance from "reality." She is "a dream within a dream" (*LE*, p. 72), dreaming her way across Africa with her mirror and notebook for companions. The narrative unfolds as a story within a story within a story. It is being told by someone else who is travelling, who has come from London and encountered Caroline along the way, giving her some addresses. Caroline turns up at one of them to meet the narrator, carrying her notebook in which she has written snippets from her travels in mirror writing. The reproductions of these entries in the notebook introduces the graphic element of *Blown Figures* into *Ladies and Escorts*, and here too we are invited to read iconically, paying attention to the visual component of the sign.

Caroline moves into the university residence on the eighth floor, high above the men's dorm. But one night an African enters by the balcony and threatens to rape her. She flees down the stairs and prepares to leave the city, seemingly unmoved by the event. We find out what happened from her notebook mirror writings which she leaves with the narrator, who holds them up to the mirror and we read, inverted, that the intruder asked Caroline why she came to Africa and, not satisfied with her answer, "for the art here" (*LE*, p. 80), demanded her total commitment to die here or have sex with him. The narrative ends on a series of visual puns constructed through the mirror. In response to his repeated statement "Are you ready for me?" Caroline answers "no" several times, then "NONONONONO" (p. 80). We are reading the page in the mirror, so we see it right way round, but as printed this word reads "ONONONONON," a positive response, rather than the intended negative. The confusion in her thinking which this suggests is borne out in the subsequent and final reply, written for us as "ƨɘY" (*LE*, p. 80), which reads like "sex," sign of Caroline's complicity. Outwardly Caroline seems unchanged by the experience, but her notebook suggests the confusion and alienation which has resulted from her encounter with the emotional crucible which is Africa. But this is also male violence against a female, rape, the most extreme form of opposition between men and women.

In several other stories in this book, including "Kill Day on the Government Wharf," the encounter of mind-bound Anglo-Saxon and violent primitive society is related to the war between the sexes. Here we first see clearly what Thomas meant when she said that she writes "to demonstrate the terrible gap between men and women" and "to show how we all delude one another" (Coupey et al., p. 98). These statements follow upon an explanation of "A Monday Dream at Alameda Park," a story in which Thomas exposes the masks and disguises worn by a middle-aged professor who has belatedly discovered his body and is now trying to keep up with a vital, young second wife. This story, and "Aquarius," about a failed writer married to a woman who admires excellence and vitality, both show this gap from the male perspective. Vibrant female sexuality seems, from the men's point of view, as threatening as the powerful energy of Skana, the killer whale, by which the writer in "Aquarius" has been thrilled and has envied for a moment. Erica, his wife, married him on the strength of a book of poems. Now he is a professor, while her storytelling about the events of their lives has become their major artistic activity. To him she embodies the fierceness of the Valkyries, while he is feminized in his weakness. This type of "reversal," which he describes in their relationship as "ugly, unnatural" (*LE*, p. 17), is the dramatic fulcrum of many of Thomas' stories: servants and mistresses, men and women, the young and the old (with respect to wisdom in "A Monday Dream at Alameda Park") all exchange places.

In "Green Stakes for the Garden" (*LE*, pp. 81–87), a story which deals with an older woman seducing a younger man in a carefully staged scene whose resonant symbolic dimensions are worthy of a Henry James or a Virginia Woolf, the mood is interrupted by someone who comes and demands to work in the garden. His threat of service is made to a woman lying prone in her garden chair. Such inversions are, of course, announced by the book's title, *Ladies and Escorts*, which puts the ladies first and the men in the subordinate position of merely accompanying them. The realities of the taverns or beer parlours where such signs are to be found are quite opposite: taverns are a man's world. The title's allusion to such places maintains from the first collection the overtones of swapping yarns over the bottle. All the more significant then is the invasion of this territory. Equally so is women's invasion of the field of writing, as the dedication makes clear. Thomas, the woman author, echoes the words of Baudelaire and Eliot, "mon semblable, mon frère," but follows these with "mon amour" (n. pag.) to mark the difference in the relationships of men to men and women to men. Lurking beneath this amiable surface, however, is the invective of the additional phrase in the original quotation, "hypocrite lecteur." Not only characters are involved in the process of deluding each other, projecting their fictions of others, but writer and reader are also involved in such games.

The most extended analysis of these complex maskings occurs in "Initram," whose title comes from a sign in one of the slides which Tony shows backwards, provoking a scolding from his estranged wife, Lydia, who seems to be under the spell of the myth of male practical competence. In turn this is associated with a story the beekeeper, present at the same "party," tells about the queen bee's nuptial flight, focusing on the destruction of her rivals and of the drones. Through cumulation, this sign is associated with the inversion of the sexes in patriarchal society and with the revenge of the colonized. More generally, however, it relates to the nonreferential status of the sign, which Thomas explores in detail in this story about storytelling, about *illudere* and *deludere*.

"Initram," which follows immediately after "Green Stakes for the Garden," begins by undermining the illusions created in the preceding story by offering five different versions of what the man was doing intruding in the garden, each prefaced by an assertion of its truth. The ontological status of the explanations varies as widely as the "painted/real" women seen by Isobel in *Blown Figures*, ranging as they do from the events being "read" in a friend's manuscript, to the man being "thought" to be there, to the narrator's inability to describe him since she was overcome by shame (p. 88). With so many different versions of the story to choose from, the burden of interpretation is placed on the reader. But by placing this material after the story, Thomas has created a catch-tale, a practical joke, like a magician enchanting us with her illusion. This assertion of the instability of the meaning of a story comes at the beginning of "Initram," forewarning us of the fact that we are also going to encounter multiple versions of this story.

"Initram" involves two women writers getting together to discuss their broken marriages. As the narrator informs us, she calls the other writer, Lydia, because she needs "a wider audience, an audience that would understand and accept [her] *exaggerations* for what they were" (*LE*, p. 89; emphasis added). As she arrives for the visit, she envisions discussion about Woolf, Proust, and the diaries of Anaïs Nin. In front of the large "mock-tudor" residence (p. 89), she remembers a soap opera from her childhood about a poor, country girl finding happiness in marriage to a rich man. Thomas' story as it unfolds is closer to the soap opera than it is to Woolf, though we are dealing here with many layers of masks all claiming to be true, the type of narrative in which Nin delights. In fact the narrator is unable to tell her story of separation because she enters into the drama of the life of Lydia, who is also currently separated from her husband — or at least she claims to be. Lydia goes through a ritual of pretence, arriving each night in the house to cook supper, organizing a party, and even sleeping in the house, her noisy love-making being experienced by the narrator as "the last line in the last paragraph of the story she'd been writing all evening" (p. 106). The doubt that hangs over the question of whether Lydia is separated or not also lingers over the question of whose story this is, since the narrative includes so many other stories embedded within it. When the narrator tells Lydia that she is thinking about writing this story, Lydia chooses this name for the character she is to play and suggests that the proposed title of "Chicken Wings" (*LE*, p. 107) be changed, as indeed it is. Is this the story Lydia composed? What exactly is the relationship between author and character when both are authors?

The mirror relationship of the two is accentuated here by the fact that both have published a book of stories and both publish a novel the same year, both have three daughters and both have participated at readings together. Indeed, one of these readings brings forth a story which is about the story of the creation of the story we are reading, an event when Lydia was too scared to read and someone else read her story:

> For there was Lydia's story, unrolling out of the mouth of another woman (whose story it was not), and there was the author herself sitting like an abandoned doll, on the floor beside the reader. The audience loved it and sent out sympathetic vibrations to her. I thought it was a con. And almost said to her, "Lydia, I think that was a very clever con," but didn't because I realized that maybe I wished I had thought of it first and why not store it away for some future date — it was a nice piece of dramatic business. (p. 92)

What we have here is a description of the recursive mechanism of this story, though as usual Thomas has not just given us Lydia's story through her narrator's voice, but has projected the narrator's story into the character of Lydia, so that mask and story are mirror matches and reversible — "Initram."

The relationship between character and author is further complicated by the autobiographical transparency of the story and by the reader's easy detection of the writer Alice Munro in the character Lydia. Our sympathy as audience is directed at both figures because of the way in which the story winks at us, signals its status as "con," and involves us in complicity as participants in the deception. It does so in ways similar to *Blown Figures*, though the frame it creates around the space of its narration is not that of playing, but that of lying. Fittingly in a story involving Munro, Thomas exposes her own obsession with paradox. Here the story is framed by the liar's paradox which appears at both the beginning and the end. The narrator commences: "Writers are terrible liars. There are nicer names for it, of course, but liars will do. They take a small incident and blow it up, like a balloon . . ." (p. 88). But then, as the stories in this collection show, people are always deluding themselves or each other. Thomas points out the impossibility of ever arriving at truth by way of representation, one thing standing for another. The word is a lie because it is different from speech, and speech though intimate with the body and breath, also distorts the nonverbal.

The introduction of the liar's paradox — the paradox of Epimenides as it is called — leads us directly into the world of *Latakia* (1979), where it is also found, both in its classical form — "All Cretans are liars" — and in its strong form: "'Michael, I love you.' It was a lie when I said it and yet as soon as I said it, it was true."[134] Such a sentence rudely violates the usually assumed dichotomy of statements into true and false. An additional twist occurs when one thinks of the functions of this sentence and the implicit assumption that its metalinguistic or self-referential element is on a higher level than the referential element. This is palpably impossible since both are communicated in the same sentence, in the same words. The sentence is thus self-contradictory, a transgression of reason. In *Latakia* Thomas explores the non-sense stemming from this paradox in language, even as in her earlier work she explored the nonsense of play, whose signalling of itself as play operates in a similar tension of metalinguistic and referential elements.

Latakia is, above all, a fiction about the difficulties of communicating through language, especially the impossibility of exchanges between men and women because of the paradoxical status of their relationships. This is clear when Rachel, the narrator of *Latakia*, rewrites Epimenides:

> I HATE YOU
> I LOVE YOU
>
> ———————————
>
> EVERYTHING ABOVE THIS
> LINE IS TRUE

(p. 29)

Along with her repeated statements about lying to Michael, this effectively renders meaningless the love letter she is writing to him in Africa from the top of her house in Crete where he has left her. This is the "longest love letter in the world" (p. 21) at two hundred pages, but paradoxically it is a hate letter too, proof of the verity of its final sentence: ". . . the best *revenge* is writing well" (p. 172; emphasis added). As well as expressing these conflicting emotions, *Latakia* explores the deceptions of language, the slippage which occurs when sensation is translated into speech, which is in turn betrayed by written language. This is dramatized in the wonderful moments of wordless communication between Rachel and her Cretan landlady, Heleni, and in other exchanges, at cross purposes, provoked by the foreign setting. The deceptions of language are also the focus of many comments by Rachel regarding her frustrations with the pen as recording instrument. This concern with the problematic relationship of language to reality and sound to sign is adumbrated in the epigraphs, which refer us variously to rules for making aural sounds coincide with visual signs,[135] to the confusing and comic multiplicity of expressions which refer to a single experience,[136] and to the primacy of sound as origin:

Epigraph 1:

No matter how we write the word *man*, whether in small letters or large, it never looks like a man, but when we read or pronounce the word, then the word *man* comes out. (n. pag.)

Here Thomas reveals her participation, along with many writers of her generation, in a dream of an Adamic language which, through the essential connection of spoken word and thing, would reinvest words with divine ancestry and power. Yet she realizes that this is dream and thus opens herself to despair at the actual separation of word and world. She sees the word as a screen which filters the world out.

The publisher's note on the back cover informs us that *Latakia* is an anti-love story, the post-mortem of a passionate affair which has involved an experiment in new social structures through a *ménage à trois*. In epistolary form, it presents the relentless analysis by Rachel, the author of four novels, of her relationship with Michael, another writer, who is eight years her junior. The third figure in this classical triangle is Hester, wife of Michael, who has neglected her career as a painter in order to give him her full attention. From Michael's perspective, however, the third angle is created by Rachel's three daughters, who are always present in her mind, and frequently in their life. Thomas paints some fine scenes of domestic discord, with vividly rendered dialogue, including fights over cleaning the toilet or cooking the food, tasks that Michael does poorly or refuses to do, demanding instead to be served — or "mothered," as Rachel insists. Indeed, so egotistical, so phallocratic is Michael as she portrays him that many readers wonder why she stays with him at all. But Rachel's behaviour is evidence of the love-hate contradiction: while her rational self is continually breaking with him, asserting independence, her body remains in subjection to him. In *Latakia* Thomas extends the range of her exploration of the body, moving from the gynecology in her earlier novels to sexual desire (though there is a sound depiction of premenstrual tension here). Each time Rachel and Michael argue, the enmity of discord is melted in the forge of passion which holds Rachel in thrall. As she suggests, Michael has given her body back to her, made her bloom again. While it is "just sex" (p. 20), as she reminds Michael, to be "physically . . . absolutely perfect mates" is "a pretty big thing" (p. 20). Their "flesh smoked" (p. 24), their "bodies cried out to another" (p. 20): they are in the grip of that most elemental force — the erotic.

In writing this tirade, Rachel incorporates material from her journal and the dream book she has been keeping, and she meanders through several narrative tenses, sketching in details of the history of their relationship from its beginning in a writing seminar. She indulges in her compulsion to "analyz[e] things to death" (p. 23) and comments about her writing, speculating on how she would develop the character Michael "if [she] were to write a novel about [him]" (p. 122). Rachel circles backward and forward, her thoughts and feelings recorded in a veritable labyrinth.[137] These are notes towards a novel, rather than the finished object itself. The threads of explanation are left untied. Rachel observes its dissolution: "The book I am working on now is about you and me (of course) — or it started out that way. . . . But there's Crete and this village and this street and all that seems much more interesting than the story of how I fell in love with you . . ." (p. 30).

The back cover of the book informs us that this is also a travelogue. For the journey — from North America to the Mediterranean as far as Latakia in Syria, back westward to Crete, then to Athens where the lovers separate — is developed in greater amplitude than in Thomas' other books, where her landscapes are almost entirely metaphorical. Indeed, one of the ironies of the book is Michael's observation that Rachel's novels are "absolutely self-centred" — ". . . that's one of their great strengths," he says (p. 118) — while Rachel herself comments on the way Crete is taking over the book she set out to write:

> Sometimes I feel like one of those Impressionist painters who cheerfully sacrificed the subject, as subject, to a study of the changing effects of light. Lovers in a landscape, perhaps, but the lovers are just part of the landscape — they are shape, tone, movement (or lack of it), not STORY. (p. 30)

Yet the narrative remains poised on the tightrope between "capturing the essence of a place" (p. 61), as travel writers like Graham Greene have done, with the "artist as transporter," as "magic carpet" (p. 61), and reducing everything to "material" (p. 109), as when dialogues with Michael and others are recorded as monologues. Rachel struggles with the traps of language, aware of literature's failure to touch reality. "I want a palette, not a pen," she writes, contrasting the sister arts of painting and writing, as Thomas did earlier in *Prospero on the Island*. "I have to say that such and such is 'like' something else — I have to take the long way around when what I *really* want to do is dip my brush directly into the ocean, the sky, the sun . . ." (p. 61). The stumbling block is metaphor. The writer must work hard to convince us of the reality of sensations which remain merely verbal constructions; the writer must make the reader "believe in the Emperor's New Clothes" (p. 124). Yet language is metaphoric. Here the private metaphors of labyrinth and Latakia refuse to transport the reader.

Thomas places the issue of "travelogue = exterior reality," "journey = private emotion" in two other contexts: a discussion of the differences between men's and women's writing, and a reflection on the arbitrariness of the linguistic sign. The latter is summed up by the city of Latakia, which becomes a private symbol for the wealth of chaotic experience which cannot be contained by language. More specifically, it is a port in Syria where the freighter which has brought Rachel and Michael from North America makes its final stop before Greece. Within this fiction, the stay in Latakia is the final episode of the narration, though it has occurred early in their travels. Latakia is in Asia, and the narrator's encounter with this Other, as with Africa in *Blown Figures*, results in the destruction of forms, a breakdown in communication caused by the gap between symbol and reality. Throughout Rachel's journey, the reader is prepared for this collapse by the language play in the text, the interjection of words in Spanish, German, and especially Greek, with its visually strange alphabet, which are interpretive puzzles for us. As Rachel writes to Michael (incidentally uniting two concerns — the problematic relationship of the sexes and the questionable status of language): ". . . you really rode your pony out into 'the Other' — me, as well as Greece and Africa" (p. 80). Their ultimate encounter with the Other occurs when they disembark in Syria and get lost, being rescued finally by an English-speaking businessman who punningly defines himself (and their experience and the book) as "Syrious" (p. 171).

When the writers leave the freighter in Latakia, they enter a confusing world where they do not speak the language and cannot even sound out the symbols of the Arabic script. "This stuff looked like decoration" (p. 169). They have relied on phonetic alphabets in a Western tradition, which prove increasingly unreliable as Thomas' macaronic translations of Greek, "Ελλάς" as "Alas" (p. 135), make clear. When they go to the temple of Baal outside the city, they see the most ancient alphabet in the world, the cuneiform Ugaritic alphabet, which is composed of lines and triangles, betraying nothing of the spoken language in their shape. This visit provokes a crisis for Rachel. She realizes that although, as rational beings, they are system makers, inventing alphabets and languages to make things clear, ". . . it doesn't really help": "Once you get beyond the letters into words, into emotions and ideas, it doesn't help at all" (p. 171). Communication is no clearer for all this effort: it still occurs mainly through "gestures and grunts" (p. 171). Throughout the book, this pressure of sensation on language is explored. Rachel advocates an "aesthetics of the flesh" (p. 171) which would inscribe sensation rather than translate it.

Rachel's "aesthetics of the flesh," her "archeology" (p. 171), which contains Michael, is of course a female aesthetic. Thomas explores some of the purported differences between men's and women's writing. Rachel suggests that for Michael, writing is an intellectual exercise, while she "write[s] with [her] whole body" (p. 124). He considers writing to be a "craft" and talks about the "arrangements" he is making (p. 123), while she refuses to consider such formal issues in an abstract way, preferring to "make" writing as one would make love. Michael, incidentally, takes umbrage at any criticism of his gestures in making love, protesting against criticism of his "technique" (p. 63). Rachel tells Michael: ". . . I don't worry as much about 'arrangements' as you do. This may be sheer laziness on my part or just greater faith in the material, that 'negative capability' idea" (p. 124). For her, the "material dictates the form" (p. 124). Later, this contrast is developed into a generalization about men setting their stories clearly in a historical framework of fairly large proportions, whereas women do not (p. 133). Thomas' novel appears to exemplify this distinction, meandering as it does through Rachel's reflections on the relationship. But the backdrop does intrude, and its historical dimension is everywhere present.

The "arrangements" present in *Latakia* are the by now familiar archetypes, although here they are explicitly female archetypes. As Rachel and Michael journey into the Mediterranean region, they move into the home territory of the Great Mother religion, and there are innumerable allusions to this archaeological past. "Archeology," Rachel writes, can only lead to the goddess, for "in the beginning Europe had no gods, only goddesses" (p. 49). In Rome, tensions between ancient and new views of women are evident. Stamps from the Vatican show a group of women sitting at the feet of Jesus, out of keeping with the celebrations for International Women's Year. In Athens, Pallas Athena's city, on Christmas day, Rachel is worried she is pregnant; her continual preoccupation with children — Rachel mourns for her children who were not — leads her to create them in her imagination. It is here, too, that the end of her affair with Michael occurs when she moves out, resulting in that unity of one, the unqualified self-possession that constitutes the new feminist romance as Quigley identifies it. Indeed, the main change which occurs in Rachel is a new recognition of her strength (p. 44). It is on the island of Crete, birthplace of goddess worship in Greece — the snake goddess at Herakleion — that Rachel writes her book under the protection of "Woman as Guardian of Culture" (p. 55). Her activity is like the weaving of the Cretan women who use their whole bodies at their large looms. And while they work, they are "talking talking talking": "The history of the street, too, is being spun, embroidered, wound by these same women" (p. 55). This women's culture is essentially oral and material, a product of their bodies. Just as they "spin" yarns, their weaving — *texere* — produces texts. Rachel is accepted into this community of creative women "because [she is] a 'mother' and the arrival of [her] daughters has become a great event" (p. 55).

On Crete is the city of Knossos, site of the labyrinth purportedly built by Daedalus for King Minos. The maze becomes a concrete metaphor for the labyrinthine structures Thomas has favoured in other novels. More specifically, it is a metaphor for a ritual dance: "A labyrinth, a maze, may possibly be a dance . . . , a ritual performed by chosen youths and maidens" (p. 104). "Was that what we were doing, the oldest dance in the world?" Rachel asks (p. 44). All threads lead to the labyrinth's centre where the minotaur is, that half-man, half-animal figure who is the symbol of the erotic dimension of love, and the fruit of the union of Pasiphaë and the bull. He is also a representation of the horned god, attendant of the Moon Goddess. Rachel and Michael are ritually reenacting this hierogamous union, as the narrative points out at various times. Michael's "cock and bull story" (p. 39) underlines his role in the ritual, as does the photograph of the two of them sitting "between the sacred bull's horns at Knossos" (p. 127). By casting aside her rational objections and entering into the cosmic dance with Michael, Rachel is empowered as a creator. By entering the labyrinth with him, she has been given back her self. Traditionally the maze guarded the entrance to the cave which was the way into Mother Earth. Here one is not lost but enters into the fullness of wisdom of the sacred Mother. At the centre of the maze, the seeker finds rebirth, often symbolized as a maiden.[138] Rachel, significantly, emerges from her Cretan experience alone and in full possession of her creative powers. By inscribing the rhythms of the labyrinth into her prose, Thomas has shown what it would be like, a writing of the female body, whose absence from literature has long been noted by a gap or hole left in meaning. "*Anon* was probably a woman," Thomas quotes Woolf (p. 47). Unlike the "legal fictions" which are the creations of paternity, as Joyce would have it, this fiction from the body of the mother remains within the private realm, in its grunts and chaos, a veritable "Latakia."

The title for Thomas' collection of stories *Real Mothers* (1981) comes from a line in *Latakia* — "... I didn't measure up to their ideal. Real mothers weren't supposed to have obsessions like writing or separate identities" (p. 51) — emphasizing the close connection between the two books, especially with respect to the linguistic slippage of meaning between men and women. Some stories deal with the creative endeavours of both partners in a relationship; others show women's revolt against myths or conventions circumscribing their lives and language. Like *Latakia* these stories are labyrinthine, though Thomas does not use typographical devices to mark the narrative divisions, not even lines as between sections of *Latakia*. This hints at a change in the direction of Thomas' work, away from visual play towards a new focus on the narrating voice.

Thomas offers her habitual play on the duplicity, the multiplicity, of language, its paradoxes and overlays opening up the space of the book and demanding an active reader to work at its meaning. The story is not in the words but in the spaces between and around them, in the play between text and context. This strategy is announced in the epigraph to "Galatea," quoted from a work on the Impressionists: "A picture must be built up by means of rhythm, calculation and selection" (*RM*, p. 35). Thomas' stories evolve through such modulation, plane grafted onto plane, perspective piled onto perspective. Much of the rich complexity, as well as the surprise, develops from the sudden shifts between perspectives — between the child's story and the mother's in "Real Mothers" (*RM*, pp. 9–22), between the husband's story of his life and the wife's in "Galatea":

> Two swans went down the river, but only one came back. The phrase kept repeating itself, over and over, the opening sentence of a fairytale or the beginning of some problem in algebra: Swan A and Swan B, moving at different speeds. (*RM*, p. 35)

Thomas' stories oscillate between these modes — between the fantastic world of the tale and a pattern of infinite regress which undercuts it.

In "Crossing the Rubicon" (*RM*, pp. 155–68), there are many levels of narrative: the story the narrator is trying to write in a self-reflexive narrative is enfolded within the story of her own life evoked through childhood memories, which are counterpointed against stories of her daughter's life and against the present interaction with the daughter, as they bake cupcakes. The first two levels focus on the breakup of a love affair, but while the self-reflexive narrative is projected into the future tense, the narrator must contend with the weight of recollected trivia from her "ragbag of a mind" (*RM*, p. 155). In the story being composed, the woman doesn't look back when she says good-bye to her lover. However, the story we actually read is about Lot's wife and the function of memory.

Characteristically, clashes between perspectives are signalled by disjunctions in language. In Montreal, where the affair ends, the sign "Arretez" (*RM*, p. 168) is ignored by the woman, who runs into the road. Other abrupt switches into a foreign language underline the difficulties of comprehension between individuals: "PAIN DORE. 'Golden pain' is the first thing that comes to her; then 'golden bread.' She stops to look it up. 'Canada: Pain doré. France: pain perdu. French Toast'" (*RM*, p. 162). Even within the French language there is no agreement: golden bread wars with lost bread. The implication is that any relationships constructed on the basis of linguistic communication are bound to falter because so much noise or static is registered between sender and receiver. The ironies of confused messages are underlined in the Italian phrase for double bed, "letto matrimoniale" (*RM*, p. 163). Although the lovers sleep there on their travels in Italy, *he* is married to someone else. This is Thomas' metaphor for the problematic nature of language: travelling in foreign countries, adrift on the cross-cultural confusions and the multiple meanings of words. The enfolding of story within story underlines these inadequacies of language. In parentheses, the daughter interjects that the lover who is idolized in the mother's story is not even nice. Expanding on Henry James's principle of reflectors, but accentuating the breaks, Thomas illustrates a facet of perception taken into account by feminist sociologists, namely, that there is *no single* story of family life or marriage; there are as many stories as there are individuals involved. Each character brings his or her story with him or her. Emphasis consequently is not on description but on the act of telling; the characters become grammatical beings, embedding their stories in the narrative as it grows through accumulation in the manner of *The Thousand and One Nights*.

To speak is to live; such is the magical power of the narrative act, a power which Thomas foregrounds in "Out in the Midday Sun" where the man writes "swiftly and easily," "automatically," with a black pen that is "magic, like the broom of the sorcerer's apprentice" (*RM*, p. 89). As this allusion makes clear, while Thomas believes in the power of language — it is a life-giving, fantastic power — this belief makes her all the more aware of the lie that is narrative. In this clash of perspectives is located Thomas' analysis and judgement of truth and lies, memory, and private and public storytelling — all potentially fallible. Thomas foregrounds this clash in a visual image, that of a stereoscope which the narrator remembers playing with as a child, a device for viewing two photographs taken at different angles to give depth at "the right distance on everything" ("Natural History," *RM*, p. 33). Memory becomes an important distancing element, and the characteristic Thomas narrator mulls over the past in an effort to attain the "illusion of solidity" (p. 34). The artist's work is based on "illusion" and "trick," as she writes in "Natural History":

> *That* was the trick. To slide it all — moon, blind girl, rat, the apple tree, her father's fingers tilting the pencil, her own solitude, the cat, the eyes of the deer, her daughter, this still moment, back/forth, back/forth, back/forth,
> until "click,"
>   until "click,"
>   until "click" —
>
> there it was: wholeness, harmony, radiance; all of it making a wonderful kind of sense, as she sat there under the apple tree, beneath the moon. (*RM*, p. 34)

And it works, this magic underneath the moon. The narrator points out, however, that night is the time to sell her beautiful house, not during the day, under the cruel, truthful light of the sun. Unlike the Joycean tripartite epiphany of modernism, harmony and radiance are generally deceptive in Thomas' world where wholeness has split apart.

"Out in the Midday Sun," despite its reference to Noel Coward, is a rewriting from an inverted female perspective of Hemingway's "The Snows of Kilimanjaro." The name of the mountain tells it all: the violence of an American bitch undoing a man. Here a series of allusions to Hemingway — the characters call themselves Papa and Mama and they quote lines from his *Green Hills of Africa*, Hemingway's pastiche of his literary father, Sherwood Anderson — sets the scene for the relevation that the woman is going to make to her husband. She has been his brilliant student, whom he has married. Although she loves him, she has lived in his house under false pretences. Not content just to be there when he wants her (she wonders whether he married her to shut her up), she has been writing in secret, and the book is about to be published. In the midst of a conversation about Hemingway's many wives, she thinks of her husband, who has had two wives before her; the implication is that he is running from the same fear of creative impotency as the American writer. As the story unfolds in Thomas' hands from the female perspective, the woman is not the destructive force. Rather, the problem lies within the male who cannot bear to have his dominancy challenged by the black pen of the apprentice sorcerer.

The play on edges occurs not just between one art form and another — between the narratives of one sex and another — but also between art and life, as in "Déjeuner sur l'herbe" (*RM*, pp. 139–54). In the famous impressionistic painting alluded to here, there is a sharp incongruity between nude figure and pastoral landscape. In the story, platonic friends visit Paris. Their lack of involvement with each other — they sleep in twin beds — reflects their touristic disinterestedness and their noninvolvement in the human suffering they witness around them. On their last day, they look for a place to picnic, deciding to eat in a cemetery, thereby flaunting their detachment. As the woman is posing with a wreath of artificial poppies for yet another tourist photo, another woman comes along empty-handed, having abandoned the kitten she had earlier been carrying. The photo is interrupted; the first woman reacts by looking for the kitten, while the man says there is nothing they can do. At this point she "snaps" and calls out tauntingly to him to end the artifice of their lives, inviting a realignment of foreground and background, a breaking of the pictorial codes by which they have been living. She throws back at him the slogans they have been seeing on walls: "DON'T TOUCH. DON'T GET INVOLVED" (*RM*, p. 143). Aestheticism divorced from human emotions and from human relationships is destructive, Thomas implies. But within the story there is no solution offered. In the final line, the man throws

back another question: "And what if you do? . . . What then?"
(p. 154).

What then indeed? As I have been suggesting, the collisions of
perspective in Thomas' work are conveyed through a series of
images of perception and through linguistic devices which open up
the gap between language and feeling. These include: the lost child,
or the word not incarnate; the foreign word, slippery, indeter-
minate in translation; and the ironic or inverted allusion, working
explicitly on convention to explode meaning. Working to effect a
similar disjunction and interrogation of the hermeneutic process are
cliché, ambiguity, and definition. Cliché, like allusion, points to the
fact that the impact of Thomas' fiction derives from her deployment
of conventions and "realistic" expectations which are then frustrated by the next section or sentence or word. Her syntax is like
that of Camus's *écriture blanche*, which Sartre once described as
writing that has a small death between each sentence; indeed, in
Thomas it may occur between each word, as "Real Mothers" (*RM*,
pp. 9–22) demonstrates.

In the title story the word "real" is an equivocal word situated at
the point where two sequences of semantic or formal associations
intersect. One set of associations comes from the sign's immediate
context, its syntactical position, and relates to the issue of being a
true mother, one who is loyal and self-sacrificing and who carries out
the tasks necessary to assure her children's well-being (i.e., all that
goes with the cliché "motherhood"). The other set of associations
comes from a wider context, from another text within the text which
develops from the mother's quest for authenticity. Her first steps
towards a life of her own, where she is involved with schoolwork and
a lover to the exclusion of her children's demands, raises the question, How can one be real and be a mother? The children's understanding of the word clashes with the mother's understanding of the
word. Within the story, the differing concepts of reality are reflected
in the mother's changing language as she moves to a new sense of
self. "Coping" is "one of her . . . new words" (*RM*, p. 10), as is
"separated" (*RM*, p. 11). The latter word opens a wider gap, since,
as the daughter Anne-Marie reflects, no one ever heard of "separated" children (though the word more appropriately describes her
psychological state than it does her mother's).

In most of these stories, the narrators or characters resort to dic-
tionaries in an attempt to stop the drift of words, seeking out the

precise meaning of a term. The futility of this exercise is revealed in the unusual definitions the dictionary yields. But the greatest onslaught on received meanings or the conventions of speech is revealed in the child's answer to her father in "Natural History": "'And what are strangers?' asked the father gently. . . . The child's reply was very serious. 'Strangers are usually men'" (*RM*, p. 33). Questions of dominance or difference leave their mark on language. It is as much a well of private experiences as it is a vehicle for public communication. One function is continuously intersecting with another.

If, as I have been suggesting, Thomas specializes in this ungrammaticality and creates structures of loss, then she offers her readers compensatory presents. There are, for instance, the joys accompanying the rediscovery of an obsolete word, a dinosaur eliminated by cultural evolution. The word "leggings," for example, dredged from the narrator's memory in "Crossing the Rubicon" (*RM*, p. 164), sent my memory spinning outside the text into visions of the green roughness that swathed my childish legs in the days when girls always wore skirts. Thomas' polishing of such lost linguistic jewels opens the texts up beyond the mimetic level to involve the reader's life story.

Again, her use of allusion invokes the same mechanisms of recall and textual explosion, though operative not in the gap between text and life, but in that between one text and another. The direct quotation of an interchange from Lawrence Durrell's *Balthazar* in "Harry and Violet" (*RM*, pp. 61–74) not only calls forth memories of reading *The Alexandria Quartet* but also foregrounds Thomas' narrative model. Durrell's intersecting, conflicting personal visions of a chain of actions — a formal analogy to the relativity proposition of physics, as his preface informs us — are reflected in the spatial and temporal relativity in Thomas' work which makes *story*, the narrative unfolding of an action, the only reality.

If I have focused on the semiotic delights of Thomas' texts, it is not to deny there are mimetic ones. On the contrary, the carefully selected and polished language is the foundation on which is built an examination of the present realities of women's lives as they struggle for a sense of selfhood ("Timbuktu"), wrestle with conflicting demands of children and husband/lovers ("Harry and Violet"), or deal with the complex web of miscomprehensions which are the conventions governing relationships between members of the opposite sex ("In the Bleak Mid-Winter" [*RM*, pp. 75–80]). In all these situations, conflicting emotional demands or role expectations are threatening to split women apart. This is the area where the struggle of contemporary women to redefine conventions is at its sharpest, because convention here coincides with our deepest emotional bonds. The danger of not being involved leads one into the grammar of family life, which in "Real Mothers" seems to deny authenticity to women. Only in the intersecting paradoxes of Thomas' narratives can these conflicting demands be reconciled. Fiction becomes a strategy for reinforcing wholeness and integration in a world that threatens to come apart. And although the fiction is a trick, an illusion of depth and solidity ("Natural History," *RM*, pp. 33–34), the careful surfaces that Thomas has created ensure that these stories appeal to the heart, just as their self-reflexive nature offers consolation of form to the mind.

To offer any final judgement on a writer whose career is still in evolution is obviously uncalled for. That Thomas is continuing to write both short and long fictional forms is, however, a fact worth probing in an attempt to forecast the future. Thomas characterizes the shorter forms as extremely demanding because the slightest error is magnified in them. Working so precisely has evidently been an important apprenticeship in the craft of writing. Continued practice has honed her use of the highly allusive word and telegraphic detail so that the traits of density and compression are to be found in Thomas' longer fiction as well. "Graven Images," a book of memoirs now in the writing, promises that Thomas will not neglect the careful polishing of detail in the future, just as its focus on memoirs promises that she will continue her exploration of the impact of perceptual frames in the creation of meaning.

NOTES

[1] Alison Appelbe, "Female Loners . . . and the Broken Marriage Syndrome," *Leisure [The Vancouver Sun]*, 31 Aug. 1973, p. 34A. All further references to this work (Appelbe) appear in the text.

[2] Don Stanley, "Stories Audrey Told Me," *Leisure [The Vancouver Sun]*, 9 Sept. 1977, p. 7A.

[3] Graeme Matheson, "Below the Surface," *Quill & Quire*, Oct. 1974, p. 3.

[4] Pierre Coupey et al., "Interview/Audrey Thomas," *The Capilano Review*, No. 7 (Spring 1975), p. 94. In all further references, this work is abbreviated as "Coupey et al."

[5] John Hofsess, "A Teller of Surprising Tales," *The Canadian [The Toronto Star]*, 6 May 1978, p. 16. All further references to this work appear in the text.

[6] There are several different versions of Thomas' beginning to write. This one comes from Eleanor Wachtel, "Interview with Audrey Thomas," CBC *Sunday Morning*, 24 Jan. 1981. She also said to David Watmough in a CBC *Anthology* interview, 1 May 1971, that she had been writing since she was a young child. To George Bowering, she stated that she began writing stories in England ("Songs and Wisdom: An Interview with Audrey Thomas," *Open Letter*, 4th ser., No. 3 [Spring 1979], p. 7). All further references to this work (Bowering) appear in the text. In the Coupey interview, she said she began writing again as a graduate student at U. B. C. (Coupey et al., p. 95).

[7] Eleanor Wachtel, "The Guts of *Mrs. Blood*," *Books in Canada*, Nov. 1979, p. 5. All further references to this work (Wachtel) appear in the text.

[8] Phil Surguy, "Initiation Writes," *Books in Canada*, April 1978, p. 8.

[9] Rev. of *Intertidal Life*, in *Canadian Book Review Annual 1984*, ed. Dean Tudor and Ann Tudor (Toronto: Simon and Pierre, 1985), p. 203.

[10] See: Donald Cameron, "The Mysterious Literary Fondness for Darkest Africa," rev. of *Mrs. Blood*, *Maclean's*, Aug. 1971, p. 64; William H. New, "Africanadiana: The African Setting in Canadian Literature," *Journal of Canadian Studies*, 6, No. 1 (Feb. 1971), 33–38; and William H. New, "Equatorial Zones and Polar Opposites," rev. of *Mrs. Blood*, by Audrey Thomas, and *The New Ancestors*, by Dave Godfrey, *Journal of Commonwealth Literature*, 7, No. 1 (June 1972), 109–13. New's article and review were merged and revised as "Equatorial Zones and Polar Opposites," in *Articulating West: Essays on Purpose and Form in Modern Canadian Literature* (Toronto: new, 1972), pp. 216–33. All further references to this work (New) appear in the text.

[11] Patricia Monk, "Shadow Continent: The Image of Africa in Three Canadian Writers," *Ariel*, 8, No. 4 (Oct. 1977), 3–25.

[12] From an interview in Jill Gardiner, "The Early Short Stories of Alice Munro," M. A. Thesis New Brunswick 1973; quoted in Linda M. Hay, "Recurring Themes in the Fiction of Audrey Thomas," M. A. Thesis New Brunswick 1975, p. xii.

[13] See, for example, Donald Stephens, "The Recent English Short Story in Canada and Its Themes," *World Literature Written in English*, 11,

No. 1 (April 1972), 49–52.

[14] Barbara Novak, "Lunar Distractions," rev. of *Real Mothers*, *Books in Canada*, Feb. 1982, p. 20.

[15] Hubert de Santana, "Wonder Women," *Today Magazine*, *[The Toronto Star]*, 13 Dec. 1980, p. 15.

[16] In "My Craft and Sullen Art: The Writers Speak," *Atlantis*, 4, No. 1 (Autumn 1978), 152.

[17] Ellen Moers, *Literary Women* (Garden City, N.Y.: Doubleday, 1976), p. 209.

[18] Audrey Thomas, "Mademoiselle Blood," rev. of *Héloise*, by Anne Hébert, *Books in Canada*, Feb. 1983, p. 11.

[19] Stanley, p. 7A.

[20] Jane Kay, "The Neglected Child of Literature," rev. of *Ten Green Bottles*, by Audrey Thomas, and four other books, *The Patriot Ledger* [Quincy, Mass.], 29 Sept. 1967, p. 30. All further references to this work (Kay) appear in the text.

[21] Anita Raskia, rev. of *Ten Green Bottles*, *News* [Savannah, Ga.], 8 Oct. 1967, n. pag. All further references to this work (Raskia) appear in the text.

[22] Nikki Moir, "A Symphony of Birth That Is Unforgettable," rev. of *Ten Green Bottles*, *The Province* [Vancouver], 12 Jan. 1968, p. 5.

[23] Donald Stephens, "Mini-Novel Excellence," rev. of *Ten Green Bottles*, *Canadian Literature*, No. 38 (Autumn 1968), p. 96. All further references to this work (Stephens) appear in the text.

[24] Laurence Lafore, "Short Turns and Encores," rev. of *Ten Green Bottles*, by Audrey Thomas, *In the Courtyards of Jerusalem*, by Chaim Brandwein, *Dear Me*, by Edita Morris, and *The Best American Short Stories 1967*, ed. Martha Foley and David Burnett, *The New York Times Book Review*, 10 Dec. 1967, p. 55.

[25] Lafore, p. 55.

[26] Rev. of *Ten Green Bottles*, *Choice*, 4 (Oct. 1967), 836.

[27] Joel Clemons, rev. of *Ten Green Bottles*, *The News and Courier* [Charleston, B. C.], 11 Feb. 1968, p. 10C.

[28] Martin Levin, rev. of *Mrs. Blood*, *The New York Times Book Review*, 3 Jan. 1971, p. 23.

[29] Barbara Bannon, rev. of *Mrs. Blood*, *Publishers' Weekly*, 198, No. 17 (26 Oct. 1970), 48.

[30] See above, note 10.

[31] Joan Coldwell, "From the Inside," rev. of *Mrs. Blood*, *Canadian Literature*, No. 50 (Autumn 1971), pp. 98–99. All further references to this

work appear in the text.

[32] Rev. of *Du Sang, Bulletin critique du livre français,* Oct. 1972, p. 1209.

[33] Anthony Boxill, "Portraits of the Artist: Three Novels by Audrey Thomas," rev. of *Mrs. Blood* and *Munchmeyer and Prospero on the Island, The Fiddlehead,* No. 95 (Fall 1972), pp. 113–17.

[34] Kildare Dobbs, "A Novelist Explores the Circles of Hell," rev. of *Munchmeyer and Prospero on the Island, The Toronto Star,* 1 April 1972, p. 59.

[35] Rev. of *Munchmeyer and Prospero on the Island,* in "Letters in Canada 1972: Fiction," *University of Toronto Quarterly,* 42 (Summer 1973), 348.

[36] "'I Cannot Wear Your Mark upon My Back,'" rev. of *Munchmeyer and Prospero on the Island, Saturday Night,* July 1972, p. 44.

[37] Judith H. McDowell, rev. of *Munchmeyer and Prospero on the Island,* by Audrey Thomas, and *Daughters of the Moon,* by Joan Haggerty, *World Literature Written in English,* 12 (April 1973), 58.

[38] Dobbs, "A Novelist Explores the Circles of Hell," p. 59.

[39] Boxill, p. 116.

[40] McDowell, p. 59.

[41] Barbara Bannon, rev. of *Songs My Mother Taught Me, Publishers' Weekly,* 204, No. 15 (8 Oct. 1973), 88.

[42] Peter Stevens, rev. of *Songs My Mother Taught Me,* by Audrey Thomas, *The Governor's Bridge Is Closed,* by Hugh Hood, *Patterns of Isolation,* by John Moss, and *Towards a View of Canadian Letters: Selected Critical Essays, 1928–1971,* by A. J. M. Smith, *World Literature Written in English,* 13 (Nov. 1974), 259.

[43] Jean Mallinson, "Song Sung Blue," rev. of *Songs My Mother Taught Me, Leisure [The Vancouver Sun],* 5 April 1974, p. 32A.

[44] "Surviving Childhood," rev. of *Songs My Mother Taught Me,* by Audrey Thomas, and *Now Molly Knows,* by Merrill Joan Gerber, *Ms.,* April 1974, p. 33.

[45] Karen Mulhallen, rev. of *Songs My Mother Taught Me, The Canadian Forum,* May–June 1974, p. 19.

[46] William Gairdner, "Realism," rev. of *Songs My Mother Taught Me, Open Letter,* 2nd ser., No. 9 (Fall 1974), pp. 119–20.

[47] Maureen Scobie, "Memories, Dreams, and Reflections," rev. of *Songs My Mother Taught Me,* by Audrey Thomas, *Night,* by Edna O'Brien, and *The Summer before the Dark,* by Doris Lessing, *Branching Out,* Preview Issue (Dec. 1973), p. 38.

[48] Mulhallen, p. 19.

[49] Gairdner, p. 119.

[50] Rev. of *Songs My Mother Taught Me*, *Quill & Quire*, Jan. 1974, p. 12.

[51] "Audrey Thomas," in *From There to Here: A Guide to English-Canadian Literature since 1960* (Erin, Ont.: Porcépic, 1974), p. 254.

[52] See above, note 12.

[53] See above, note 4.

[54] George Bowering, "The Site of Blood," rev. of *Blown Figures*, *Canadian Literature*, No. 65 (Summer 1975), p. 90.

[55] "It Had to Be the Scrambler," rev. of *Blown Figures*, *The Globe and Mail*, 5 April 1975, p. 37.

[56] Linda Sandler, rev. of *Blown Figures*, *The Malahat Review*, No. 36 (Oct. 1975), p. 142.

[57] Rev. of *Blown Figures*, *Publishers' Weekly*, 208, No. 18 (3 Nov. 1975), 63.

[58] Margaret Atwood, rev. of *Blown Figures*, *The New York Times Book Review*, 1 Feb. 1976, p. 8.

[59] Michele Turin, rev. of *Blown Figures*, *Best Sellers*, 36 (April 1976), 5.

[60] O. H. T. Rudzick, rev. of *Blown Figures*, in "Letters in Canada 1974: Fiction," *University of Toronto Quarterly*, 44 (Summer 1975), 309.

[61] Eleanor Wachtel, "The Image of Africa in the Fiction of Audrey Thomas," *Room of One's Own*, 2, No. 4 (1977), 21–28.

[62] George Bowering, "Snow Red: The Short Stories of Audrey Thomas," *Open Letter*, 3rd ser., No. 5 (Summer 1976), pp. 28–39.

[63] See above, note 11.

[64] Dolores Gros-Louis, "Pens and Needles: Daughters and Mothers in Recent Canadian Fiction," *Kate Chopin Newsletter*, 2, No. 3 (1976–77), 8–15. As an example of the slight shifts involved in these articles, this one, by offering an "images of women" approach and by comparing Thomas' *Songs My Mother Taught Me* with other Canadian female *Bildungsromane* invites us to see Clara Cleary, the protagonist's mother who is trapped by the nurturing role, as a negative model of woman against whom Isobel Cleary revolts.

[65] William H. New, "Fiction," in *Literary History in Canada: Canadian Literature in English*, 2nd ed., gen. ed. and introd. Carl F. Klinck (Toronto: Univ. of Toronto Press, 1976), III, 271–72.

[66] Deborah Scharbach, "Audrey Thomas," rev. of *Ten Green Bottles* and *Ladies and Escorts*, *Brick: A Journal of Reviews*, No. 4 (Fall 1978), p. 49.

[67] Marion McCormick, "Love, Marriage and Related Disasters," rev. of *Ladies and Escorts, Quill & Quire*, July 1977, p. 5.

[68] Margaret Atwood, rev. of *Ten Green Bottles* and *Ladies and Escorts, The Globe and Mail*, 16 April 1977, p. 25. All further references to this work (Atwood) appear in the text.

[69] Sam Solecki, rev. of *Ladies and Escorts*, in "Letters in Canada 1977: Fiction," *University of Toronto Quarterly*, 47 (Summer 1978), 329. See also Ken Adachi, "Stories Echo with Anguish, Torment," rev. of *Ten Green Bottles* and *Ladies and Escorts, The Toronto Star*, 30 April 1977, Sec. H, p. 9.

[70] Eleanor Wachtel, rev. of *Ten Green Bottles* and *Ladies and Escorts, Room of One's Own*, 3, No. 4 (1978), 50.

[71] Susan Walker, rev. of *Latakia, Quill & Quire*, Feb. 1980, p. 41.

[72] Edna Barker, rev. of *Latakia, Canadian Book Review Annual 1979*, ed. Dean Tudor, Nancy Tudor, and Kathy Vanderlinden (Toronto: Peter Martin, 1980), p. 114.

[73] Constance Rooke, rev. of *Latakia, Canadian Women's Studies*, 2, No. 4 (1980), 108.

[74] Ken Adachi, "New Dispatches from the Front," rev. of *Latakia, The Toronto Star*, 2 Dec. 1979, Sec. B, p. 7.

[75] Rev. of *Latakia*, in "Letters in Canada 1979: Fiction," *University of Toronto Quarterly*, 49 (Summer 1980), 325.

[76] Rev. of *Latakia, The Globe and Mail*, 22 Dec. 1979, Sec. Entertainment, p. 10.

[77] Barbara Godard, rev. of *Latakia, The Fiddlehead*, No. 126 (Summer 1980), pp. 121–23.

[78] Rooke, p. 107.

[79] "The Divided Self," *Atlantis*, 5, No. 2 (Spring 1980), 52–67.

[80] Ellen Quigley, "Redefining Unity and Dissolution in *Latakia*," *Essays on Canadian Writing*, No. 20 (Winter 1980–81), pp. 201–19.

[81] Robert Kroetsch, "The Exploding Porcupine: Violence of Form in English-Canadian Fiction," in *Papers from the Conference on Violence in the Canadian Novel since 1960*, ed. Virginia Harger-Grinling and Terry Goldie (St. John's, Nfld.: Memorial Univ., 1981), pp. 194, 195.

[82] Robert Diotte, "The Romance of Penelope: Audrey Thomas' Isobel Carpenter Trilogy," *Canadian Literature*, No. 86 (Autumn 1980), pp. 60–68.

[83] "Memory Organized: The Novels of Audrey Thomas," *Canadian Literature*, No. 92 (Summer 1982), pp. 46–56.

[84] See above, note 6.

[85] Helen Hoy, rev. of *Real Mothers*, in "Letters in Canada 1981: Fiction," *University of Toronto Quarterly*, 51 (Summer 1982), 322.

[86] Eleanor Wachtel, "Contemporary Triangles," rev. of *Real Mothers* and *Two in the Bush and Other Stories, Saturday Night*, April 1982, p. 52.

[87] Urjo Kareda, "Sense and Sensibility," rev. of *Intertidal Life, Saturday Night*, Jan. 1985, p. 50. All further references to this work (Kareda) appear in the text.

[88] "A Novel of Riches," rev. of *Intertidal Life, The Globe and Mail*, 22 Dec. 1984, p. E20.

[89] David Staines, "Feminist Matter Fashioned into Fine Novel Mapping the New War between the Sexes," rev. of *Intertidal Life, The Gazette* [Montreal], 12 Jan. 1985, p. H12.

[90] Katherine Govier, "The Flotsam and Jetsam on Thomas's Island," rev. of *Intertidal Life, Quill & Quire*, Nov. 1984, p. 39.

[91] Burt Heward, "Thomas's Heroine to Cherish," rev. of *Intertidal Life, The Citizen* [Ottawa], 17 Nov. 1984, p. C2.

[92] Judith Fitzgerald, "Audrey Thomas: Her Time Has Come," rev. of *Intertidal Life, The Whig-Standard* [Kingston], 17 Nov. 1984, p. 19.

[93] Judith Fitzgerald, "Audrey Thomas Taps Motherlode," rev. of *Intertidal Life, The Toronto Star*, 2 Dec. 1984, p. H13.

[94] Introd., *Goodbye Harold, Good Luck* (Toronto: Viking, 1986), p. xvi.

[95] Joel Yanofsky, "Thinking Small," rev. of *Goodbye Harold, Good Luck, Books in Canada*, June–July 1986, p. 14; emphasis added.

[96] Barbara Gunn, "Writer with Dazzling Gift for Short Fiction," rev. of *Goodbye Harold, Good Luck, The Vancouver Sun*, 14 June 1986, p. E15.

[97] Ronald Hatch, "Stories for Now," rev. of *Goodbye Harold, Good Luck, The Canadian Forum*, Aug.–Sept. 1986, p. 34.

[98] Anne Archer, "Real Mummies," *Studies in Canadian Literature*, 9 (1984), 214.

[99] Archer, p. 215.

[100] Wendy Keitner, "Real Mothers Don't Write Books: A Study of the Penelope-Calypso Motif in the Fiction of Audrey Thomas and Marian Engel," in *Present Tense: A Critical Anthology*, ed. and introd. John Moss, *The Canadian Novel*, No. 4 (Toronto: NC, 1985), p. 185.

[101] Frank Davey, "Alternate Stories: The Short Fiction of Audrey Thomas and Margaret Atwood," *Canadian Literature*, No. 109 (Summer 1986), pp. 5–14. All further references to this work appear in the text.

[102] Brigitte G. Bossanne, "Audrey Thomas and Lewis Carroll: Two Sides of the Looking Glass," *North Dakota Quarterly*, 52, No. 3 (Summer

1984), 223; Joan Coldwell, "Natural Herstory and *Intertidal Life*," *Room of One's Own*, 10, No. 3–4 (March 1986), 140–49.

[103] Lorna Irvine, "The Hieroglyphics of *Mrs. Blood*," in *Sub/version: Canadian Fictions by Women* (Toronto: ECW, 1986), p. 35. All further references to this work appear in the text.

[104] "Delusion and Dream in Thomas' *Blown Figures*," in *Sub/version*, pp. 55–72.

[105] Barbara Godard, "Dispossession," rev. of *Blown Figures*, *Open Letter*, 3rd ser., No. 5 (Summer 1976), pp. 81–82.

[106] Louis K. MacKendrick, "A Peopled Labyrinth of Walls: Audrey Thomas' *Blown Figures*," in Moss, ed., *Present Tense*, p. 183; emphasis added.

[107] Coral Ann Howells, "No Sense of an Ending: *Real Mothers*," *Room of One's Own*, 10, No. 3–4 (March 1986), 111.

[108] Howells, "No Sense of an Ending," p. 111.

[109] Coral Ann Howells, "Margaret Laurence: *The Diviners* and Audrey Thomas: *Latakia*," *Canadian Woman Studies*, 6, No. 1 (Fall 1984), 99.

[110] Howells, "Margaret Laurence," p. 99.

[111] Pauline Butling, "Thomas and Her Rag-Bag," *Canadian Literature*, No. 102 (Autumn 1984), p. 195. All further references to this work appear in the text.

[112] For discussion of this, see my articles "Other Fictions: Robert Kroetsch's Criticism," *Open Letter*, 5th ser., No. 8–9 (Summer–Fall 1984), pp. 5–21, and "Structuralism/Post-Structuralism: Language, Reality and Canadian Literature," in *Future Indicative: Literary Theory and Canadian Literature*, ed. and introd. John Moss (Ottawa: Univ. of Ottawa Press, 1987), pp. 25–51.

[113] Pauline Butling, "The Cretan Paradox or Where the Truth Lies in *Latakia*," *Room of One's Own*, 10, No. 3–4 (March 1986), 108. All further references to this work appear in the text.

[114] Susan Rudy Dorscht, "On Blowing Figures . . . and Bleeding: Post-structuralist Feminism and the 'Writing' of Audrey Thomas," *Canadian Fiction Magazine*, No. 57 (1986) [*Tessera*, No. 3], p. 68. This is an abbreviated version of Dorscht's thesis, in the writing of which she had access to the manuscript of this text.

[115] Chantal Zabus, "A Calibanic Tempest in Anglophone and Francophone New World Writing," *Canadian Literature*, No. 104 (Spring 1985), p. 49. See also Diana Brydon, "Re-Writing *The Tempest*," *World Literature Written in English*, 23 (Winter 1984), 80.

[116] Arnold E. Davidson, "Reading between the Texts in Audrey

Thomas' *Munchmeyer and Prospero on the Island,*" *The American Review of Canadian Studies,* 15, No. 4 (Winter 1985), 421.

[117] Davidson, p. 422.

[118] Audrey Thomas, "Omo," in *Ten Green Bottles* (1967; rpt. Ottawa: Oberon, 1977), p. 56. All further references to this work (*TGB*) appear in the text.

[119] Elizabeth Komisar, "Audrey Thomas: A Review/Interview," rev. of *Blown Figures, Open Letter,* 3rd ser., No. 3 (Late Fall 1975), p. 59.

[120] "Déjeuner sur l'herbe," in *Real Mothers* (Vancouver: Talonbooks, 1981), pp. 139–54. All further references to this work (*RM*) appear in the text.

[121] *Mrs. Blood* (1970; rpt. Vancouver: Talonbooks, 1975), p. 220. All further references to this work appear in the text.

[122] Wachtel, "Interview with Audrey Thomas," 24 Jan. 1981.

[123] The various manuscript drafts are deposited in the Thomas papers, Special Collections, Univ. of British Columbia library.

[124] Audrey Thomas, "Henry James in the Palace of Art: A Survey and Evaluation of James' Aesthetic Criteria as Shown in His Criticism of Nineteenth Century Painting," M. A. Thesis British Columbia 1963, p. 4.

[124A] *Munchmeyer and Prospero on the Island* (New York: Bobbs-Merrill, 1971), p. 10. All further references to this work appear in the text.

[125] *Songs My Mother Taught Me* (Vancouver: Talonbooks, 1973), p. 93; emphasis added. All further references to this work appear in the text.

[126] Jacques Ehrmann, "Homo Ludens Revisited," in *Game, Play, Literature,* ed. Jacques Ehrmann (1968; rpt. Boston: Beacon, 1971), p. 56.

[127] In *Ladies and Escorts* (Ottawa: Oberon, 1977), pp. 19–30. All further references to this work (*LE*) appear in the text.

[128] *Blown Figures* (Vancouver: Talonbooks, 1974), p. 318. All further references to this work appear in the text.

[129] Bowering, "The Site of Blood," p. 86.

[130] The particular fairy tale Thomas invokes here is Hans Christian Andersen's "The Snow Queen," which has additional significance as an intertextual play with Daphne Marlatt's first book, *Frames of a Story* (1968), which is based on this tale. In this way, *Blown Figures* spirals out indefinitely. The allusion to Marlatt's work makes especially clear the attention paid to framing and breaking frame in Thomas' fiction. For identification of the fairy story in Marlatt and Thomas, see Quigley, pp. 201–19.

[131] For more background, see my "Dispossession," pp. 81–82, where much of this material has previously appeared, and John H. Stape, "Dr.

Jung at the Site of Blood: A Note on *Blown Figures*," *Studies in Canadian Literature*, 2 (Summer 1977), 124–26.

[132] "Closing Statement: Linguistics and Poetics," in *Style in Language*, ed. Thomas A. Sebeok (Cambridge, Mass.: M.I.T. Press, 1960), p. 357.

[133] Gregory Bateson, *Steps to an Ecology of Mind* (New York: Ballantine, 1972), p. 180. This section was developed from ideas expressed in Erving Goffman, *Frame Analysis* (New York: Harper Colophon, 1974), and Johan Huizinga, *Homo Ludens* (1950; rpt. Boston: Beacon, 1955).

[134] *Latakia* (Vancouver: Talonbooks, 1979), pp. 29, 45. All further references to this work are indicated in parentheses.

[135] Epigraph 3:

"When two vowels go walking,
The first one does the talking"

(Old Rhyme Used in Elementary Schools to Explain the Pronunciation of Words like 'Goat') (*Latakia*, n. pag.)

[136] Epigraph 4:

English: I can't get over it
Now I've seen everything

France: J'n'en reviens pas
J'aurai tout vu
J'en ai assez

Canada: J'ai mon voyage

from *The Practical Handbook of Canadian French* (*Latakia*, n. pag.)

[137] For a development of this labyrinth metaphor, see Pauline Butling, rev. of *Latakia*, *Periodics*, No. 7–8 (Winter 1981), pp. 186–88.

[138] W.F. Jackson Knight, *Virgil: Epic and Anthropology* (London: George Allen and Unwin, 1967), p. 267.

SELECTED BIBLIOGRAPHY

Primary Sources

Thesis

Thomas, Audrey. "Henry James in the Palace of Art: A Survey and Evaluation of James' Aesthetic Criteria as Shown in His Criticism of Nineteenth Century Painting." M. A. Thesis British Columbia 1963.

Books

Thomas, Audrey. *Ten Green Bottles*. 1967; rpt. Ottawa: Oberon, 1977.
———. *Mrs. Blood*. 1970; rpt. Vancouver: Talonbooks, 1975.
———. *Munchmeyer and Prospero on the Island*. New York: Bobbs-Merrill, 1971.
———. *Songs My Mother Taught Me*. Vancouver: Talonbooks, 1973.
———. *Blown Figures*. Vancouver: Talonbooks, 1974.
———. *Ladies and Escorts*. Ottawa: Oberon, 1977.
———. *Latakia*. Vancouver: Talonbooks, 1979.
———. *Real Mothers*. Vancouver: Talonbooks, 1981.
———. *Two in the Bush and Other Stories*. New Canadian Library, No. 163. Toronto: McClelland and Stewart, 1981.
———. *Intertidal Life*. Toronto: Stoddart, 1984.
———. *Goodbye Harold, Good Luck*. Toronto: Viking, 1986.

Contributions to Periodicals

Thomas, Audrey. In "My Craft and Sullen Art: The Writers Speak." *Atlantis*, 4, No. 1 (Autumn 1978), 152–54.
———. "Untouchables: A Memoir." *Room of One's Own*, 7, No. 3 (1982), 2–17.
———. "Mademoiselle Blood." Rev. of *Héloise*, by Anne Hébert. *Books in Canada*, Feb. 1983, pp. 11–12.

Secondary Sources

Adachi, Ken. "Stories Echo with Anguish, Torment." Rev. of *Ten Green Bottles* and *Ladies and Escorts*. *The Toronto Star*, 30 April 1977, Sec. H, p. 9.

———. "New Dispatches from the Front." Rev. of *Latakia*. *The Toronto Star*, 22 Dec. 1979, Sec. B, p. 7.

Appelbe, Alison. "Female Loners . . . and the Broken Marriage Syndrome." *Leisure [The Vancouver Sun]*, 31 Aug. 1973, p. 34A.

Archer, Anne. "Real Mummies." *Studies in Canadian Literature*, 9 (1984), 214–23.

Atwood, Margaret. Rev. of *Blown Figures*. *The New York Times Book Review*, 1 Feb. 1976, p. 8.

———. Rev. of *Ten Green Bottles* and *Ladies and Escorts*. *The Globe and Mail*, 16 April 1977, p. 25.

Bannon, Barbara. Rev. of *Mrs. Blood*. *Publishers' Weekly*, 198, No. 17 (26 Oct. 1970), 48.

———. Rev. of *Songs My Mother Taught Me*. *Publishers' Weekly*, 204, No. 15 (8 Oct. 1973), 88.

———. Rev. of *Blown Figures*. *Publishers' Weekly*, 208, No. 18 (3 Nov. 1975), 63.

Barker, Edna. Rev. of *Latakia*. In *Canadian Book Review Annual 1979*. Ed. Dean Tudor, Nancy Tudor, and Kathy Vanderlinden. Toronto: Peter Martin, 1980, p. 114.

Bilan, R. P. Rev. of *Latakia*. In "Letters in Canada 1979: Fiction." *University of Toronto Quarterly*, 49 (Summer 1980), 325.

Bossanne, Brigitte G. "Audrey Thomas and Lewis Carroll: Two Sides of the Looking Glass." *North Dakota Quarterly*, 52, No. 3 (Summer 1984), 215–34.

Bowering, George. "The Site of Blood." Rev. of *Blown Figures*. *Canadian Literature*, No. 65 (Summer 1975), pp. 86–90.

———. "Snow Red: The Short Stories of Audrey Thomas." *Open Letter*, 3rd ser., No. 5 (Summer 1976), pp. 28–39.

———. "Songs and Wisdom: An Interview with Audrey Thomas." *Open Letter*, 4th ser., No. 3 (Spring 1979), pp. 7–31.

Boxill, Anthony. "Portraits of the Artist: Three Novels by Audrey Thomas." Rev. of *Mrs. Blood* and *Munchmeyer and Prospero on the Island*. *The Fiddlehead*, No. 95 (Fall 1972), pp. 113–17.

Brydon, Diana. "Re-writing *The Tempest*." *World Literature Written in English*, 23 (Winter 1984), 75–88.

Butling, Pauline. Rev. of *Latakia*. *Periodics*, No. 7–8 (Winter 1981), pp. 186–88.

———. "Thomas and Her Rag-Bag." *Canadian Literature*, No. 102 (Autumn 1984), pp. 195–99.

———. "The Cretan Paradox or Where the Truth Lies in *Latakia*." *Room of One's Own*, 10, Nos. 3–4 (March 1986), 105–10.

Cameron, Donald. "The Mysterious Literary Fondness for Darkest Africa." Rev. of *Mrs. Blood. Maclean's*, Aug. 1971, p. 64.

Clemons, Joel. Rev. of *Ten Green Bottles. The News and Courier* [Charleston, B. C.], 11 Feb. 1968, p. 10C.

Coldwell, Joan. "From the Inside." Rev. of *Mrs. Blood. Canadian Literature*, No. 50 (Autumn 1971), pp. 98–99.

———. "Memory Organized: The Novels of Audrey Thomas." *Canadian Literature*, No. 92 (Spring 1982), pp. 46–56.

———. "Natural Herstory and *Intertidal Life*." *Room of One's Own*, 10, Nos. 3–4 (March 1986), 140–49.

Cooper-Clark, Diana. "Audrey and Rachel." Rev. of *Latakia. Canadian Literature*, No. 91 (Winter 1981), pp. 104–06.

Coupey, Pierre, Gladys Hindmarch, Wendy Pickell, and Bill Schermbrucker. "Interview/Audrey Thomas." *The Capilano Review*, No. 7 (Spring 1975), pp. 87–109.

Davey, Frank. "Audrey Thomas." In *From There to Here: A Guide to English-Canadian Literature since 1960*. Erin, Ont.: Porcépic, 1974, pp. 254–57.

———. "Alternate Stories: The Short Fiction of Audrey Thomas and Margaret Atwood." *Canadian Literature*, No. 109 (Summer 1986), pp. 5–14.

Davidson, Arnold E. "Reading between the Texts in Audrey Thomas' *Munchmeyer and Prospero on the Island*." *The American Review of Canadian Studies*, 15, No. 4 (Winter 1985), 421–31.

de Santana, Hubert. "Wonder Women." *Today Magazine [The Toronto Star]*, 13 Dec. 1980, pp. 14–17.

Diotte, Robert. "The Romance of Penelope: Audrey Thomas's Isobel Carpenter Trilogy." *Canadian Literature*, No. 86 (Autumn 1980), pp. 60–68.

Dobbs, Kildare. "A Novelist Explores the Circles of Hell." Rev. of *Munchmeyer and Prospero on the Island. The Toronto Star*, 1 April 1972, p. 59.

———. "It Had to Be the Scrambler." Rev. of *Blown Figures. The Globe and Mail*, 5 April 1975, p. 37.

Dorscht, Susan Rudy. "On Blowing Figures . . . and Bleeding: Poststructuralist Feminism and the 'Writing' of Audrey Thomas." *Canadian Fiction Magazine*, No. 57 (1986) [*Tessera*, No. 3], pp. 61–69.

Fitzgerald, Judith. "Audrey Thomas: Her Time Has Come." Rev. of *Intertidal Life*. *The Whig-Standard Magazine* [Kingston], 17 Nov. 1984, pp. 19–20.

———. "Audrey Thomas Taps Motherlode." Rev. of *Intertidal Life*. *The Toronto Star*, 2 Dec. 1984, p. H13.

Gairdner, William. "Realism." Rev. of *Songs My Mother Taught Me*. *Open Letter*, 2nd ser., No. 9 (Fall 1974), pp. 119–20.

Galloway, Priscilla. Rev. of *Intertidal Life*. In *Canadian Book Review Annual 1984*. Ed. Dean Tudor and Ann Tudor. Toronto: Simon and Pierre, 1985, pp. 202–03.

Godard, Barbara. "Dispossession." Rev. of *Blown Figures*. *Open Letter*, 3rd ser., No. 5 (Summer 1976), pp. 81–82.

———. Rev. of *Latakia*. *The Fiddlehead*, No. 126 (Summer 1980), pp. 121–23.

———. Rev. of *Real Mothers*. *The Fiddlehead*, No. 135 (Jan. 1983), pp. 110–14.

Govier, Katherine. "The Flotsam and Jetsam on Thomas's Island." Rev. of *Intertidal Life*. *Quill & Quire*, Nov. 1984, p. 39.

Gros-Louis, Dolores. "Pens and Needles: Daughters and Mothers in Recent Canadian Fiction." *Kate Chopin Newsletter*, 2, No. 3 (1976–77), 8–15.

Gunn, Barbara. "Writer with Dazzling Gift for Short Fiction." Rev. of *Goodbye Harold, Good Luck*. *The Vancouver Sun*, 14 June 1986, p. E15.

Hatch, Ronald. "Stories for Now." Rev. of *Goodbye Harold, Good Luck*. *The Canadian Forum*, Aug.–Sept. 1986, pp. 34–35.

Hay, Linda MacKinley. "Recurring Themes in the Fiction of Audrey Thomas." M. A. Thesis New Brunswick 1975.

Heward, Burt. "Thomas's Heroine to Cherish." Rev. of *Intertidal Life*. *The Citizen* [Ottawa], 17 Nov. 1984, p. C2.

Hofsess, John. "A Teller of Surprising Tales." *The Canadian* [*The Toronto Star*], 6 May 1978, pp. 16–18.

Howells, Coral Ann. "Margaret Laurence: *The Diviners* and Audrey Thomas: *Latakia*." *Canadian Woman Studies/Les Cahiers de la femme*, 6, No. 1 (Fall 1984), 98–100.

———. "No Sense of an Ending: *Real Mothers*." *Room of One's Own*, 10, Nos. 3–4 (March 1986), 111–23.

Hoy, Helen. Rev. of *Real Mothers*. In "Letters in Canada 1981: Fiction." *University of Toronto Quarterly*, 51 (Summer 1982), 321–22.

Irvine, Lorna. "Delusion and Dream in Thomas' *Blown Figures*." In *Sub/version: Canadian Fictions by Women*. Toronto: ECW, 1986, pp. 55–72.

——. "The Hieroglyphics of *Mrs. Blood*." In *Sub/version: Canadian Fictions by Women*. Toronto: ECW, 1986, pp. 21–36.

Kareda, Urjo. "Sense and Sensibility." Rev. of *Intertidal Life*. *Saturday Night*, Jan. 1986, pp. 50–51.

Kay, Jane. "The Neglected Child of Literature." Rev. of *Ten Green Bottles*, by Audrey Thomas, and four other books. *The Patriot Ledger* [Quincy, Mass.], 29 Sept. 1967, p. 30.

Keitner, Wendy. "Real Mothers Don't Write Books: A Study of the Penelope-Calypso Motif in the Fiction of Audrey Thomas and Marian Engel." In *Present Tense: A Critical Anthology*. Ed. and introd. John Moss. The Canadian Novel, No. 4. Toronto: NC, 1985, pp. 185–204.

Komisar, Elizabeth. "Audrey Thomas: A Review/Interview." Rev. of *Blown Figures. Open Letter*, 3rd ser., No. 3 (Late Fall 1975), pp. 59–64.

Kroetsch, Robert. "The Exploding Porcupine: Violence of Form in English-Canadian Fiction." In *Papers from the Conference on Violence in the Canadian Novel since 1960*. Ed. Virginia Harger-Grinling and Terry Goldie. St. John's, Nfld.: Memorial Univ., 1981, pp. 191–99.

Lafore, Laurence. "Short Turns and Encores." Rev. of *Ten Green Bottles*, by Audrey Thomas, *In the Courtyards of Jerusalem*, by Chaim Brandwein, *Dear Me*, by Edita Morris, and *The Best American Short Stories 1967*, ed. Martha Foley and David Burnett. *The Book Review*, 10 Dec. 1967, p. 55.

Levin, Martin. Rev. of *Mrs. Blood. The New York Times Book Review*, 3 Jan. 1971, p. 23.

MacKendrick, Louis K. "A Peopled Labyrinth of Walls: Audrey Thomas' *Blown Figures*." In *Present Tense: A Critical Anthology*. Ed. and introd. John Moss. The Canadian Novel, No. 4. Toronto: NC, 1985, pp. 168–84.

Mallinson, Jean. "Song Sung Blue." Rev. of *Songs My Mother Taught Me. Leisure [The Vancouver Sun]*, 5 April 1974, p. 32A.

Matheson, Graeme. "Below the Surface." *Quill & Quire*, Oct. 1974, p. 3.

McAlpine, Mary. "'I Cannot Wear Your Mark upon My Back.'" Rev. of *Munchmeyer and Prospero on the Island. Saturday Night*, July 1972, pp. 44–45.

McCormick, Marion. "Love, Marriage and Related Disasters." Rev. of *Ten Green Bottles* and *Ladies and Escorts. Quill & Quire*, July 1977, p. 5.

McDowell, Judith H. Rev. of *Munchmeyer and Prospero on the Island*, by Audrey Thomas, and *Daughters of the Moon*, by Joan Haggerty. *World Literature Written in English*, 12 (April 1973), 57–59.

McMullen, Lorraine. "The Divided Self." *Atlantis*, 5, No. 2 (Spring 1980), 52–67.

Moir, Nikki. "A Symphony of Birth That Is Unforgettable." Rev. of *Ten Green Bottles*. *The Province* [Vancouver], 12 Jan. 1968, p. 5.

Monk, Patricia. "Shadow Continent: The Image of Africa in Three Canadian Writers." *Ariel*, 8, No. 4 (Oct. 1977), 3–25.

Mulhallen, Karen. Rev. of *Songs My Mother Taught Me*. *The Canadian Forum*, May–June 1974, pp. 18–19.

New, William H. "Africanadiana: The African Setting in Canadian Literature." *Journal of Canadian Studies*, 6, No. 1 (Feb. 1971), 33–38.

——. "Equatorial Zones and Polar Opposites." Rev. of *Mrs. Blood*, by Audrey Thomas, and *The New Ancestors*, by Dave Godfrey. *Journal of Commonwealth Literature*, 7, No. 1 (June 1972), 109–13. Rpt. (rev.) in *Articulating West: Essays on Purpose and Form in Modern Canadian Literature*. Toronto: new, 1972, pp. 216–33.

——. "Fiction." In *Literary History of Canada: Canadian Literature in English*. 2nd ed. Gen. ed. and introd. Carl F. Klinck. Toronto: Univ. of Toronto Press, 1976. III, 238–83.

Novak, Barbara. "Lunar Distractions." Rev. of *Real Mothers*. *Books in Canada*, Feb. 1982, pp. 18–20.

Quigley, Ellen. "Redefining Unity and Dissolution in *Latakia*." *Essays on Canadian Writing*, No. 20 (Winter 1980–81), pp. 201–19.

Raskia, Anita. Rev. of *Ten Green Bottles*. *News* [Savannah, Ga.], 8 Oct. 1967.

——. Rev. of *Du sang*. *Bulletin critique du livre français*, oct. 1972, p. 1209.

——. Rev. of *Ten Green Bottles*. *Choice*, 4 (Oct. 1967), 836.

Rooke, Constance. Rev. of *Latakia*. *Canadian Women's Studies*, 2, No. 4 (1980), 107–08.

Rudzick, O. H. T. Rev. of *Munchmeyer and Prospero on the Island*. In "Letters in Canada 1972: Fiction." *University of Toronto Quarterly*, 42 (Summer 1973), 348.

——. Rev. of *Blown Figures*. In "Letters in Canada 1974: Fiction." *University of Toronto Quarterly*, 44 (Summer 1975), 308–09.

Rule, Jane. Rev. of *Latakia*. *The Globe and Mail*, 22 Dec. 1979, Sec. Entertainment, p. 10.

Sandler, Linda. Rev. of *Blown Figures*. *The Malahat Review*, No. 36 (Oct.

1975), pp. 140–42.

Scharbach, Deborah. "Audrey Thomas." Rev. of *Ten Green Bottles* and *Ladies and Escorts. Brick: A Journal of Reviews*, No. 4 (Fall 1978), pp. 49–51.

Scobie, Maureen. "Memories, Dreams, and Reflections." Rev. of *Songs My Mother Taught Me*, by Audrey Thomas, *Night*, by Edna O'Brien, and *The Summer before the Dark*, by Doris Lessing. *Branching Out*, Preview Issue (Dec. 1973), pp. 38–39.

Shulman, Alix Kates. "Surviving Childhood." Rev. of *Songs My Mother Taught Me*, by Audrey Thomas, and *Now Molly Knows*, by Merrill Joan Gerber. *Ms.*, April 1974, pp. 33–35.

Solecki, Sam. Rev. of *Ladies and Escorts*. In "Letters in Canada 1977: Fiction." *University of Toronto Quarterly*, 47 (Summer 1978), 328–29.

Staines, David. "Feminist Matter Fashioned into Fine Novel Mapping the New War between the Sexes." Rev. of *Intertidal Life. The Gazette* [Montreal], 12 Jan. 1985, p. H12.

Stanley, Don. "Stories Audrey Told Me." *Leisure [The Vancouver Sun]*, 9 Sept. 1977, p. 7A.

Stape, John H. "Dr. Jung at the Site of Blood: A Note on *Blown Figures*." *Studies in Canadian Literature*, 2 (Summer 1977), 124–26.

Stephens, Donald. "Mini-Novel Excellence." Rev. of *Ten Green Bottles*. *Canadian Literature*, No. 38 (Autumn 1968), pp. 94–96.

——. "The Recent English Short Story in Canada and Its Theme." *World Literature Written in English*, 11, No. 1 (April 1972), 49–52.

Stevens, Peter. Rev. of *Songs My Mother Taught Me*, by Audrey Thomas, *The Governor's Bridge Is Closed*, by Hugh Hood, *Patterns of Isolation*, by John Moss, and *Towards a View of Canadian Letters: Selected Critical Essays, 1928–1971*, by A. J. M. Smith. *World Literature Written in English*, 13 (Nov. 1974), 253–60.

Surguy, Phil. "Initiation Writes." *Books in Canada*, April 1978, pp. 7–9.

Turin, Michele. Rev. of *Blown Figures. Best Sellers*, 36 (April 1976), 5.

Wachtel, Eleanor. "The Image of Africa in the Fiction of Audrey Thomas." *Room of One's Own*, 2, No. 4 (1977), 21–28.

——. Rev. of *Ten Green Bottles* and *Ladies and Escorts. Room of One's Own*, 3, No. 4 (1978), 50–52.

——. "The Guts of *Mrs. Blood*." *Books in Canada*, Nov. 1979, pp. 3–6.

——. "Interview with Audrey Thomas." CBC *Sunday Morning*, 24 Jan. 1981.

——. "Contemporary Triangles." Rev. of *Real Mothers* and *Two in the Bush and Other Stories. Saturday Night*, April 1982, pp. 51–52.

Walker, Susan. Rev. of *Songs My Mother Taught Me*. *Quill & Quire*, Jan. 1974, p. 12.

——. Rev. of *Latakia*. *Quill & Quire*, Feb. 1980, p. 41.

Watmough, David. "Interview." CBC *Anthology*, 1 May 1971.

Wigston, Nancy. "A Novel of Riches." Rev. of Intertidal Life. *The Globe and Mail*, 22 Dec. 1984, p. E20.

Yanofsky, Joel. "Thinking Small." Rev. of *Goodbye Harold, Good Luck*. *Books in Canada*, June–July 1986, pp. 12–14.

Zabus, Chantal. "A Calibanic Tempest in Anglophone and Francophone New World Writing." *Canadian Literature*, No. 104 (Spring 1985), pp. 35–50.

INDEX